LeGette's
*Calorie*
ENCYCLOPEDIA

# Le Gette's Calorie ENCYCLOPEDIA

## Bernard Le Gette

Greenwich House
Distributed by Crown Publishers, Inc.
New York

This 1984 edition is published by
Greenwich House, a division of Arlington
House, Inc. distributed by Crown Publishers,
Inc. by arrangement with Warner Books, Inc.


Manufactured in the United States of
America

**Library of Congress Cataloging in Publication Data**

Le Gette, Bernard.
  Le Gette's calorie counter.

    1. Food—Caloric content—Tables. I. Title.
TX551.L36  1984        641.1′042        84-22285
ISBN: 0-517-455935

h g f e d c b a

# Contents

v

# Contents

# *Introduction*

Losing weight is simple. It's not easy—but it's simple.
You cut the intake of your calories, and then
you lose weight. Everything else you've ever heard
is icing on the cake you can't eat. Carbohydrates,
cholesterol, volume, protein, metabolism, exercise,
are all very interesting, and confusing, to think
about, though none of these things plays a big role
in how much you weigh or how little you can
weigh.

But even when people cut calories they
usually don't do a very good job of it. You have
probably gone on diets, wondered why they
didn't work and wandered off them again, or maybe
they did work, but your will power collapsed—

the constant pressure of not eating so many delicious foods caved you right in.

There are two reasons why most people fail. The first is that they don't really know how many calories they're consuming. They estimate how many calories are in each food, estimate how much of each food they ate, and constantly say things like, "That was only a little snack—two or three crackers." Sound familiar? And of course they're always rejecting potatoes.

Well I'll tell you right now, there is no way you can estimate. You can't estimate the size, you can't estimate the number of calories and you can't estimate the number of times you snacked. You can't estimate a thing. You aren't that smart. Nobody is.

You have to count the pieces, weigh them, and check every time how many calories you just ate. And then you have to write it down. Every calorie. Every day.

Now I know this is more inconvenient than being fat, and hating yourself every day, and being tired, and having heart attacks. But that's the way it is. It does have the advantage of being one inconvenience instead of many, and it is also only one simple way to lose weight—instead of many complicated ways not to—which brings us to the second reason most people fail.

It's because losing weight tends to get very vague in people's minds. It's a hidden enemy that has to be strained against every day. And that's very disheartening—which means it won't work. Any constant general restriction on your life, that has no definite limits and no clear procedure, is just not going to work. That's why specific diets are so successful in the short term—they remove the vagueness, the guesswork, the doubt. But we aren't talking about the short term. We're talking about weighing whatever you like for the rest of your life.

Fortunately, you don't have to fight hidden enemies. You don't even have to use much will power. You only have to know how to count— calories.

The purpose of this book and the years of research that went into it is to give you—in one place—the calories of all the foods you might ever eat. Whether it's fresh, or a commercially packaged brand, or a meal you ate in a restaurant or prepared at home, or a snack you ate at a drive-in—it's here. The portions listed are as standardized as is practical, so you don't have to bring your calculator. There are no extra columns of things that won't help you lose weight, and there is as little repetition as possible. You won't find listings of Thingamajigs—25 calories; Thingamajigs on a stick—25 calories; Thingamajigs sliced—25 calories, and so on. If thingamajigs are 25 calories, that's all you need to read—very simple.

The chapters are in a logical order chosen to

help you remember where things are listed. If everything were listed alphabetically you wouldn't know if some fish would be found under fillet, or haddock, or Mrs. Paul's, and even when you found it you couldn't compare it to others of its kind. So everything is in these fourteen basic groupings.

And the fifteenth chapter is the Fingertip Low Calorie Guide. This is an innovation which I hope will enable you to find a variety of low calorie foods at a glance. They are listed in calorie groups so you can plan your shopping, your meals, even your snacks with a specific number of calories in mind. It is also a pretty thorough list of the low calorie foods available. As you'll see in the rest of the book, being called *low calorie* or *dietetic* is no guarantee that a food is low in calories.

Everything is listed for normal usage. That is, if a food is made from a mix, say, the quantity and the calories listed are for the food after it's been prepared according to the package instructions. Likewise, it is of no use to know how many calories are in a pound of spinach while it is still frozen, so that is not listed. Now some things are listed as containing 0 calories for one tsp, and that is accurate; it is also reasonably accurate for one tbs. I can't guarantee, however, that there are no calories in three lbs. of sweetener. There just might be a few.

## Introduction

So how do you lose weight? Eat *what* you want, though of course a balanced diet is always best. It's not what, but *how many* that counts. Remember, virtually all foods have calories. The question is, how much satisfaction and/or nutrition are you getting from a particular food? For the calories in it, a plain potato contains a phenomenal variety of nutrients— you can probably live longer on potatoes than on any other single food—and that would suit some people fine. Others, however, would like to go quickly on apples, which contain neither calories nor nutrients in any marked degree.

But however you do it—eat fewer calories. Measure every portion. It's quite easy. Just put your chicken, or your potato, on a scale, see what the scale says, and compare that to the portion listed in this book. Write down the number of calories for each meal. Add them up at the end of the day, and in the morning write down how much you weigh next to yesterday's calorie total.

But you have to do it every time. It won't do you any good sometimes. And if after awhile you think you can remember most foods' calories, you're wrong. You have to measure. You have to count. The reason you're fat (which is why you bought this book) is you don't know how to play it by eye. You were brought up to eat too much, your aggression makes you hungry, your metabolism is rotten, whatever. It doesn't matter. You want to be thin. I just told you how. If you really *want* to be thin, that's what you'll do. Otherwise you'll continue to play at it and make excuses.

Now if you want to look good and be completely healthy *in addition* to being thin, you'll also exercise, though the exercise won't do either of those things for you if you're overweight. And it won't help you to lose much weight either. The relation between calories and exercise is straightforward. The harder it is, the more calories you burn. There are 3,600 calories in 1 pound of fat. Roughly, you'll burn 100 calories by:

| | | |
|---|---|---|
| skating (either kind) | 45 | minutes |
| skiing (either kind) | 35 | " |
| football | 30 | " |
| handball | 22 | " |
| walking | 19 | " |
| rowing | 18 | " |
| bicycling | 15 | " |
| chopping wood | 13 | " |
| swimming | 12 | " |
| jumping rope | 11 | " |
| jogging | 10 | " |
| running | 6 | " |

or (even more roughly) 18 holes of golf (on foot) or two sets of tennis.

So if you want to lose that pound of fat, it's easier not to eat the 3,600 calories than to jump

rope for 7 hours. What will help the most is a
regular, steady approach to food and calories.
This book can be your guide to help you look and
feel the person you really want to be.

| | |
|---|---|
| 1 quart | = 4 cups |
| 1 cup | = 8 fluid ounces (oz) |
| 1 cup | = ½ pint |
| 1 cup | = 16 tablespoons |
| 1 ounce | = 2 tablespoons |
| 1 tablespoon (tbs.) | = 3 teaspoons |
| 1 jigger, or shot | = 1½ ounces |
| | |
| 1 pound (lb.) | = 16 ounces |

Remember, a fluid ounce is a measure of volume, not weight.

---

ALL listings are for food *as prepared* for normal usage. That means that after it's been prepared with all the normal ingredients, and it's ready to eat—that's what the calories are for.

# CHAPTER 1

# Beverages

## SPIRITS, WINES, LIQUEURS, COCKTAILS, BRANDIES, AND COCKTAIL MIXES

Note: The number of calories in distilled spirits depends entirely on the alcoholic content—the higher the proof, the higher the calories. This is true for bourbon, gin, rum, Scotch, tequila, vodka, and almost anything called whiskey.

# 1

## Distilled Spirits, 1 oz

| | |
|---|---|
| 80 proof | 65 |
| 90 proof | 75 |
| 100 proof | 85 |
| 150 proof | 125 |

## Cocktails, canned or bottled, alcoholic, 1 oz

**Amaretto Sour**
*Mr. Boston*   40
**Apricot Sour**
*Party Tyme*   33
**Banana Daiquiri**
*Party Tyme*   33
**Daiquiri**
*Hiram Walker*   59
*Mr. Boston*   33
*Party Tyme*   33
*Calvert*   63
**Gimlet**
*Party Tyme*   40
**Gin & Tonic**
*Party Tyme*   28
**Mai Tai**
*Lemon Hart*   60
*Mr. Boston*   36
*Party Tyme*   33

## Manhattan
*Calvert*     54
*Mr. Boston*     40
*Party Tyme*     37

## Margarita
*Calvert*     59
*Mr. Boston*     35
*Mr. Boston strawberry*     45
*Party Tyme*     33

## Martini, Gin
*Calvert*     63
*Hiram Walker*     55
*Mr. Boston*     33
*Party Tyme*     41

## Martini, Vodka
*Calvert*     63
*Hiram Walker*     49
*Mr. Boston*     34
*Party Tyme*     36

## Old Fashioned
*Hiram Walker*     55

## Piña Colada
*Mr. Boston*     60
*Party Tyme*     32

## Rum & Cola
*Party Tyme*     28

## Screwdriver
*Mr. Boston*     39
*Party Tyme*     35

**Sour, Gin**
*Calvert*      65
**Sour, Scotch**
*Party Tyme*      33
**Sour, Tequila**
*Calvert*      65
**Sour, Whiskey**
*Calvert*      60
*Hiram Walker*      60
*Mr. Boston*      40
**Tequila Sunrise**
*Mr. Boston*      40
**Tom Collins**
*Calvert*      65
*Party Tyme*      29
**Vodka Tonic**
*Party Tyme*      27
**Wallbanger**
*Mr. Boston*      34

# Cocktail Mixes, bottled and dry, nonalcoholic, 1 oz or 1 premeasured packet

**Alexander**
*Holland House*      69
**Amaretto**
*Holland House*      79
**Banana Daiquiri**
*Holland House*      66

**Beverages**

**Mint Julep**
*Holland House* 67

**Old Fashioned**
*Holland House* 9
*Party Tyme* 28

**Piña Colada**
*Holland House* 60
*Party Tyme* 50

**Pink Squirrel**
*Holland House* 69

**Planter's Punch**
*Party Tyme* 37

**Screwdriver**
*Holland House* 69
*Party Tyme* 21

**Sidecar**
*Holland House* 17

**Sour, Blackberry**
*Holland House* 50

**Sour, Virgin**
*Party Tyme* 50

**Sour, Whiskey**
*Canada Dry* 11
*Holland House* 53
*Holland House* low calorie 9
*Party Tyme* 29
*Party Tyme* instant 53

**Sip 'n Slim**
*Holland House* 10

**Strawberry Sting**
 *Holland House*     35
**Tom Collins**
 *Holland House*     58
 *Party Tyme*      44
 *Party Tyme* instant    58

# Cocktails, standard recipe, alcoholic, 1 oz alcohol, unless noted

| | |
|---|---|
| **Bacardi** | 155 |
| **Bloody Mary** | 140 |
| **Brandy Alexander** | 225 |
| **Bourbon Highball (1½ oz bourbon)** | |
|  with soda | 125 |
|  with ginger ale | 180 |
| **Cuba Libre** | 224 |
| **Daiquiri** | 135 |
| **Gimlet** | 136 |
| **Gin Fizz** | 172 |
| **Grasshopper** | 235 |
| **Irish Coffee** | 214 |
| **Manhattan** | 177 |
| **Martini, Gin or Vodka** | 115 |
| **Mint Julep** | 209 |
| **Old Fashioned** | 144 |
| **Orange Blossom** | 153 |
| **Pink Lady** | 190 |
| **Rob Roy** | 199 |

**1**

| | |
|---|---|
| Rum Cola (see Cuba Libre) | 224 |
| Screwdriver | 168 |
| Side Car | 161 |
| Sloe Gin Fizz | 155 |
| Stinger | 149 |
| Tom Collins | 170 |
| Whiskey Sour | 142 |

## Wines, 4 oz

**Alsatian**
| | |
|---|---|
| *Wilm* | 88 |

**Altar, red**
| | |
|---|---|
| *Gold Seal* | 132 |
| *Henri Marchant* | 132 |

**Blackberry**
| | |
|---|---|
| *Manischewitz* | 180 |

**Bordeaux**
red
| | |
|---|---|
| *B&G Margaux* | 83 |
| *B&G Prince Noir* | 81 |
| *B&G Saint-Emilion* | 84 |
| *Chanson* | 108 |
| *Cruse* | 92 |
| *Cruse Saint-Emilion* | 92 |
| *Cruse Saint-Julien* | 92 |
| *Cruse Médoc* | 96 |
| *Cruse Château La Garde* | 108 |

**1**

**1**

| | |
|---|---:|
| *Gold Seal* blanc de blancs | 98 |
| brut | 81 |
| dry | 91 |
| *Great Western* brut | 100 |
| dry | 104 |
| pink | 108 |
| *Henri Marchant* blanc de blancs | 88 |
| brut | 91 |
| dry | 98 |
| *Lejon* | 94 |
| *Korbel* | 104 |
| *Manischewitz* | 88 |
| *Mumm's* brut | 88 |
| dry | 111 |
| *Taylor* brut | 101 |
| dry | 104 |
| pink | 108 |
| *Veuve Clicquot* | 104 |

**Chianti**

| | |
|---|---:|
| *Brolio* | 88 |
| *Gancia* | 88 |
| *Italian Swiss Colony* | 87 |

**Claret**

| | |
|---|---:|
| *Gold Seal* | 109 |
| *Inglenook* | 80 |
| *Italian Swiss Colony* | 86 |
| *Louis Martini* | 126 |
| *Taylor* | 96 |

**Cold Duck**

| | |
|---|---:|
| *Gold Seal* | 97 |

# 1

| | |
|---|---|
| *Great Western* | 121 |
| *Taylor* | 120 |
| **Concord** | |
| *Gold Seal* | 132 |
| *Henri Marchant* | 132 |
| *Manischewitz* | |
| red | 160 |
| white | 130 |
| medium dry | 120 |
| dry | 85 |
| *Mogen David* | 160 |
| **Kosher** | |
| *Manischewitz* | |
| sweet | 170 |
| medium | 112 |
| dry | 91 |
| **Labrusca** | |
| *Gold Seal* | 130 |
| *Henri Marchant* | 132 |
| **Lake Country** | |
| *Taylor* | 106 |
| **Liebfraumilch** | |
| *Anheuser & Fehrs* | 80 |
| *Dienhard* | 95 |
| **Malaga** | |
| *Manischewitz* | 180 |
| **Moselle** | |
| *Dienhard* | 95 |
| *Julius Kayser* | 77 |

**1**

**1**

| | |
|---|---:|
| *B&G* | 93 |
| **Riesling** | |
| *Dienhard* | 96 |
| *Gold Seal* | 92 |
| *Henri Marchant* | 92 |
| *Inglenook* | 82 |
| *Louis Martini* | 120 |
| **Rosé** | |
| *Cruse* | 96 |
| *Gold Seal* | 99 |
| *Henri Marchant* | 96 |
| *Italian Swiss Colony* | 86 |
| *Taylor* | 92 |
| **Sake** | 151 |
| **Sancerre** | |
| *B&G* | 80 |
| **Sauterne** | |
| *Gallo* | 67 |
| *Gallo* Haut | 83 |
| *Gold Seal* | 97 |
| *Gold Seal* Haut | 109 |
| *Great Western* | 105 |
| *Henri Marchant* | 109 |
| *Italian Swiss Colony* | 77 |
| *Louis Martini* | 120 |
| *Mogen David* cream | 59 |
| *Mogen David* dry | 39 |
| *Taylor* | 105 |
| **Soave** | |
| *Antinori* | 110 |

**1**

**Thunderbird**
Gallo                              139
**Valpolicella**
Antinori                        109
**Zinfandel**
Inglenook                       76
Italian Swiss Colony          80
Louis Martini                  120

# Aperitif and Dessert Wines, 4 oz

**Asti Spumante**
Gancia                          168
**Aquavit**
Leroux                          300
**Campari**                      66
Dubonnet Blonde               151
Dubonnet Red                  190
**Madeira**
Gold Seal                       144
Henri Marchant                144
Leacock                         160
Sandeman                       168
**Muscatel**
Gallo                           144
Gold Seal                       210
**Pernod**
Julius Wyle                     315

### Port

| | |
|---|---|
| *Gallo* | 146 |
| *Gold Seal* | 185 |
| *Great Western* | 178 |
| *Italian Swiss Colony* | 170 |
| *Louis Martini* | 215 |
| *Robertson* | 180 |
| *Sandeman* | 184 |
| *Taylor* | 195 |

### Sherry

| | |
|---|---|
| *Gallo* | 104 |
| *Gold Seal* | 185 |
| *Great Western* | 156 |
| *Taylor* | 200 |
| *Dry Sack* | 160 |

### Sherry, cream

| | |
|---|---|
| *Gallo* | 150 |
| *Gold Seal* | 205 |
| *Great Western* | 180 |
| *Louis Martini* | 175 |
| *Taylor* | 178 |

### Sherry, dry

| | |
|---|---|
| *Gallo* | 110 |
| *Gold Seal* | 162 |
| *Great Western* | 140 |
| *Italian Swiss Colony* | 132 |
| *Louis Martini* | 180 |
| *Sandeman* | 145 |
| *Taylor* | 152 |

**Vermouth, dry**

| | |
|---|---|
| C&P | 148 |
| Gallo | 100 |
| Gancia | 168 |
| Great Western | 113 |
| Lejon | 129 |
| Noilly Pratt | 136 |
| Taylor | 136 |

**Vermouth, sweet**

| | |
|---|---|
| C&P | 156 |
| Gallo | 150 |
| Gancia | 185 |
| Great Western | 172 |
| Lejon | 174 |
| Noilly Pratt | 172 |
| Taylor | 175 |

# Cordials and Liqueurs, 1 oz

| | |
|---|---|
| **Amaretto** | 80 |
| **Anise** | 82 |
| **Anisette** | |
| Bols | 111 |
| DuBouchett | 85 |
| DeKuyper | 95 |
| Garnier | 82 |
| Mr. Boston | 90 |
| Mr. Boston Connoisseur | 64 |

**Apricot**
| | |
|---|---|
| *Bols* | 96 |
| *Dolfi* | 100 |
| *DuBouchett* | 65 |

**B & B** 94

**Benai** 110

**Benedictine** 110

**Blackberry**
| | |
|---|---|
| *Bols* | 90 |
| *Dolfi* | 89 |
| *DuBouchett* | 68 |

**Brandy, flavored**
| | |
|---|---|
| *Bols* | 100 |
| *DuBouchett* | 87 |
| *Garnier* | 6 |
| *Leroux* | 90 |
| *Mr. Boston* | 100 |
| *Mr. Boston Connoisseur* | 75 |

**Cherry liqueur**
| | |
|---|---|
| *Bols* | 96 |
| *DeKuyper* | 75 |
| *Dolfi* | 87 |
| *DuBouchett* | 72 |
| *Hiram Walker* | 82 |
| *Leroux* | 82 |

**Chocolate**
| | |
|---|---|
| *Vandermint* | 90 |

**Claristine**
| | |
|---|---|
| *Leroux* | 114 |

**1**

## Coffee
*Tia Maria*     92
*Pasha*     100
## Crème de almond
*DuBouchett*     100
## Crème de apricot
*Mr. Boston*     90
*Mr. Boston Connoisseur*     65
## Crème de banana
*Garnier*     90
*Mr. Boston*     90
*Mr. Boston Connoisseur*     65
## Crème de cacao
*Bols*     100
*Dolfi*     100
*DuBouchett*     100
*Garnier*     100
*Hiram Walker*     100
*Mr. Boston*     90
*Mr. Boston Connoisseur*     65
## Crème de cassis
*Leroux*     87
*Mr. Boston*     90
## Crème de menthe     100
## Crème de noisette     90
## Crème de noyaux
*Bols*     115
*Mr. Boston*     99
## Crème de peach
*Mr. Boston Connoisseur*     65

**1**

| | |
|---|---|
| **Curaçao** | 100 |
| **Drambuie** | 110 |
| **Grenadine** | 81 |
| **Kirsch** | 80 |
| **Kümmel** | |
| *DuBouchett* | |
| 48 proof | 65 |
| 70 proof | 83 |
| *Garnier* | 75 |
| *Hiram Walker* | 71 |
| *Leroux* | 75 |
| *Mr. Boston* | 78 |
| **Lochon Ora** | |
| *Leroux* | 89 |
| **Peach Liqueur** | |
| *Bols* | 96 |
| *DeKuyper* | 82 |
| *Dolfi* | 103 |
| *DuBouchett* | 67 |
| *Hiram Walker* | 81 |
| *Leroux* | 85 |
| **Raspberry Liqueur** | |
| *Dolfi* | 80 |
| *DuBouchett* | 56 |
| **Rock & Rye** | |
| *DuBouchett* | |
| 60 proof | 78 |
| 70 proof | 86 |
| *Garnier* | 83 |
| *Mr. Boston* | 90 |

# 1

| | |
|---|---:|
| Mr. Boston Connoisseur | 65 |
| **Schnapps, peppermint** | |
| DuBouchett | 85 |
| Garnier | 83 |
| Hiram Walker | 78 |
| Leroux | 87 |
| Mr. Boston | 77 |
| **Sloe Gin** | |
| Bols | 85 |
| DeKuyper | 70 |
| Dolfi | 114 |
| DuBouchett | 70 |
| Garnier | 83 |
| Mr. Boston | 67 |
| **Triple Sec** | |
| Bols | 104 |
| Dolfi | 107 |
| DuBouchett | 61 |
| Garnier | 83 |
| Hiram Walker | 105 |
| Leroux | 104 |
| Mr. Boston | 100 |

# BEER, ALE, MALT LIQUOR,
## 12 oz

| | |
|---|---:|
| Andeker | 160 |
| Black Horse Ale | 162 |
| Brauhaus | 150 |

| | |
|---|---|
| *Buckeye* | 144 |
| *Budweiser* | 156 |
| *Budweiser Malt Liquor* | 160 |
| *Busch Bavarian* | 155 |
| *Carling Black Label* | 160 |
| *Carlsberg Light* | 159 |
| *Carlsberg Dark* | 240 |
| *Champale Malt Liquor* | 157 |
| *Country Club Malt Liquor* | 163 |
| *Coors* | 138 |
| *Eastside Lager* | 145 |
| *Falstaff* | 150 |
| *Gablinger's* | 99 |
| *Goebel* | 145 |
| *Grand Union* | 150 |
| *Grenzquell* | 150 |
| *Hamms* | 138 |
| *Heidelberg* | 133 |
| *Heidelberg Light* | 129 |
| *Heileman's* | 158 |
| *Kingsbury* | 146 |
| *Knickerbocker* | 160 |
| *Meister Brau* | 144 |
| *Meister Brau Draft* | 144 |
| *Meister Brau Lite* | 96 |
| *Michelob* | 160 |
| *Michelob Light* | 134 |
| *Miller* | 150 |
| *Miller Lite* | 96 |
| *Natural Light* | 110 |

| | |
|---|---|
| *Old Dutch* | 150 |
| *Old Milwaukee* | 144 |
| *Old Ranger* | 150 |
| *Pabst Blue Ribbon* | 150 |
| *Pabst Light* | 100 |
| *Pabst Extra Light* | 70 |
| *Pearl* | 145 |
| *Pilser's* | 152 |
| *Red Cap Ale* | 159 |
| *Rheingold* | 160 |
| *Schaefer* | 158 |
| *Schlitz* | 148 |
| *Schlitz Light* | 96 |
| *Schmidt's* | 142 |
| *Stag* | 151 |
| *Stroh Bohemian* | 136 |
| *Stroh Bock* | 155 |
| *Stroh Light* | 115 |
| *Tuborg USA* | 140 |
| *Tudor* | 150 |

# Near Beer, 12 oz

| | |
|---|---|
| *Goetz Pale* | 78 |
| *Kingsbury* | 45 |

# 1

## Nonalcoholic Beer, 12 oz

| | |
|---|---:|
| *Maltcrest* | 70 |
| *Metbrew* | 70 |
| *Zing* | 65 |

# SOFT DRINKS, 8 oz

Note: Virtually all sodas that are called *low calorie*, *sugar free*, or *dietetic* contain 2 calories or less.

| | |
|---|---:|
| **Aspen** | 105 |
| **Birch Beer** | |
| *Canada Dry* | 110 |
| *Pennsylvania Dutch* | 109 |
| *Yukon Club* | 116 |
| **Bitter lemon** | |
| *Canada Dry* | 104 |
| *Schweppes* | 128 |
| **Bitter orange** | |
| *Schweppes* | 124 |
| ***Bubble Up*** | 97 |
| ***Cactus Cooler*** | 120 |
| **Cherry** | |
| *Cott* | 123 |
| *Crush* | 121 |

| | |
|---|---:|
| *Fanta* | 117 |
| *Mission* | 122 |
| **Club soda, all brands** | 0 |
| **Coconut** | |
| *Yoo-Hoo* | 117 |
| **Coffee** | |
| *Hoffman* | 88 |
| **Cola** | |
| *Canada Dry* | 110 |
| *Coca-Cola* | 96 |
| *Pepsi-Cola* | 104 |
| *Royal Crown* | 109 |
| *Pepsi Light* | 47 |
| *Shasta* | 90 |
| **Cream** | |
| *Canada Dry* | 127 |
| *Fanta* | 130 |
| *Shasta* | 90 |
| *Schweppes* | 115 |
| **Dr. Brown's Cel-Ray Tonic** | 89 |
| **Dr. Nehi** | 98 |
| **Dr. Pepper** | 98 |
| **Fruit punch** | |
| *Shasta* | 110 |
| **Fruit mix** | |
| *Wyler's* | 88 |
| **Ginger Ale** | |
| *Canada Dry* | 85 |
| *Fanta* | 85 |
| *Nehi* | 91 |

| | |
|---|---:|
| *Schweppes* | 88 |
| **Ginger Beer** | |
| *Schweppes* | 96 |
| **Grape** | |
| *Canada Dry* | 130 |
| *Crush* | 120 |
| *Fanta* | 114 |
| *Nehi* | 116 |
| *Patio* | 128 |
| *Schweppes* | 129 |
| *Shasta* | 114 |
| **Grapefruit** | |
| *Fanta* | 115 |
| *Shasta* | 103 |
| **Half and Half** | 110 |
| *Hi Spot* | 100 |
| *Kick* | 118 |
| *Kool Aid*, all flavors | 93 |
| **Lemon** | |
| *Hi-C* | 123 |
| *Shasta* | 97 |
| **Lemon-Lime** | |
| *Shasta* | 93 |
| **Lime** | |
| *Canada Dry* | 130 |
| *Mello-Yello* | 115 |
| *Mr. PiBB* | 93 |
| *Mountain Dew* | 118 |
| **Orange** | |
| *Canada Dry* | 130 |

**Beverages**

| | |
|---|---|
| *Crush* | 120 |
| *Fanta* | 114 |
| *Hi-C* | 101 |
| *Nedick's* | 121 |
| *Nehi* | 124 |
| *Patio* | 128 |
| *Schweppes* | 118 |
| *Shasta* | 114 |
| *Sunkist* | 125 |

**Pineapple**
| | |
|---|---|
| *Canada Dry* | 110 |

**Purple Passion**
| | |
|---|---|
| *Canada Dry* | 120 |

**Quinine Water**
| | |
|---|---|
| *Canada Dry* | 95 |
| *Fanta* | 84 |
| *Schweppes* | 88 |

**Rondo**
| | |
|---|---|
| *Schweppes* | 100 |

**Root Beer**
| | |
|---|---|
| *A&W* | 114 |
| *Berks County* | 116 |
| *Canada Dry Barrelhead* | 110 |
| *Canada Dry Rooti* | 110 |
| *Dad's* | 105 |
| *Fanta* | 103 |
| *Hires* | 100 |
| *On Tap* | 105 |
| *Patio* | 110 |
| *Royal Crown* | 113 |

| | |
|---|---:|
| *Schweppes* | 105 |
| *Shasta* | 100 |
| **7-Up** | 97 |
| **Sprite** | 95 |
| **Squirt** | 91 |
| **Strawberry** | |
| *Canada Dry* | 120 |
| *Crush* | 121 |
| *Fanta* | 121 |
| *Nehi* | 116 |
| *Shasta* | 94 |
| *Yoo-Hoo* | 124 |
| **Sun-Drop** | 118 |
| **Teem** | 93 |
| **Tahitian Treat** | |
| *Canada Dry* | 130 |
| **Tiki** | 100 |
| **Tonic** | |
| *Canada Dry* | 90 |
| *Schweppes* | 88 |
| *Shasta* | 66 |
| **Upper 10** | 101 |
| **Vanilla** | |
| *Yoo-Hoo* | 125 |
| **Vanilla Cream** | |
| *Canada Dry* | 130 |
| **Wild Cherry** | |
| *Canada Dry* | 130 |
| **Wink** | 120 |

# 1

# COFFEE AND TEA, 6 oz

**Coffee**

| | |
|---|---:|
| regular | 2 |
| instant | 4 |
| flavored | |
|    *General Foods* | |
|      *Cafe Francais* | 60 |
|      *Cafe Vienna* | 60 |
|      *Orange Cappuccino* | 60 |
|      *Suisse Mocha* | 60 |
| **Postum** | 10 |
| **Tea, bags or loose** | 1 |
| **Tea, bottled or canned** | |
|   *Lipton* | 84 |
|     sugar free | 1 |
|     No-Cal | 0 |
| **Tea, instant** | |
|   *Lipton lemon-flavored* | 3 |
|   *100% Tea* | 0 |
|   *Nestea* | 1 |
|   *Tender Leaf* | 1 |
| **Tea, mix, iced, lemon-flavored** | |
|   *Our Own (A&P)* | 62 |
|   *Lipton* | 40 |
|   *Nestea* | 15 |
|     with sugar | 70 |

| | |
|---|---|
| *Salada* | 57 |
| *Wyler's* | 56 |

# FRUIT AND VEGETABLE
# JUICES, 6 oz

## Fresh

| | |
|---|---|
| **Grapefruit** | 70 |
| **Lemon or Lime** | 45 |
| **Lemon or Lime, 1 Tbsp** | 3 |
| **Orange** | |
| California | 85 |
| Florida | 80 |
| Valencia | 85 |
| **Peach Nectar** | 90 |
| **Tangerine** | 80 |

## Bottled and Canned

| | |
|---|---|
| **Apple** | |
| *Ann Page* | 90 |
| *Heinz* | 75 |

**1**

| | |
|---|---:|
| *Musselman's* | 80 |
| *Mott's* | 80 |
| *Pillsbury* | 60 |
| *Seneca* | 80 |
| *Welch's* | 90 |
| **Apple-Cranberry** | |
| *Lincoln* | 104 |
| **Apricot nectar** | |
| *Del Monte* | 100 |
| *Heart's Delight* | 194 |
| *Heinz* | 104 |
| *Libby's* | 110 |
| *Seneca* | 75 |
| **Cranberry-Apple** | |
| *Cranapple* | 120 |
| **Fig** | |
| *Real Fig* | 135 |
| **Fig and Prune** | |
| *Fig 'n' Prune* | 135 |
| **Grape** | |
| *Heinz* | 120 |
| *Seneca* | 110 |
| *Welch's* | 120 |
| **Grapefruit** | |
| *Del Monte* | 70 |
| *Heinz* | 70 |
| *Libby's* | 75 |
| *Ocean Spray* | 70 |
| *Seneca* | 55 |
| *Stokely-Van Camp* | 60 |

*Welch's* 75
**Grapefruit-Orange**
*Seneca* 77
**Grenadine syrup, nonalcoholic, 1 oz.**
*Garnier* 100
*Giroux* 104
**Lemon, 1 Tbsp**
*ReaLemon* 4
*Rose's* 5
**Lime, 1 Tbsp**
*ReaLime* 6
**Orange**
*Del Monte* 80
*Heinz* 75
*Libby's* 90
*Welch's* 90
**Orange-Grapefruit**
*Del Monte* 80
*Libby's* 80
*Stokely-Van Camp* 70
**Peach Nectar**
*Del Monte* 100
*Libby's* 90
*Heart's Delight* 89
**Pear Nectar**
*Del Monte* 110
*Libby's* 100
*Heart's Delight* 95
**Pineapple**
*Del Monte* 100

# 1

**1**

| | |
|---|---|
| *Welch's* | 38 |
| **Vegetable** | |
| *Campbell V-8* | 35 |
| *Vegemato* | 32 |

# Frozen Juice

| | |
|---|---|
| **Grape** | |
| *Minute Maid* | 99 |
| *Snow Crop* | 99 |
| **Grapefruit** | |
| *Bird's Eye* | 68 |
| *Minute Maid* | 75 |
| *Snow Crop* | 75 |
| **Lemon** | |
| *Minute Maid* | 40 |
| **Orange** | |
| *Bright and Early* | 90 |
| *Minute Maid* | 90 |
| *Snow Crop* | 120 |
| *Stokely-Van Camp* | 90 |
| **Orange-Grapefruit** | |
| *Bird's Eye* | 72 |
| *Minute Maid* | 76 |
| **Pineapple** | |
| *Dole* | 101 |
| *Minute Maid* | 92 |

**Pineapple-orange**
| | |
|---|---|
| *Minute Maid* | 94 |
| *Dole* | 77 |

**Tangerine**
| | |
|---|---|
| *Minute Maid* | 86 |
| *Snow Crop* | 85 |

# Dairy-Packed Juice, 8 oz

**Grapefruit**
| | |
|---|---|
| *Tropicana* | 75 |

**Orange**
| | |
|---|---|
| *Borden* | 96 |
| *Kraft* | 90 |
| *Sealtest* | 96 |
| *Tropicana* | 83 |

**Orange-Grapefruit**
| | |
|---|---|
| *Kraft* | 90 |

**Orange-Pineapple**
| | |
|---|---|
| *Ann Page* | 87 |
| *Hi-C* | 94 |
| *Kraft* | 96 |

# 1

# FRUIT-FLAVORED DRINKS, ALL TYPES, 6 oz

**Apple**
| | |
|---|---|
| *Ann Page* | 90 |
| *Hi-C* | 90 |

**Apple-Grape**
| | |
|---|---|
| *Mott's* | 90 |
| *Welch's* | 92 |

**Apricot-Apple**
| | |
|---|---|
| *BC* | 92 |

**Cherry**
| | |
|---|---|
| *Ann Page* | 90 |
| *Hi-C* | 75 |

**Citrus Cooler**
| | |
|---|---|
| *Ann Page* | 90 |
| *Hi-C* | 90 |

**Cranberry**
| | |
|---|---|
| *Ann Page* | 120 |
| *Ocean Spray* | 105 |
| *Seneca* | 120 |
| *Welch's* | 105 |

**Cranberry-Apple**
| | |
|---|---|
| *Ann Page* | 135 |
| *Lincoln* | 103 |
| *Mott's* | 95 |
| *Ocean Spray* | 135 |

**Cranberry-Apricot**
*Ocean Spray*                                    105
**Cranberry-Grape**
*Ocean Spray*                                    105
*Welch's*                                        120
**Cranberry-Orange**
*Knox*                                            59
**Cranberry-Prune**
*Ocean Spray*                                    120
**Grape**
*Ann Page*                                        90
*Hi-C*                                            90
*Welch's*                                         90
**Grape-Apple**
*BC*                                             107
**Grapefruit**
*Ann Page*                                        80
*Sealtest*                                        90
*Tropicana*                                       70
**Lemon**
*Sealtest*                                        90
**Lemonade**
*Bird's Eye*                                      74
*Borden*                                          78
*Country Time*                                    67
*Hi-C*                                            75
*Minute Maid*                                     75
*ReaLemon*                                        76
*Sealtest*                                        80
*Snow Crop*                                       75

| | |
|---|---|
| *Stokely-Van Camp* | 80 |
| *Wyler's* | 67 |
| **Lemon-Limeade** | |
| *Minute Maid* | 75 |
| *Snow Crop* | 75 |
| **Limeade** | |
| *Bird's Eye* | 75 |
| *Minute Maid* | 75 |
| *Snow Crop* | 75 |
| **Orange** | |
| *A&P* | 80 |
| *Ann Page* | 90 |
| *Bird's Eye* | 105 |
| *Borden* | 85 |
| *Hi-C* | 125 |
| *Minute Maid* | 125 |
| *Start* | 120 |
| *Stokely-Van Camp* | 114 |
| *Tang* | 120 |
| *Tropicana* | 93 |
| *Welch's* | 135 |
| **Orange-Pineapple** | |
| *Ann Page* | 120 |
| *BC* | 120 |
| *Start* | 120 |
| **Peach** | |
| *Hi-C* | 120 |
| **Pineapple-Grapefruit** | |
| *Dole* | 120 |

**1**

## Punch
| | |
|---|---|
| *Ann Page* | 120 |
| *Hawaiian Punch* | 120 |
| *Hi-C* | 130 |
| *Mott's* | 120 |
| *Stokely-Van Camp* | 114 |
| *Tropicana* | 93 |
| *Welch's* | 130 |
| *Wyler's* | 85 |

**Raspberry**
| | |
|---|---|
| *Wyler's* | 85 |

**Strawberry**
| | |
|---|---|
| *Hi-C* | 120 |
| *Wyler's* | 85 |

**Tangerine**
| | |
|---|---|
| *Hi-C* | 120 |

**Wild Berry**
| | |
|---|---|
| *Ann Page* | 120 |
| *Hi-C* | 115 |

# CHAPTER 2

# *Dairy*

## BUTTER AND MARGARINE

**Butter**
  ½ cup (¼ lb)                  815
  1 Tbsp                      100
**Butter, whipped**
  ½ cup                      540
  1 Tbsp                      65
**Margarine, 1 Tbsp**
  Imitation
    *Mazola*                   50
    *Parkay*                   50
    *Weight Watchers*         50

| | |
|---|---|
| Regular and Soft, all brands | 100 |
| Diet, all brands | 50 |
| Spread | |
| *Blue Bonnet* | 80 |
| *Fleishmann* | 80 |
| *Parkay* | 70 |
| Whipped, all brands | 70 |

# CHEESE, 1 oz unless noted

| | |
|---|---|
| **American** | |
| *Borden* | 104 |
| *Kraft* | 90 |
| **Blue** | |
| *Borden* | 105 |
| *Casino* | 100 |
| *Kraft* | 99 |
| **Brie** | |
| *Dorman* | 100 |
| *Kraft* | 100 |
| **Camembert** | |
| *Borden* | 85 |
| *Kraft* | 85 |
| **Caraway** | |
| *Kraft* | 111 |
| **Cheddar** | |
| *Borden* | 113 |
| *Kraft* | 113 |

**2**

## Colby

| | |
|---|---|
| *Borden* | 111 |
| *Kraft* | 111 |

## Cottage, 1 cup

creamed

| | |
|---|---|
| *Borden* | 240 |
| *Breakstone* | 230 |
| *Breakstone* low-fat | 180 |
| *Foremost* | 212 |
| *Friendship* | 360 |
| *Kraft* | 214 |
| *Lucerne* | 240 |
| *Meadow Gold* | 134 |
| *Sealtest* | 114 |

partly creamed

| | |
|---|---|
| *Meadow Gold* | 204 |
| *Sealtest* | 176 |

uncreamed, potstyle

| | |
|---|---|
| *Borden* | 196 |
| *Breakstone* | 170 |
| *Kraft* | 206 |
| *Sealtest* | 180 |

low fat

| | |
|---|---|
| *Borden* | 180 |
| *Breakstone* | 180 |
| *Friendship* | 200 |
| *Lucerne* | 200 |
| *Viva* | 200 |
| *Weight Watchers* | 180 |

**Cream cheese**
| | |
|---|---|
| *Borden* | 96 |
| *Kraft Philadelphia Brand* | 98 |

**Edam**
| | |
|---|---|
| *Dorman* | 105 |
| *House of Gold* | 105 |

**Farmer's**
| | |
|---|---|
| *Breakstone* | 30 |
| *Dutch Garden* | 100 |
| *Friendship* | 38 |
| *Wispride* | 100 |

**Fondue**
| | |
|---|---|
| *Swiss Knight* | 60 |

**Fontina**
| | |
|---|---|
| *Kraft* | 114 |

**Frankenmuth**
| | |
|---|---|
| *Kraft* | 113 |

**Gjetost**
| | |
|---|---|
| *Kraft* | 135 |

**Gorgonzola**
| | |
|---|---|
| *Kraft* | 112 |

**Gouda**
| | |
|---|---|
| *Borden* | 86 |
| *Kraft* | 108 |

**Gruyère**
| | |
|---|---|
| *Borden* | 101 |
| *Kraft* | 108 |
| *Swiss Knight* | 101 |

**Leyden**
| | |
|---|---|
| *Kraft* | 80 |

**Liederkranz**
  *Borden* ..... 86
**Limburger**
  *Borden* ..... 97
  *Dorman* ..... 100
  *Kraft* ..... 98
  *Mountain Valley* ..... 100
**Monterey Jack**
  *Borden* ..... 103
  *Casino* ..... 100
  *Kraft* ..... 103
**Mozzarella**
  *Borden* ..... 79
  *Kraft* ..... 79
  *Dorman* ..... 85
**Muenster**
  *Borden* ..... 85
  *Dorman* ..... 90
  *Kraft* ..... 100
**Neufchâtel**
  *Borden* ..... 73
  *Kraft* ..... 69
**Nuworld**
  *Kraft* ..... 104
**Parmesan, grated, 1 Tbsp**
  *Buitoni* ..... 23
  *Kraft* ..... 27
  *La Rosa* ..... 33
  *Lucerne* ..... 25

**Parmesan & Romano, grated, 1 Tbsp**
   *Borden*   30
   *Kraft*   30
**Pimiento**
   *Borden*   104
   *Kraft*   104
**Port Salut**
   *Dorman*   100
   *Kraft*   100
**Premost**
   *Kraft*   134
**Provolone**
   *Borden*   93
   *Kraft*   99
**Ricotta**
   *Borden*   42
   *Kraft*   99
**Romano, grated, 1 Tbsp**
   *Buitoni*   21
   *Kraft*   26
**Roquefort**
   *Borden*   107
   *Kraft*   105
**Sap Sago**
   *Kraft*   76
**Sardo Romano**
   *Kraft*   110
**Scamorze**
   *Kraft*   100

⎡**2**

## Swiss
   *Borden*     104
   *Dorman*     90
   *Kraft*     104
## Sage
   *Kraft*     113
## Tilsit
   *Dorman*     95

# Cheese Food

## American
   *Borden*     92
   *Kraft*     77
## Blue
   *Borden*     82
   *Borden Vera Blue*     91
   *Wispride*     100
## Cheddar
   *Wispride*     100
## Jalapeno pepper
   *Kraft*     93
## Munst-ett
   *Kraft*     101
## Pimiento
   *Borden*     91
   *Pauley Swiss*     90
   *Velveeta*     90
## Pizza
   *Kraft*     80

**Sharp**
  *Kraft*                                        93
**Swiss**
  *Borden*                                       91
  *Kraft*                                        91


# Cheese Spread

**American**
  *Borden*                                       85
  *Kraft*                                        77
  *Kraft Old English*                            97
**American with Bacon**
  *Borden*                                       80
  *Kraft*                                        92
**Blue**
  *Borden*                                       82
  *Roka*                                         80
  *Wispride*                                     92
**Cheddar**
  *Snack Mate*                                   85
  *Wispride*                                     97
**Garlic**
  *Borden*                                       82
  *Kraft*                                        86
**Limburger**
  *Borden*                                       82

⌐2

| | |
|---|---|
| *Mohawk Valley* | 70 |
| *Moose* | 70 |
| **Pimiento** | |
| *Cheez Whiz* | 76 |
| *Kraft* | 77 |
| *Snack Mate* | 90 |
| **Smoked** | |
| *Borden* | 80 |
| *Velveeta* | 80 |

# CREAM, 1 Tbsp

| | |
|---|---|
| **half and half** | |
| *Borden* | 19 |
| *Meadow Gold* | 27 |
| *Sealtest* | 20 |
| **light** | |
| *Borden* | 25 |
| *Foremost* | 30 |
| *Sealtest* | 35 |
| **medium** | |
| *Borden* | 41 |
| *Sealtest* | 42 |
| **heavy (whipping)** | |
| *Borden* | 52 |

| | |
|---|---|
| *Foremost* | 52 |
| *Lucerne* | 10 |
| *Sealtest* | 52 |

## Sour Cream, 1 Tbsp

| | |
|---|---|
| **Borden** | 29 |
| **Borden** half and half | 29 |
| **Borden** imitation | 25 |
| **Foremost** | 30 |
| **Sealtest** | 29 |

## Non-Dairy Creamers, 1 Tsp

**coffee creamers**

| | |
|---|---|
| *Carnation Coffee-Mate* | 11 |
| *Meadow Gold* | 9 |
| *Pet Cremora* | 11 |

**whipped toppings**

| | |
|---|---|
| *Reddi-Whip* | 7 |
| *Sta-Whip* | 8 |

# EGGS

**Chicken**

raw, boiled, or poached

| | |
|---|---|
| medium | 72 |
| large | 82 |
| extra large | 94 |

raw, white only

| | |
|---|---|
| medium | 15 |
| large | 18 |
| extra large | 20 |
| 1 cup | 125 |

raw, yolk only

| | |
|---|---|
| medium | 53 |
| large | 60 |
| extra large | 68 |

fried

| | |
|---|---|
| medium | 85 |
| large | 97 |
| extra large | 113 |

scrambled or omelet

| | |
|---|---|
| medium | 99 |
| large | 110 |
| extra large | 127 |

| | |
|---|---|
| **Duck, raw** | 130 |
| **Goose, raw** | 266 |
| **Turkey, raw** | 135 |

# 2

# Egg Mixes, Commercial

**Imitation**
  *Morningstar Farms Scramblers*, ½ cup     130
  *Tillie Lewis Eggstra*, 1 pkt     101
  *Fleishmann Egg Beaters*, ½ cup     81
**Omelets, 1 pkt**
  Plain
    *Durkee*     604
    *Durkee* dry mix     112
  with bacon
    *Durkee*     620
    *Durkee* dry mix     125
  with cheese
    *Durkee*     617
    *Durkee* dry mix     127
    *McCormick*     130
    *Schilling*     128
  Western
    *Durkee*     604
    *Durkee* dry mix     112
    *McCormick*     115
    *Schilling*     115
**Scrambled**
  *Durkee*     124
  with bacon
    *Durkee*     180
  with sausage and potatoes
    *Swanson*     452

# MILK, 8 oz

**Buttermilk**
  *Borden*
    .1% fat                                      88
    .5% fat                                      90
    1% fat                                      107
    1.5% fat                                    110
    2% fat                                      122
    3% fat                                      158
  *Friendship* 1.4% fat                         120
  *Golden Nugget* .8%                            92
  *Light 'n Lively* .8% fat                      95
  *Lucerne* 1.5% fat                            120
  *Sealtest* 2% fat                             114
**Skim**
  *Borden* .1% fat                               81
  *Lucerne*
    0% fat                                       90
    1% fat                                      110
    2% fat                                      130
  *Meadow Gold*
    .5% fat                                      87
    2% fat                                      130
  *Sealtest* .1% fat                             79
**Skim Fortified**
  *Borden*                                       81
  *Borden Lite Line*                            117
  *Borden Hi Protein*                           132

| | |
|---|---|
| *Gail Borden* | 81 |
| *Light 'n Lively* | 114 |
| *Sealtest* | 137 |
| **Whole** | |
| *Borden* | 160 |
| *Foremost* | 154 |
| *Lucerne* | 160 |
| *Meadow Gold* | 166 |
| *Sealtest* | 150 |
| **Whole Fortified** | |
| *Gail Borden* | 159 |
| *Sealtest Multivitamin* | 151 |

## Milk Beverages, 8 oz unless noted

| | |
|---|---|
| **Cherry-vanilla** | |
| *Borden* | 291 |
| **Chocolate** | |
| *Borden* | 210 |
| *Meadow Gold* | 190 |
| *Sealtest* | 175 |
| **Chocolate fudge** | |
| *Borden* | 284 |
| **Chocolate mixes** | |
| *Carnation Instant*, 1 pkt | 130 |
| *Carnation Slender*, 1 pkt | 110 |
| *Nestle's Quik* | 215 |

**2**

*Ovaltine*, 1 oz      105
*Pillsbury*, 1 pkt      295
*Safeway*, 2 tsp      215
*Sealtest*      195
**Chocolate malt mix**
*Carnation Instant*, 1 pkt      130
*Carnation Slender*, 1 pkt      110
**Eggnog, dairy packed**
*Borden*
  4.7% fat      260
  6% fat      302
  8% fat      375
*Carnation*, 1 pkt      130
*Meadow Gold*      327
*Sealtest*      324
**Malt**
*Borden*      80
*Carnation*      90
*Ovaltine*      100
**Mocha**
*Borden*      291
**Strawberry**
*Borden*      287
*Carnation*, 1 pkt      130
*Pillsbury*, 1 pkt      290
**Vanilla**
*Borden*      291
*Carnation*, 1 pkt      130

# YOGURT, 8 oz

**Plain**

| | |
|---|---|
| *Borden Lite-Line* | 140 |
| *Borden Swiss Style* | 167 |
| *Breakstone* | 144 |
| *Dannon* | 150 |
| *Light 'n Lively* | 140 |
| *Lucerne* | 160 |
| *Pet* | 157 |
| *Viva* | 180 |

**Flavored, all flavors**

| | |
|---|---|
| *Borden* | 270 |
| *Breyer's* | 270 |
| *Dannon* | 210 |
| *Light 'n Lively* | 240 |
| *Meadow Gold* | 270 |
| *Viva* | 250 |

**Frozen**

*Danny*

| | |
|---|---|
| In-A-Cup, 8 oz. | 180 |
| On-A-Stick, uncoated | 65 |

# CHAPTER 3

# *Breads, Crackers, Flour*

## BREAD, 1 slice, approximately 1 oz unless noted

**Bran**
  *Brownberry*                                    75
**Corn & Molasses**
  *Pepperidge Farm*                               71
**Cinnamon Raisin**
  *Thomas*                                        60
**Cracked Wheat**
  *Pepperidge Farm*                               66

| | |
|---|---:|
| *Tasty Bake* | 70 |
| **Date Nut** | |
| *Thomas* | 100 |
| **French** | |
| *Pepperidge Farm* | 79 |
| *Wonder* | 75 |
| **Garlic** | |
| *Stouffer* | 80 |
| **Gluten** | |
| *Thomas* | 32 |
| *Hollywood* | 70 |
| **Honey Bran** | |
| *Pepperidge Farm* | 58 |
| **Honey Wheatberry** | |
| *Arnold* | 90 |
| *Pepperidge Farm* | 60 |
| **Italian** | |
| *Pepperidge Farm* | 81 |
| *Naturel* | |
| *Arnold* | 65 |
| **Nut** | |
| *Brownberry* | 85 |
| **Oatmeal** | |
| *Brownberry* | 82 |
| *Pepperidge Farm* | 66 |
| *Profile* | 52 |
| **Protein** | |
| *Thomas* | 45 |
| **Pumpernickel** | |
| *Arnold* | 75 |

$\overline{3}$

| | |
|---|---|
| *Pepperidge Farm* | 79 |
| **Raisin** | |
| Plain | |
| *Arnold* | 75 |
| *Thomas* | 66 |
| with cinnamon | |
| *Brownberry* | 85 |
| *Pepperidge Farm* | 75 |
| *Thomas* | 65 |
| with nuts | |
| *Brownberry* | 95 |
| **Rice Cakes** | |
| *Spiral* | 36 |
| **Rye** | |
| *Arnold* | 50 |
| Jewish | 75 |
| soft | 75 |
| *Brownberry* | 65 |
| *Pepperidge Farm* | 82 |
| *Tasty Bake* | 91 |
| *Wonder* | 75 |
| **Sourdough** | |
| *Di Carlo* | 71 |
| **Wheat** | |
| *Arnold* | |
| *Granary* | 71 |
| *Branola* | 90 |
| *Brick Oven* | 60 |
| *Melba* Thin | 40 |
| *Brownberry* | 85 |

**3**

| | |
|---|---|
| *Buckwheat* | 75 |
| *Colonial* | 72 |
| *Home Pride* | 75 |
| *Pepperidge Farm* | 70 |
| *Pepperidge Farm* Very Thin | 40 |
| *Thomas* | 50 |
| *Wonder* | 75 |

**Wheat Germ**
| | |
|---|---|
| *Pepperidge Farm* | 69 |

**White**
| | |
|---|---|
| *Arnold* | |
|    *Brick Oven,* .8 oz slice | 65 |
|    *Brick Oven,* 1.1 oz slice | 85 |
|    *Country* | 95 |
|    *Hearthstone Country* | 70 |
|    *Melba* Thin | 40 |
| *Brownberry Sandwich* | 75 |
| *Brownberry Thin* | 70 |
| *Butternut* | 75 |
| *Colonial* | 75 |
| *Daffodil Farm* | 58 |
| *Fresh Horizons* | 50 |
| *Hart* | 75 |
| *Heartstone* | 85 |
| *Home Pride* | 75 |
| *Homestyle* | 75 |
| *Manor* | 75 |
| *Pepperidge Farm* | 75 |
| *Pepperidge Farm* Sandwich | 72 |
| *Sweetheart* | 75 |

**3**

| | |
|---|---|
| *Tasty Bake* | 72 |
| *Thomas* | 64 |
| *Weight Watchers* | 35 |
| *Wonder* | 75 |
| **Whole Wheat** | |
| *Pepperidge Farm* | 61 |
| *Thomas* | 65 |

# Bread, Canned, ½ inch slice

| | |
|---|---|
| **Banana Nut** | |
| *Dromedary* | 71 |
| **Brown** | |
| *B&M* | 52 |
| **Chocolate Nut** | |
| *Cross & Blackwell* | 65 |
| *Dromedary* | 87 |
| **Date Nut** | |
| *Dromedary* | 75 |
| **Fruit and Nut** | |
| *Cross & Blackwell* | 77 |
| **Orange Nut** | |
| *Cross & Blackwell* | 76 |
| *Dromedary* | 78 |
| **Spice Nut** | |
| *Cross & Blackwell* | 65 |

# 3

## Bread Mixes

**White, ¼ loaf**
*Pillsbury*     460
**Cornbread, 1 pkg**
*Pillsbury*     320
*Aunt Jemima*     330

# BISCUITS, MUFFINS AND ROLLS

## Biscuits, Baking Powder, 1 biscuit

*1869 Brand*     105
prebaked     100
*Pillsbury*     70
*Tenderflake*     60

## Biscuits, refrigerated, 1 biscuit

**Plain**
*Ballard*     50
*Borden*     59
*Hungry Jack*     95
Flaky     90

## 3

| | |
|---|---|
| *Pillsbury* | 55 |
| Flaky Baking Powder | 67 |
| *Tenderflake* | |
| Baking Powder | 60 |
| **Buttermilk** | |
| *Hungry Jack* | |
| Extra Rich | 65 |
| Flaky | 80 |
| Fluffy | 100 |
| *Pillsbury* | 50 |
| Big Country | 95 |
| Extra Light | 55 |
| *Tenderflake* | 55 |
| **Corn Bread** | |
| *Pillsbury* | 95 |

# Muffins, frozen, 1 muffin

| | |
|---|---|
| **Blueberry** | |
| *Thomas* | 110 |
| *Howard Johnson* | 121 |
| *Morton* | 120 |
| *Rounds* | 110 |
| *Pepperidge Farm* | 130 |
| **Corn** | |
| *Howard Johnson* | 118 |
| *Morton* | |
| regular | 130 |

| | |
|---|---|
| Rounds | 125 |
| *Pepperidge Farm* | 140 |
| *Thomas* | 120 |
| **English** | |
| *Thomas* | 130 |
| **Orange** | |
| *Howard Johnson* | 115 |
| **Raisin Bran** | |
| *Pepperidge Farm* | 130 |

## Muffins, Mix, 1 muffin

| | |
|---|---|
| **Apple Cinnamon** | |
| *Betty Crocker* | 160 |
| **Banana Nut** | |
| *Betty Crocker* | 185 |
| **Blueberry** | |
| *Betty Crocker* | 120 |
| **Corn** | |
| *Betty Crocker* | 160 |
| **Orange** | |
| *Betty Crocker* | 155 |
| **Pineapple** | |
| *Betty Crocker* | 125 |

**3**

# Muffins, packaged

**Bran**
*Thomas* 118
**Cinnamon Raisin**
*Pepperidge Farm* 140
**Corn**
*Thomas* 180
*Toast-r-Cakes* 120
**English**
*Di Carlo* 145
*Hostess* 145
*Thomas* 140
*Wonder* 144
**Honey Butter**
*Arnold Orowheat* 150
**Onion**
*Thomas* 130
**Raisin**
*Wonder* 155
**Sourdough**
*Wonder* 130
**Wheat**
*Home Pride* 140

# 3)

## Muffins, refrigerated, 1 muffin

**Apple Cinnamon**
*Pillsbury* 155
**Corn**
*Pillsbury* 130

## Rolls, 1 roll

**Hard Rolls**
*Pepperidge Farm* 120
French, 3 oz 264
French, 5 oz 395
*Hearth* 64
Sesame Crisp 76
*Wonder* 82
**Sandwich and Hamburger Rolls**
*Arnold*
Dutch Egg Buns 130
*Francisco* 180
Soft 110
Hamburger 110
Hot Dog 110
*Colonial* 160
*Pepperidge Farm* 120
*Wonder* 160
**Soft Rolls**
*Arnold*

**3**

| | |
|---|---|
| *Deli-Twist* | 110 |
| Finger, 24's and 12's | 55 |
| *Francisco* | 100 |
| Refrigerator | 95 |
| *Ballard* | 95 |
| *Borden* | |
| Gem Flake | 70 |
| Onion | 95 |
| *Colonial* | 80 |
| *Home Pride* | 90 |
| *Pepperidge Farm* | |
| Butter Crescent | 130 |
| Dinner | 65 |
| Finger | 60 |
| Golden Twist | 120 |
| Old Fashioned | 37 |
| Parkerhouse | 60 |
| Party | 35 |
| *Pillsbury* | |
| Butterflake | 110 |
| Crescent | 95 |
| Hot Roll Mix | 95 |
| *Wonder* | |
| Buttermilk | 85 |
| Pan | 105 |
| **Sweet Rolls, refrigerated** | |
| Caramel | |
| *Pillsbury* | 160 |
| Cinnamon | |
| *Ballard* | 100 |

*Hungry Jack*     145
*Pillsbury*     114
Orange
    *Pillsbury*     130
Scones
    *Hostess*     188

# CRACKERS, 1 piece

**Bacon Flavored**
    *Keebler*     15
    *Nabisco Bacon Thins*     11
**Barbecue**
    *Chit Chat*     14
    *Sunshine*     17
**Butter**
    *Hi-Ho*     17
    *Keebler*
       Butter Thins     17
       Club     15
       Townhouse     19
    *Nabisco*     15
    *Ritz*     17
    *Tam-Tams*     13
**Butter-cheese**
    *Ritz*     18

**3**

**Caraway**
*Caraway Crazy* 15
**Cheese**
*Cheese-Nips* 5
*Cheese Tid-Bits* 4
*Cheez-It* 6
*Che-Zo* 5
*Keebler* 11
*Pepperidge Farm* 12
**Cheese-peanut Butter**
*Keebler* 14
**Chicken**
*Chicken In a Biskit* 10
**Club**
*Keebler* 15
**Flings Curls**
*Nabisco* 10
**Gold Fish**
*Pepperidge Farm, 1 oz* 140
**Ham**
*Nabisco* 12
**Hi-Ho**
*Sunshine* 18
**Kavli Flatbread** 35
**Matzos**
*Goodman's Square* 110
*Goodman's Tea* 75
*Horowitz-Margareten* 130
*Manischewitz*
　Egg 132

| | |
|---|---|
| Egg 'N Onion | 113 |
| Regular | 110 |
| Tam Tams | 14 |
| Tasteas | 115 |
| Thin Tea | 110 |
| Whole Wheat | 122 |

**Onion**
| | |
|---|---|
| *Keebler* | 15 |
| *Manischewitz* | 13 |
| *Nabisco* | 13 |
| French Onion | 12 |
| *Pepperidge Farm* | 12 |

**Potato**
| | |
|---|---|
| *Chippers* | 14 |
| *Potato Piffles* | 17 |

**Ritz**
| | |
|---|---|
| *Nabisco* | 17 |

**Rye**
| | |
|---|---|
| *Keebler* Rye Toast | 18 |
| *Peek Frean* | 30 |
| *Ry Krisp* | 24 |

**Saltines**
| | |
|---|---|
| *Jacob's* | |
| Biscuits for Cheese | 35 |
| English Cream | 110 |
| *Keebler* | |
| Salt-Free | 15 |
| Saltines | 14 |
| Sea Toast | 60 |
| Whole Wheat Sea Toast | 58 |

*Nabisco*
  Premium                       12
  Royal Lunch                   54
  Uneeda                        22
*Sunshine*                      11

**Sesame**
  *Keebler*                     16
  *Meal Mates*                  22
  *Sesame Sillys*               15
  *Sunshine*                    24

**Shapies**                     10

**Sip'N Chips**                 10

**Sociables**
  Nabisco                       10

**Toasts**
  *Dutch Rusk*                  60
  *Holland Rusk*                39
  *Keebler*                     15
  *Old London*                  11
  *Pepperidge Farm*             11
  *Sunshine All-Rye*            21

**Soda and water crackers**
  *Huntley & Palmer*            35
  *Jacob's Golden Puffs*        34
  *Keebler Milk Lunch*          27
  *Waldorf*                     18
  *Zesta*                       14

**Tomato-onion**
  *Sunshine*                    15

**Town House**
  *Keebler*                                    15
**Triangle Thins**
  *Nabisco*                                     8
**Twig?**
  *Nabisco*                                    14
**Waffle crackers**                            22
**Waverly wafers**
  *Nabisco*                                    18
**Wheat**
  *Nabisco*
    *Wheat Toast*                              15
    *Wheat Thins*                               9
**Zwieback**
  *Nabisco*                                    31

# OTHER BREAD PRODUCTS

**Breadcrumbs, 1 cup**                        450

*Contadina*                                   450
*4C* plain                                    410
*4C* seasoned                                 400

# Breadsticks, 1 piece

**onion**
  *Stella D'Oro*    35
**plain**
  *Stella D'Oro*    40
**sesame**
  *Stella D'Oro*    38
**dietetic**
  *Stella D'Oro*    43

# Croutons, ½ cup unless noted

**bacon**
  *Bel Air*    80
  *Brownberry*    90
**cheese and garlic**
  *Bel Air*    100
**garlic**
  *Bel Air*    80
**Italian cheese**
  *Bel Air*    100
**plain**
  *Bel Air*    60
**seasoned**
  *Bel Air*    90
  *Brownberry*    90

## Stuffing, mixes, 1 pkg

| | |
|---|---|
| *Pepperidge Farm* | 110 |
| *Stove Top* | 170 |
| *Uncle Ben's* | 120 |

# FLOURS, 1 cup

| | |
|---|---|
| **Buckwheat** | |
| dark | 325 |
| light | 340 |
| **Cake** | 370 |
| **Carob** | 250 |
| **Corn** | 485 |
| **Corn Starch, 1 Tbsp** | 35 |
| **Lima Bean** | 430 |
| **Peanut** | 225 |
| **Rye** | |
| light | 315 |
| medium | 310 |
| dark | 420 |
| **Soybean, defatted** | 325 |
| full fat | 300 |
| low fat | 310 |
| **Tortilla** | |
| corn | 410 |

3

| | |
|---|---|
| wheat | 450 |
| **Wheat, all purpose** | 485 |
| bread | 500 |
| cake | 430 |
| gluten | 530 |
| self-rising | 440 |
| whole wheat | 400 |
| **White** | 400 |
| **Unbleached** | 400 |

## Meal, 1 cup

| | |
|---|---|
| **Almond** | 696 |
| **Corn** | 433 |
| **Cracker** | 450 |
| **Graham cracker** | 465 |
| **Matzo** | 444 |

# CHAPTER 4

# Cereal, Pancakes, Waffles and French Toast

## CEREAL, ready to eat, 1 cup

**bran**

| | |
|---|---|
| All-Bran, *Kellogg's* | 190 |
| 40% Bran Flakes, *Kellogg's* | 140 |
| 100% Bran Flakes, *Nabisco* | 150 |
| 40% Bran Flakes, *Post* | 125 |
| Bran Chex, *Ralston Purina* | 165 |
| Bran & Prune Flakes, *Post* | 120 |
| Bran & Raisin Flakes, *General Mills* | 125 |
| Raisin Bran, *Kellogg's* | 200 |
| Raisin Bran, *Ralston Purina* | 200 |
| Raisin Bran, *Safeway* | 200 |

| | |
|---|---:|
| Raisin Bran with Sugar Coating, *Post* | 178 |
| Bran-Buds with wheat germ, *Kellogg's* | 200 |

**corn**

| | |
|---|---:|
| Country Corn Flakes, *General Mills* | 80 |
| Kix, *General Mills* | 75 |
| Corn Flakes, *Kellogg's* | 110 |
| Toasties Corn Flakes, *Post* | 110 |
| Corn Chex, *Ralston Purina* | 110 |
| Corn Flakes, *Ralston Purina* | 110 |
| Corn Flakes, *Safeway* | 110 |
| Corn Flakes & Blueberries, *Post* | 110 |
| Corn Flakes & Strawberries, *Post* | 110 |
| Sugar Frosted Flakes, *Kellogg's* | 144 |
| Sugar Pops, *Kellogg's* | 105 |
| Honeycomb Corn, *Post* | 85 |
| Sugar Sparkled Flakes, *Post* | 149 |
| Cocoa Puffs, *General Mills* | 110 |
| Trix, *General Mills* | 111 |

**corn and oats**

| | |
|---|---:|
| Sugar Sparkled Twinkies, *General Mills* | 112 |
| Cap'n Crunch, *Quaker* | 163 |
| Crisp, *Quaker* | 105 |

**oats**

| | |
|---|---:|
| Cheerios, *General Mills* | 110 |
| OK's, *Kellogg's* | 83 |
| Alpha-Bits, *Post* | 110 |
| Crispy Critters, *Post* | 110 |
| Fortified Oat Flakes, *Post* | 165 |
| Life, *Quaker* | 160 |
| Lucky Charms, *General Mills* | 110 |

**4**

| | |
|---|---|
| Frosty O's, *General Mills* | 110 |
| Sugar Jets, *General Mills* | 111 |
| Stars, *Kellogg's* | 112 |
| Fruit Loops, *Kellogg's* | 112 |

**rice**

| | |
|---|---|
| Rice Krispies, *Kellogg's* | 105 |
| Puffed Rice, *Quaker* | 45 |
| Crispy Rice, *Ralston Purina* | 110 |
| Rice Chex, *Ralston* | 110 |
| Crispy Rice, *Safeway* | 110 |
| Puffa Puffa Rice, *Kellogg's* | 120 |
| Rice Honeys, *Nabisco* | 150 |
| Rice Krinkles, *Post* | 127 |
| Cocoa Crispies, *Kellogg's* | 113 |

**wheat**

| | |
|---|---|
| Buc Wheats, *General Mills* | 146 |
| Total, *General Mills* | 110 |
| Wheat Stax, *General Mills* | 81 |
| Wheaties, *General Mills* | 108 |
| Crumbles, *Kellogg's* | 140 |
| Pep, *Kellogg's* | 106 |
| Shredded Wheat, *Kellogg's* 1 biscuit | 63 |
| Shredded Wheat, *Nabisco* 1 biscuit | 92 |
| Grape Nuts Flakes, *Post* | 150 |
| Puffed Wheat, *Quaker* | 38 |
| Shredded Wheat, *Quaker* 1 biscuit | 68 |
| Wheat Chex, *Ralston Purina* | 165 |
| Sugar Crisp, *Kellogg's* | 147 |
| Sugar Smacks, *Kellogg's* | 110 |
| Wheat Honeys, *Nabisco* | 153 |

**4**

**mixed grains**

| | |
|---|---|
| Concentrate, *Kellogg's* | 310 |
| Product 19, *Kellogg's* | 106 |
| Special K, *Kellogg's* | 70 |
| Apple Jacks, *Kellogg's* | 112 |
| Team Flakes, *Nabisco* | 83 |
| Grape Nuts, *Post* | 400 |
| Quake, *Quaker* | 118 |

# Cereal, cooked, 1 cup

**barley**

| | |
|---|---|
| *Quaker* | 172 |

**corn meal mush**

| | |
|---|---|
| *Quaker* | 128 |

**farina**

*Cream of Wheat*

| | |
|---|---|
| Instant | 133 |
| Mix'N Eat | 140 |
| Quick | 133 |
| Regular | 133 |
| *H-O* | 168 |
| *Pillsbury* | 120 |
| *Quaker* | 100 |

**grits**

*Quaker*

| | |
|---|---|
| Instant | 79 |

**4**

| | |
|---|---|
| Instant with cheese flavor, 1 pkt | 105 |
| Instant with imitation bacon, 1 pkt | 100 |
| Instant with imitation ham, 1 pkt | 100 |
| *3-Minute Brand*, ¼ cup | 150 |
| **oats** | |
| *H-O* | 150 |
| *Quaker* | 160 |
| **oatmeal** | |
| *Quaker* | 143 |
| **rice** | |
| *Cream of Rice* | 145 |
| **rye** | |
| *Con Agra* | 360 |
| **whole wheat** | |
| *Quaker* Pettilohns | 145 |

# PANCAKES, FRENCH TOAST, WAFFLES AND OTHER BREAKFASTS, 1 piece unless noted

| | |
|---|---|
| **Breakfast Bars, frozen** | |
| *Carnation* | 210 |
| *General Mills* | 190 |

**4**

**Crepes, mix, 6″ crepe**
*Aunt Jemima*    55

**French Toast, frozen**
*Aunt Jemima*    85
   with cinnamon    100
*Downyflake*    135
*Swanson,* with sausage, 1 pkg    335

**French Toast, mix**
*McCormick*    119

**Fritters, frozen**
*Mrs. Paul's*    120

**Pancakes, frozen**
*Downyflake*    75
*Swanson,* with sausage, 1 pkg    500

**Pancakes, frozen batter**
*Aunt Jemima*    70

**Pancakes, mix, 4″ pancake**
*Aunt Jemima*
   Easy Pour    60
   buckwheat    80
   buttermilk    70
*Betty Crocker*    70
*Hungry Jack*    75
   blueberry    112
   buttermilk    80
   Extra Lights    60

**Pancake-Waffle, mix**
*Aunt Jemima*    70
   buttermilk    100
   whole wheat    80

$$\overline{\phantom{xx}4}$$

| | |
|---|---|
| *Log Cabin* | 60 |
| buttermilk | 75 |
| **Waffle, mix** | |
| *Aunt Jemima* | 100 |
| *Downyflake* | 60 |
| Jumbo | 89 |

# CHAPTER 5

# *Beans, Pasta and Rice*

## BARLEY, 1 cup

| | |
|---|---|
| pearled, light | 698 |
| pearled, Pot or Scotch | 696 |

## BEANS DRIED,
### 1 cup unless noted

| | |
|---|---|
| Broadbeans, raw, immature seeds, 8 oz | 238 |
| Broadbeans, raw, mature seeds, 8 oz | 768 |

**5**

| | |
|---|---|
| Black, dry, uncooked, 8 oz | 768 |
| Chick peas | |
|   8 oz | 817 |
|   1 cup | 720 |
| Great Northern | 212 |
| Lima, immature seeds | 190 |
| Lima, mature seeds, dried | 262 |
| Mung, dried | 714 |
| Pea or Navy, dried | 224 |
| Pinto (red Mexican), uncooked | 663 |
| Red Kidney | 220 |
| White, dried | 224 |

## Baked Beans, ½ cup

| | |
|---|---|
| *B & M* | 180 |
| *Campbell* | 148 |
|   barbecue | 171 |
|   with franks | 181 |
|   with pork | 147 |
| *Heinz* | 140 |
|   *Campside* | 180 |
|   with franks | 184 |
|   with pork | 150 |
| *Howard Johnson's* | 163 |
| *Morton House* | 160 |

5

# PASTA, 1 cup unless noted

## Dry

**egg noodles**

| | |
|---|---|
| *Goodman's* | 175 |
| *La Rosa* | 190 |
| *La Rosa* spinach | 200 |
| *Pennsylvania Dutch* | 200 |
| *Prince* | 190 |
| *Ronzoni* | 200 |

**macaroni**

| | |
|---|---|
| *Goodman's* | 170 |
| *La Rosa* | 180 |
| *Prince* | 170 |
| *Ronzoni* | 175 |

**spaghetti**

| | |
|---|---|
| *Buitoni* | 175 |
| *Goodman's* | 160 |
| *La Rosa* | 165 |
| *Prince* | 160 |
| *Ronzoni* | 165 |

# 5

# Macaroni, canned, bagged, frozen and mixes

**with beef**

| | |
|---|---|
| *Banquet* | 260 |
| *Chef Boy-Ar-Dee* | 235 |
| *Franco-American* | 220 |
| *Green Giant Boil-in-Bag*, 1 pkg | 240 |
| *Morton* | 260 |
| *Stouffer's*, 1 pkg | 380 |

**with beef and cheese**

| | |
|---|---|
| *Banquet* | 300 |
| *Green Giant Boil-in-Bag*, 1 pkg | 330 |
| *Hormel*, 7½ oz can | 340 |
| *Howard Johnson's* | 330 |
| *Morton* | 215 |
| *Mac-A-Roni & Cheddar* | 290 |
| *Pennsylvania Dutch* | 310 |
| *Stouffer's*, 1 pkg | 520 |
| *Swanson* | 200 |

**with cheese sauce**

| | |
|---|---|
| *Franco-American* | 225 |
| *Heinz* | 230 |
| *MacaroniO's* | 180 |
| *Noodle-Roni* | 290 |
| *Scallop-A-Roni* | 275 |

**with chili sauce**

| | |
|---|---|
| *Fiesta Mac-A-Roni* | 270 |

**creole style**

| | |
|---|---|
| *Heinz*, 8¾-oz can | 169 |

**5**

# Noodles, canned, frozen and mixes

**Almondine**
 *Betty Crocker,* 1 pkg       960
**with beef**
 *Heinz,* 8½ oz can       170
**with beef in gravy**
 *College Inn*       238
**with beef in tomato sauce**
 *College Inn*       238
**with beef**
 *Hormel,* 7½-oz can       240
**with beef sauce**
 *Pennsylvania Dutch*       260
 *Betty Crocker*       170
**with butter sauce**
 *Pennsylvania Dutch*       300
**with cheese**
 *Noodle-Roni*       650
**with cheese sauce**
 *Pennsylvania Dutch*       300
**with cheese sauce and sour cream**
 *Noodle-Roni Romanoff*       362
**with chicken**
 *Dinty Moore,* 7½-oz can       215
**with chicken sauce**
 *Noodle-Roni*       250
 *Pennsylvania Dutch*       300
 *Twist-A-Roni*       250

**Romanoff**
| | |
|---|---:|
| *Betty Crocker,* 1 pkg | 800 |
| *Stouffer's,* 1 pkg | 500 |

**Stroganoff**
| | |
|---|---:|
| *Betty Crocker,* 1 pkg | 900 |
| *Pennsylvania Dutch* | 630 |

**with tuna**
| | |
|---|---:|
| *Stouffer's,* 1 pkg | 400 |

# Noodles, Italian style, canned, frozen and mixes

**Cannelloni, 8 oz**
| | |
|---|---:|
| *Weight Watchers* | 275 |

**Eggplant Parmigiana, 8 oz**
| | |
|---|---:|
| *Buitoni* | 421 |
| *Weight Watchers* | 172 |

**Lasagna, 8 oz unless noted**
| | |
|---|---:|
| *Buitoni* | 250 |
| with meat sauce | 340 |
| *Chef Boy-Ar-Dee* | |
| canned | 241 |
| mix | 265 |
| *Golden Grain,* 1 pkg | 720 |
| *Green Giant* | |
| *Boil-in-Bag,* 1 pkg | 310 |
| *Oven Bake,* 1 pkg | 300 |
| *Hormel* | |
| 7½-oz can | 270 |
| 10-oz can | 370 |

| | |
|---|---|
| *Lean Cuisine,* 11 oz | 260 |
| *Lean Line,* 10 oz | 270 |
| *Roman* | 274 |
| *Stouffer's,* 1 pkg | 385 |
| *Swanson,* 1 pkg | 540 |
| *Weight Watchers* | 215 |

**Manicotti, 8 oz**
| | |
|---|---|
| *Buitoni* | 395 |
| with sauce | 350 |
| *Lean Line* | 270 |

**Ravioli, 8 oz**
| | |
|---|---|
| *Buitoni* | |
| cheese | 575 |
| meat | 680 |
| *Chef Boy-Ar-Dee* | |
| cheese | 263 |
| meat | 210 |
| *Franco-American,* 7½-oz can | 220 |
| *La Rosa* | |
| cheese | 205 |
| meat | 218 |
| *Roman* | |
| cheese | 496 |
| meat | 552 |

**Ravioli Parmigiana, 8 oz**
| | |
|---|---|
| *Buitoni* | |
| cheese | 301 |
| meat | 381 |

**Rotini**

| | |
|---|---|
| *Franco-American*, 7½-oz can | 200 |
| with meatballs | 230 |

**Shells**

| | |
|---|---|
| *Buitoni*, 8 oz | 235 |
| *Lean Line*, 11 oz | 270 |

**Spaghetti, all with tomato sauce, 1 cup unless noted**

| | |
|---|---|
| *Banquet* with meatballs | 212 |
| *Betty Crocker*, 1 pkg | 170 |
| *Buitoni* | |
| with meatballs | 250 |
| with mushrooms | 170 |
| *Chef Boy-Ar-Dee* | |
| with cheese sauce | 180 |
| with meat | 260 |
| with meat sauce | 250 |
| with meatballs | 250 |
| with mushrooms | 225 |
| *Franco-American* | |
| with cheese sauce | 200 |
| with meat | 290 |
| with meatballs | 260 |
| *Spaghetti-Os* | |
| with cheese | 200 |
| with meatballs | 228 |
| *Golden Grain* | 275 |
| *Green Giant, Boil-in-Bag* | |
| with meatballs | 280 |

*Heinz*
| | |
|---|---|
| with cheese sauce | 175 |
| with franks | 310 |
| with meat sauce | 173 |

*Hormel*
| | |
|---|---|
| with meat | 280 |
| with meat sauce | 205 |

| | |
|---|---|
| *Kraft* | 260 |
| *La Rosa* with meatballs | 230 |
| *Lean Cuisine* | 280 |
| *Libby's* with meatballs | 95 |
| *Morton*, frozen, 1 pkg | 220 |
| *Stouffer's*, 1 pkg | 445 |
| *Swanson*, 1 pkg | 290 |

**Ziti**
| | |
|---|---|
| *Buitoni*, 8 oz | 270 |
| *Lean Line*, 10 oz | 270 |
| *Weight Watchers*, 1 pkg | 350 |

# RICE, 1 cup unless noted

**Plain**
| | |
|---|---|
| *Ann Page*, whole pkg | 1000 |
| *Bird's Eye* | 260 |
| *Carolina* | 200 |

| | |
|---|---|
| *Green Giant* | 230 |
| *Minute* | 300 |
| *Rice-A-Roni,* whole pkg | 780 |
| *River* | 200 |
| *Uncle Ben's* | 200 |
| *Uncle Ben's,* brown | 250 |

**Flavored**

beef
  *Uncle Ben's* 210

beef and cracked rice
  *Betty Crocker* 416

beef and vermicelli
  *Minute* 300
  *Rice-A-Roni* 315

beef and cheese sauce
  *Betty Crocker* 350

chicken
  *Uncle Ben's* 210

chicken with crumb topping
  *Betty Crocker* 365

chicken and vermicelli
  *Minute* 300
  *Rice-A-Roni* 321

curry
  *Uncle Ben's* 205

fried Chinese and vermicelli
  *Rice-A-Roni* 375

ham and vermicelli
  *Rice-A-Roni* 300

**5**

pilaf
   *Uncle Ben's*     290
**Frozen**
   *Green Giant*     160
     Medley     220
     Pilaf     240
     Verdi     140
**Spanish, canned**
   *Heinz*     190
   *La Rosa*     155
   *Libby's*     57
   *Stokely-Van Camp*     180

# Bulgur (parboiled wheat), 1 cup

**Club Wheat, dry**     630
**Hard Red Winter Wheat, dry**     605
   canned, unseasoned     225
   seasoned     246
**White Wheat, dry**     555

# CHAPTER 6

# *Soup*

## CANNED OR FROZEN,
### 1 cup unless noted

97

with bacon

| | |
|---|---:|
| *Ann Page* | 140 |
| *Campbell's* | 174 |
| *Town House* | 155 |

with hot dogs

| | |
|---|---:|
| *Campbell's* | 168 |

with smoked pork

| | |
|---|---:|
| *Heinz* | 160 |

**Bean, black**

| | |
|---|---:|
| *Campbell's* | 95 |
| *Crosse & Blackwell* | 118 |

**Bean, lima**

| | |
|---|---:|
| *Manischewitz* | 93 |

**Beef**

plain

| | |
|---|---:|
| *Campbell's* | 105 |
| *Lipton* | 200 |

with barley

| | |
|---|---:|
| *Manischewitz* | 83 |
| *Wyler's* | 72 |

with cabbage

| | |
|---|---:|
| *Manischewitz* | 62 |

with low sodium

| | |
|---|---:|
| *Campbell's*, 7¼-oz can | 170 |

mushroom

| | |
|---|---:|
| *Lipton* | 45 |

with noodles

| | |
|---|---:|
| *Campbell's* | 69 |
| *Heinz* | 74 |
| *Manischewitz* | 65 |

**6**

| | |
|---|---|
| *Lipton* | 67 |
| *Souptime*, 1 envelope | 30 |
| *Town House* | 75 |
| *Wyler's* | 50 |
| with vegetables | |
| *Manischewitz* | 61 |
| **Borscht** | |
| *Manischewitz* | 72 |
| *Rokeach* | 75 |
| **Bouillon, 1 cube** | |
| beef | |
| *Herb-Ox* | 6 |
| *Knorr-Swiss* | 15 |
| *Maggi* | 6 |
| *Wyler's* | 7 |
| chicken | |
| *Herb-Ox* | 6 |
| *Knorr-Swiss* | 17 |
| *Maggi* | 7 |
| *Wyler's* | 8 |
| onion | |
| *Herb-Ox* | 10 |
| *Wyler's* | 8 |
| vegetable | |
| *Herb-Ox* | 6 |
| *Wyler's* | 6 |
| **Bouillon, instant, 1 tsp** | |
| beef | |
| *Maggi* | 6 |
| *Wyler's* | 10 |

chicken
*Maggi*                                           7
*Wyler's*                                         6
**Broth**
beef
*Campbell's*                                      26
*College Inn*                                     15
*Swanson*, 6¾-oz can                             25
*Weight Watchers*, 1 pkt                          10
chicken
*Campbell's*                                      43
*College Inn*                                     32
*Richardson & Robbins*                           17
*Swanson*, 6¼-oz can                             25
chicken with noodles
*College Inn*                                     45
chicken with rice
*College Inn*                                     45
*Richardson & Robbins*                           45
**Celery, cream of**
*Ann Page*                                        60
*Campbell's*                                      160
*Heinz*                                           180
*Town House*                                      100
**Cheddar cheese**
*Campbell's*                                      150
**Chickarina**
*Progresso*                                       100
**Chicken**
*Lipton*                                          220

**Chicken alphabet**
*Campbell's*                                     88
**Chicken with barley**
*Manischewitz*                                   83
**Chicken, cream of**
*Ann Page*                                       90
*Lipton*                                        106
*Souptime*, 1 pkt                               100
*Town House*                                     95
**Chicken with dumplings**
*Campbell's*                                    100
**Chicken gumbo**
*Campbell's*                                     59
**Chicken with kasha**
*Manischewitz*                                   41
**Chicken with low sodium**
*Campbell's*, 7½-oz can                         170
**Chicken noodle**
*A & P*                                          67
*Ann Page*                                       70
*Campbell's*                                     66
*Golden Grain*                                   74
*Heinz*                                          35
*Lipton*                                         54
*Manischewitz*                                   46
*Souptime*, 1 pkt                                30
*Town House*                                     75
*Wyler's*                                        44
**Chicken with rice**
*Ann Page*                                       50

| | |
|---|---|
| *Campbell's* | 51 |
| *Heinz* | 58 |
| *Lipton* | 59 |
| *Manischewitz* | 48 |
| *Town House* | 60 |
| *Wyler's* | 49 |

**Chicken with stars**

| | |
|---|---|
| *Ann Page* | 65 |
| *Campbell's* | 60 |

**Chicken with vegetables**

| | |
|---|---|
| *Ann Page* | 80 |
| *Campbell's* | 73 |
| *Heinz* | 85 |
| *Lipton* | 70 |
| *Manischewitz* | 55 |
| *Town House* | 85 |
| *Wyler's*, mix | 28 |

**Chili, with beef**

| | |
|---|---|
| *Campbell's* | 165 |
| *Heinz* | 160 |
| *Town House* | 160 |

**Chowder**

clam, Manhattan

| | |
|---|---|
| *Campbell's* | 77 |
| *Doxsee* | 62 |
| *Heinz* | 74 |
| *Howard Johnson's* | 104 |
| *Crosse & Blackwell* | 75 |

clam, New England

| | |
|---|---|
| *Campbell's* | 206 |

**Mushroom**
Plain
| | |
|---|---|
| *Campbell's* | 80 |
| *Golden Grain* | 95 |
| *Souptime* | 80 |
| *Wyler's* | 151 |

with barley
| | |
|---|---|
| *Manischewitz* | 72 |

bisque
| | |
|---|---|
| *Crosse & Blackwell* | 127 |

cream of
| | |
|---|---|
| *Ann Page* | 120 |
| *Campbell's* | 217 |
| *Heinz* | 200 |
| *Knorr-Swiss* | 116 |
| *Lipton* | 92 |
| *Town House* | 124 |
| *Wyler's* | 151 |

**Noodle**
| | |
|---|---|
| *Lipton* | 50 |

with chicken broth
| | |
|---|---|
| *Ann Page*, 1 pkt | 225 |
| *Lipton* | 60 |

with ground beef
| | |
|---|---|
| *Campbell's* | 98 |

**Onion**
| | |
|---|---|
| *Ann Page*, 1 pkt | 125 |
| *Crosse & Blackwell* | 57 |
| *Golden Grain* | 33 |

**6**

| | |
|---|---|
| *Knorr-Swiss* | 45 |
| *Lipton* | 35 |
| *Souptime,* 1 pkt | 20 |
| *Wyler's* | 146 |
| **Onion with mushroom** | |
| *Lipton* | 35 |
| **Oriental style** | |
| *Lipton* | 210 |
| **Oyster stew** | |
| *Campbell's* | |
| canned | 146 |
| frozen | 196 |
| **Pea** | |
| green | |
| *Campbell's* | 148 |
| *Golden Grain* | 73 |
| *Knorr-Swiss* | 71 |
| *Lipton* | 136 |
| *Souptime* low sodium, 1 pkt | 70 |
| with ham | |
| *Campbell's* | 130 |
| low sodium, 7½-oz can | 150 |
| split | |
| *Manischewitz* | 133 |
| split with ham | |
| *Ann Page* | 180 |
| *Campbell's* | 180 |
| *Heinz* | 150 |
| *Town House* | 154 |

**Pepper pot**
  *Campbell's*      105
**Petite Marmite**
  *Crosse & Blackwell*      41
**Potato**
  Plain
    *Lipton*      100
  cream of
    *Campbell's*      190
  with leek
    *Wyler's*      155
**Schav**
  *Manischewitz*      11
  *Rokeach*      12
**Scotch broth**
  *Campbell's*      90
**Senegalese**
  *Crosse & Blackwell*      75
**Shrimp, cream of**
  *Crosse & Blackwell*      113
  *Campbell's*      230
**Sirloin burger**
  *Campbell's*      177
**Steak and potato**
  *Campbell's*      160
**Stockpot**
  vegetable
    *Lipton*      220
  vegetable-beef
    *Campbell's*      96

**Tomato**
| | |
|---|---|
| Ann Page | 80 |
| Campbell's | 84 |
| Heinz | 87 |
| Lipton | 93 |
| Manischewitz | 61 |
| Progresso | 110 |
| Souptime, 1 pkt | 70 |
| Town House | 87 |

**Tomato bisque**
| | |
|---|---|
| Campbell's | 126 |

**Tomato**
low sodium
| | |
|---|---|
| Campbell's 7¼-oz can | 130 |

with rice
| | |
|---|---|
| Ann Page | 90 |
| Campbell's | 106 |
| Manischewitz | 78 |

with vegetables
| | |
|---|---|
| Golden Grain | 86 |
| Lipton | 69 |

**Tuna Creole**
| | |
|---|---|
| Crosse & Blackwell | 70 |

**Turkey**
Plain
| | |
|---|---|
| Campbell's | 138 |

with noodles
| | |
|---|---|
| Ann Page | 75 |

| | |
|---|---:|
| *Heinz* | 83 |
| *Lipton* | 74 |
| *Town House* | 83 |
| low sodium | |
| *Campbell's,* 7¼-oz can | 60 |
| with vegetables | |
| *Ann Page* | 60 |
| *Campbell's* | 78 |
| **Vegetable** | |
| Plain | |
| *Ann Page* | 70 |
| *Campbell's* | 83 |
| Old Fashioned | 74 |
| *Lipton* | 70 |
| Italian | 100 |
| *Knorr-Swiss* | 56 |
| *Manischewitz* | 63 |
| *Town House* | 83 |
| *Wyler's* | 81 |
| with beef | |
| *Ann Page* | 80 |
| *Campbell's* | 81 |
| low sodium, 7¼-oz can | 80 |
| Old Fashioned | 79 |
| *Heinz* | 66 |
| *Lipton* | 53 |
| *Town House* | 66 |
| cream of | |
| *Souptime,* 1 pkt | 80 |

Soup

$\sqrt{6}$

# CHAPTER 7

# Meat, Poultry and Seafood

## MEAT, FRESH

Retail cuts of meat are frequently weighed with bone first, *then* they are trimmed, cooked and weighed for their yield. So for instance 1 lb. of pork loin chops are weighed raw with bone, but after they are trimmed and cooked, their yield is 5.9 oz.

# 7

## Beef, choice-grade, retail cuts

**Chuck, arm, roast, or steak; boneless, lean with fat**
raw, 1 lb     1,012
braised, drained
    10.7 oz (yield from 1 lb)     879
    4 oz     328
    1 cup, chopped     405
    1 cup, ground     318
**Chuck, arm, roast, or steak, lean only**
braised, drained
    9.1 oz (yield from 1 lb)     498
    4 oz     219
    1 cup, chopped     270
    1 cup, diced     212
**Chuck, rib roast or steak, lean with fat**
raw, 1 lb     1,597
braised, drained
    10.7 oz (yield from 1 lb)     1,298
    4 oz     484
    1 cup, chopped     598
    1 cup, ground     470
**Chuck, stewing; boneless, lean with fat**
raw, 1 lb     1,166
stewed, drained
    10.7 oz (yield from 1 lb)     994
    4 oz     371
    1 cup, chopped     458
**Chuck, stewing; boneless, lean only**
raw, 1 lb     717

**7**

| | |
|---|---:|
| stewed, drained | |
| 10.7 oz (yield from 1 lb) | 651 |
| 4 oz | 243 |
| 1 cup, chopped | 300 |
| **Club steak, 16% bone, lean with fat** | |
| raw, 1 lb | 1,443 |
| broiled | |
| 9.8 oz (yield from 1 lb raw) | 1,262 |
| 4 oz without bone | 515 |
| **Club steak, 16% bone, lean only** | |
| broiled | |
| 5.7 oz (yield from 1 lb) | 393 |
| 4 oz without bone | 277 |
| **Flank steak, boneless, lean only** | |
| raw, 1 lb | 653 |
| braised, drained | |
| 10.7 oz (yield from 1 lb) | 596 |
| 4 oz | 222 |
| **Ground, lean with 10% fat** | |
| raw, 1 lb | 812 |
| broiled, 12 oz (yield from 1 lb) | 745 |
| **Ground, lean with 21% fat** | |
| raw, 1 lb | 1,216 |
| broiled, 11.5 oz (yield from 1 lb) | 932 |
| **Plate, boneless, lean with fat** | |
| raw, 1 lb | 1,216 |
| simmered, drained | |
| 10.7 oz (yield from 1 lb) | 1,313 |
| 4 oz | 490 |

**Plate, boneless, lean only**
  simmered, drained
    6.5 oz (yield from 1 lb)      368
    4 oz      226
**Porterhouse steak, 9% bone, lean with fat**
  raw, 1 lb      1,603
  broiled
    10.6 oz (yield from 1 lb)      1,400
    4 oz without bone      527
**Porterhouse steak, 9% bone, lean only**
  broiled
    6.1 oz (yield from 1 lb)      385
    4 oz without bone      254
**Rib roast, boneless, lean with fat**
  raw, 1 lb      1,819
  roasted
    11.7 oz (yield from 1 lb)      1,456
    4 oz      499
    1 cup, chopped      616
    1 cup, ground      484
**Rib roast, boneless, lean only**
  roasted
    7.5 oz (yield from 1 lb)      511
    4 oz      273
    1 cup, chopped      337
    1 cup, ground      265
**Round steak, boneless, lean with fat**
  raw, 1 lb      894
  braised or broiled
    11.1 oz (yield from 1 lb)      820

| | |
|---|---:|
| 4 oz | 296 |

**Round steak, boneless, lean only**
braised or broiled

| | |
|---|---:|
| 9.5 oz (yield from 1 lb) | 507 |
| 4 oz | 296 |

**Rump roast, boneless, lean with fat**

| | |
|---|---:|
| raw, 1 lb | 1,374 |

roasted

| | |
|---|---:|
| 11.7 oz (yield from 1 lb) | 1,149 |
| 4 oz | 394 |
| 1 cup, chopped | 486 |
| 1 cup, ground | 382 |

**Rump roast, boneless, lean only**
roasted

| | |
|---|---:|
| 8.8 oz (yield from 1 lb) | 516 |
| 4 oz | 236 |
| 1 cup, chopped | 291 |
| 1 cup, ground | 229 |

**Sirloin steak, double bone, 18% bone, lean with fat**

| | |
|---|---:|
| raw, 1 lb | 1,240 |

broiled

| | |
|---|---:|
| 9.6 oz (yield from 1 lb) | 1,110 |
| 4 oz without bone | 463 |

**Sirloin steak, double bone, 18% bone, lean only**
broiled

| | |
|---|---:|
| 6.3 oz (yield from 1 lb) | 372 |
| 4 oz without bone | 272 |

**Sirloin steak, round-bone, 7% bone, lean with fat**

| | |
|---|---:|
| raw, 1 lb | 1,316 |

broiled

| | |
|---|---:|
| 10.9 oz (yield from 1 lb) | 1,192 |
| 4 oz without bone | 439 |

**Sirloin steak, round-bone, 7% bone, lean only**
broiled

| | |
|---|---:|
| 7.2 oz (yield from 1 lb) | 420 |
| 4 oz without bone | 235 |

**T-bone steak, 11% bone, lean with fat**

| | |
|---|---:|
| raw, 1 lb | 1,596 |

broiled

| | |
|---|---:|
| 10.4 oz (yield from 1 lb) | 1,395 |
| 4 oz without bone | 537 |

**T-bone steak, 11% bone, lean only**
broiled

| | |
|---|---:|
| 5.8 oz (yield from 1 lb) | 368 |
| 4 oz without bone | 253 |

# Beef, prepared and specialty cuts

**Beef, corned**

| | |
|---|---:|
| raw, 1 lb | 1,596 |

cooked

| | |
|---|---:|
| 10.7 oz (yield from 1 lb) | 1,131 |
| 4 oz | 422 |

**Beef, dried, creamed, home recipe**

| | |
|---|---:|
| 8 oz | 350 |

**Beef, hearts, lean only**
raw

| | |
|---|---:|
| 8 oz | 245 |

| | |
|---|---|
| braised | |
| 4 oz | 213 |
| 1 cup, chopped | 273 |
| **Beef, kidneys** | |
| raw, 8 oz | 294 |
| braised | |
| 4 oz | 286 |
| 1 cup, chunks | 353 |
| **Beef, liver** | |
| raw, 1 lb | 635 |
| fried, 4 oz | 260 |
| **Beef pancreas, raw, 4 oz** | |
| fat | 358 |
| medium fat | 321 |
| lean | 160 |
| **Beef suet, raw, 1 oz** | 242 |
| **Beef sweetbreads (thymus)** | |
| yearlings, raw, 1 lb | 939 |
| yearlings, braised, 4 oz | 365 |
| **Beef, tongue** | |
| very fat, raw, trimmed, 8 oz | 615 |
| fat, raw, trimmed, 8 oz | 524 |
| medium-fat, raw, trimmed | |
| 8 oz | 470 |
| braised, 4 oz | 277 |
| **Beef, tripe, 4 oz** | |
| commercial | 113 |
| pickled | 70 |

# 7

## Lamb, fresh

**Leg, lean with fat**
raw, with bone, 1 lb                                  845
roasted, with bone
    9.4 oz (yield from 1 lb)                       745
raw, boneless, 1 lb                                 1,007
roasted, boneless
    11.2 oz (yield from 1 lb)                       887
    4 oz                                             317
    1 cup, chopped                                   391
**Leg, lean**
roasted, with bone
    7.8 oz (yield from 1 lb with fat)               411
roasted, boneless
    9.7 oz (yield from 1 lb with fat)               491
    4 oz                                             211
    1 cup, chopped                                   260
**Loin chops, with bone, lean with fat**
raw, 1 lb                                           1,146
broiled
    10.1 oz (yield from 1 lb)                      1,023
    4 oz                                             407
    1 chop, 3.4 oz                                   341
    1 chop, 2.5 oz                                   255
**Loin chops, with bone, lean only**
broiled
    6.9 oz (yield from 1 lb)                         368
    4 oz                                             213
    1 chop, 2.3 oz                                   122

| | |
|---|---:|
| 1 chop, 1.7 oz | 92 |
| **Rib chops with bone, lean with fat** | |
| raw, 1 lb | 1,229 |
| broiled | |
| 9.5 oz (yield from 1 lb) | 1,091 |
| 4 oz | 462 |
| 1 chop, 3.1 oz | 362 |
| 1 chop, 2.4 oz | 273 |
| **Rib chops with bone, lean only** | |
| broiled | |
| 6 oz (yield from 1 lb) | 361 |
| 4 oz | 239 |
| 1 chop, 2 oz | 120 |
| 1 chop, 1.5 oz | 91 |
| **Shoulder, lean with fat** | |
| raw with bone, 1 lb | 1,082 |
| roasted, with bone | |
| 9.5 oz (yield from 1 lb) | 913 |
| raw, boneless, 1 lb | 1,275 |
| roasted, boneless | |
| 11.2 oz (yield from 1 lb) | 1,075 |
| 4 oz | 383 |
| 1 cup, chopped | 473 |
| **Shoulder, lean only** | |
| roasted, with bone | |
| 7 oz (yield from 1 lb) | 410 |
| roasted, boneless | |
| 8.3 oz (yield from 1 lb) | 482 |
| 4 oz | 233 |
| 1 cup, chopped | 287 |

**7**

**Lamb's quarters**

| | |
|---|---:|
| raw, trimmed, 1 lb | 195 |
| boiled, drained | |
| 4 oz | 36 |
| 1 cup | 64 |

**Lamb hearts**

| | |
|---|---:|
| raw, 8 oz | 368 |
| braised | |
| 4 oz | 295 |
| 1 cup, chopped | 377 |

**Lamb kidneys**

| | |
|---|---:|
| raw, 8 oz | 238 |

**Lamb liver**

| | |
|---|---:|
| raw, 1 lb | 617 |
| broiled, 4 oz | 296 |

**Lamb tongue**

| | |
|---|---:|
| raw, trimmed, 8 oz | 452 |
| braised, 4 oz | 288 |

**Lamb sweetbreads (thymus), 4 oz**

| | |
|---|---:|
| raw | 106 |
| braised | 200 |

# Ham, retail cuts (see also Pork)

| | |
|---|---:|
| Boiled, 8 oz (about 8 slices) | 531 |
| Fresh, lean with fat | |
| raw, 1 lb with bone and skin | 1,188 |

baked
| | |
|---|---|
| 9.2 oz (yield from 1 lb) | 980 |
| raw, 1 lb without bone and skin | 1,397 |

baked
| | |
|---|---|
| 10.9 oz (yield from 1 lb) | 1,152 |
| 4 oz | 424 |
| 1 cup, chopped | 524 |
| 1 cup, ground | 411 |

**Fresh, lean only**
baked, with bone and skin
| | |
|---|---|
| 6.8 oz (yield from 1 lb) | 421 |

baked, without bone and skin
| | |
|---|---|
| 8.1 oz (yield from 1 lb with fat) | 495 |
| 4 oz | 246 |
| 1 cup, chopped | 304 |
| 1 cup, ground | 239 |

**Light-cured, lean with fat**
| | |
|---|---|
| raw, with bone and skin, 1 lb | 1,100 |

baked, with bone and skin
| | |
|---|---|
| 11.3 oz (yield from 1 lb) | 925 |
| raw, without bone and skin, 1 lb | 1,279 |

baked, without bone and skin
| | |
|---|---|
| 13.1 oz (yield from 1 lb) | 1,075 |
| 4 oz | 328 |
| 1 cup, chopped | 405 |
| 1 cup, ground | 318 |

**Light-cured, lean only**
baked, with bone and skin
| | |
|---|---|
| 8.7 oz (yield from 1 lb with fat) | 460 |

**7**

baked, without bone and skin
    10.2 oz (yield from 1 lb with fat)      539
baked, without bone and skin
    4 oz      328
    1 cup, chopped      405
    1 cup, ground      318
**Long-cured, dry, unbaked**
    medium-fat, lean with fat, with bone and skin,
    4 oz      384
    lean, lean with fat, with bone and skin, 4 oz 302
**Ham, minced, 4 oz**      259

## Pork, fresh

**Boston butt, shoulder, with bone and skin, lean with fat**
    raw, 1 lb      1,220
    roasted, 10.2 oz (yield from 1 lb)      1,024
**Boston butt, shoulder, without bone and skin, lean with fat**
    raw, 1 lb      1,302
    roasted
        10.9 oz (yield from 1 lb)      1,087
        1 cup, chopped      494
        1 cup, ground      388
**Boston butt, shoulder, with bone and skin, lean only**
    roasted, 8.1 oz (yield from 1 lb with fat)      559

**7**

**Boston butt, shoulder, without bone and skin, lean only**
  roasted

| | |
|---|---:|
|     8.6 oz (yield from 1 lb with fat) | 595 |
|     1 cup, chopped | 342 |
|     1 cup, ground | 268 |

**Loin chops, with bone, lean with fat**

| | |
|---|---:|
|   raw, 1 lb | 1,065 |
|   broiled | |
|     8.2 oz (yield from 1 lb) | 911 |
|     1 chop, 2.7 oz | 305 |
|     1 chop, 2 oz | 227 |

**Loin chops without bone, lean with fat**

| | |
|---|---:|
|   raw, 1 lb | 1,352 |
|   broiled | |
|     10.4 oz (yield from 1 lb) | 1,153 |
|     4 oz | 411 |

**Loin chops, with bone, lean only**

| | |
|---|---:|
|   broiled | |
|     5.9 oz (yield from 1 lb with fat) | 454 |
|     1 chop, 2 oz | 151 |
|     1 chop, 1.5 oz | 113 |

**Loin chops, without bone, lean with fat**

| | |
|---|---:|
|   raw, 1 lb | 1,065 |
|   baked or roasted, 8.6 oz (yield from 1 lb) | 883 |

**Loin roast, without bone, lean with fat**

| | |
|---|---:|
|   raw, 1 lb | 1,352 |
|   baked or roasted | |
|     10.9 oz (yield from 1 lb) | 1,115 |
|     4 oz | 411 |
|     1 cup, chopped | 507 |

**7**

**Loin roast, with bone, lean only**
baked or roasted
    6.9 oz (yield from 1 lb with fat) — 495
    1 cup, chopped — 356
**Loin roast, without bone, lean only**
baked or roasted
    8.7 oz (yield from 1 lb with fat) — 627
    4 oz — 288
    1 cup, chopped — 356
**Picnic, shoulder, with bone and skin, lean with fat**
raw, 1 lb — 1,083
simmered, 8.4. oz (yield from 1 lb) — 890
**Picnic, shoulder, without bone and skin, lean with fat**
raw, 1 lb — 1,315
simmered
    10.2 oz (yield from 1 lb) — 1,085
    4 oz — 424
    1 cup, chopped — 524
**Picnic, shoulder, with bone and skin, lean only**
simmered, 6.2 oz (yield from 1 lb with fat) — 373
**Picnic, shoulder, without bone and skin, lean only**
simmered
    7.6 oz (yield from 1 lb with fat) — 456
    4 oz — 241
    1 cup, chopped — 297
**Spareribs, with bone, lean with fat**
raw, 1 lb — 976
braised
    6.3 oz (yield from 1 lb) — 792
    4 oz — 499

# Pork, specialty cuts, hog

**Hearts**
| | |
|---|---|
| raw, 4 oz | 128 |
| braised, 4 oz | 221 |
| braised, 1 cup | 283 |
| **Kidneys, raw, 8 oz** | 240 |

**Liver**
| | |
|---|---|
| raw, 1 lb | 594 |
| fried, 4 oz | 205 |
| **Pancreas (Sweetbreads), 4 oz** | 274 |
| **Spleen, raw, 4 oz** | 122 |

**Tongue, 4 oz**
| | |
|---|---|
| raw, trimmed | 244 |
| braised | 287 |


# Pork, specialty cuts, pig, 4 oz

| | |
|---|---|
| **Feet, pickled** | 227 |
| Salt Pork | |
| with skin | 1,137 |
| without skin | 888 |
| **Stomach, scalded** | 274 |

# 7

## Pork, cured, retail shoulder cuts (for other cured cuts see Bacon and Ham)

**Boston butt, with bone and skin, lean with fat**
    unbaked, 1 lb     1,277
    baked or roasted, 11 oz (yield from 1 lb)    1,030
**Boston butt, without bone and skin, lean with fat**
    unbaked, 1 lb     1,320
    baked or roasted
        11.8 oz from 1 lb     1,109
        4 oz     374
        1 cup, chopped     462
        1 cup, ground     363
**Boston butt, with bone and skin, lean only**
    baked or roasted, 9.1 oz (yield from 1 lb with fat)  629
**Boston butt without bone and skin, lean only**
    baked or roasted
        9.8 oz (yield from 1 lb with fat)     678
        4 oz     276
        1 cup, chopped     340
        1 cup, ground     267
**Picnic, with bone and skin, lean with fat**
    unbaked, 1 lb     1,060
    baked or roasted, 9.7 oz (yield from 1 lb)    888
**Picnic, without bone and skin, lean with fat**
    unbaked, 1 lb     1,293
    baked or roasted
        11.8 oz (yield from 1 lb)     1,085
        4 oz     366
        1 cup, chopped     452

| | |
|---|---:|
| 1 cup, ground | 355 |
| **Picnic, with bone and skin, lean only** | |
| baked or roasted, 6.8 oz (yield from 1 lb with fat) | 405 |
| **Picnic, without bone and skin, lean only** | |
| baked or roasted | |
| 8.3 oz (yield from 1 lb with fat) | 496 |
| 4 oz | 239 |
| 1 cup, chopped | 295 |
| 1 cup, ground | 232 |
| **Bacon, Canadian** | |
| uncooked, 1 lb | 980 |
| fried, drained | |
| 12 oz (approx. yield from 1 lb) | 921 |
| 4 oz | 311 |
| 1 slice 3⅜" wide | 58 |
| **Bacon, cured** | |
| raw, 1 lb | 3,016 |
| fried, drained | |
| 5.1 oz (approx. yield from 1 lb) | 860 |
| 1 thick slice | 72 |
| 1 medium slice | 43 |
| 1 thin slice | 30 |

# Veal, fresh, retail cuts

**Chuck cuts and boneless for stew, lean with fat**

| | |
|---|---:|
| raw, with bone, 1 lb | 628 |
| stewed, with bone, 8.4 oz (yield from 1 lb) | 564 |

| | |
|---|---:|
| raw, without bone, 1 lb | 785 |
| stewed, without bone | |
| 10.6 oz (yield from 1 lb) | 703 |
| 4 oz | 267 |
| 1 cup, chopped | 329 |
| **Loin cuts, lean with fat** | |
| raw, with bone, 1 lb | 681 |
| braised, or broiled, with bone | |
| 9.5 oz (yield from 1 lb) | 629 |
| raw, without bone, 1 lb | 821 |
| braised or broiled, without bone | |
| 11.4 oz (yield from 1 lb) | 758 |
| 4 oz | 245 |
| 1 cup, chopped | 328 |
| **Plate (breast of veal), lean with fat** | |
| raw, with bone, 1 lb | 828 |
| braised or stewed, with bone, | |
| 8.3 oz (yield from 1 lb) | 718 |
| raw, without bone, 1 lb | 1,048 |
| braised or stewed, without bone | |
| 10.6 oz (yield from 1 lb) | 906 |
| 4 oz | 344 |
| **Rib roast, lean with fat** | |
| raw, with bone, 1 lb | 723 |
| roasted, with bone, 8.5 oz (yield from 1 lb) | 648 |
| raw, without bone, 1 lb | 939 |
| roasted, without bone | |
| 11 oz (yield from 1 lb) | 842 |
| 4 oz | 305 |
| 1 cup, chopped | 377 |

| | |
|---|---|
| 1 cup, ground | 296 |

**Round with rump (roasts and leg cutlets), lean with fat**

| | |
|---|---|
| raw, with bone, 1 lb | 573 |
| braised or broiled, with bone | |
| 8.7 oz (yield from 1 lb) | 534 |
| raw, without bone, 1 lb | 744 |
| braised or broiled, without bone | |
| 11.3 oz (yield from 1 lb) | 693 |
| 4 oz | 245 |
| 1 cup, chopped | 302 |

# Veal, specialty cuts

**Calf hearts**

| | |
|---|---|
| raw, 4 oz | 140 |
| braised, 4 oz | 236 |
| 1 cup | 302 |
| **Calf kidneys, raw, 8 oz** | 256 |

**Calves' liver**

| | |
|---|---|
| raw, 4 oz | 212 |
| fried, 4 oz | 296 |
| **Calf pancreas, 4 oz, raw** | 183 |

**Calf tongue, 4 oz**

| | |
|---|---|
| raw, trimmed | 143 |
| braised | 181 |

**Calf sweetbreads (thymus), 4 oz**

| | |
|---|---|
| raw | 106 |
| braised | 192 |

# 7

# Cold Cuts, Sausages and other meats

| | |
|---|---|
| **Beaver, roasted, 8 oz.** | 563 |
| **Bockwurst** | |
| 1 lb (approx 7 links) | 1,198 |
| 1 link (approx 2.3 oz) | 172 |
| **Bologna** | |
| without binders | |
| chub, 1 slice (3″ x ⅛″) | 36 |
| ring, 12 oz ring (15″ x 1⅜″) | 942 |
| sliced, 1 slice (approx 1 oz) | 79 |
| with cereal | |
| chub, 1 slice | 34 |
| ring, 12 oz ring | 891 |
| sliced, 1 slice | 74 |
| **Brains, all types, fresh, raw, 8 oz** | 284 |
| **Capicola** | |
| 1 oz | 141 |
| 1 slice | 105 |
| **Cervelat, dry** | |
| 1 oz | 128 |
| 4 slices | 54 |
| **Frankfurter's without binders** | |
| 1 lb | 1,343 |
| 1 frank (5″ x ¾″) | 133 |
| **Frog's legs, raw** | |
| whole, with bone, 1 lb | 215 |
| meat only, 4 oz | 83 |
| **Meat Loaf, 4 oz** | 227 |

| | |
|---|---:|
| **Muskrat, roasted, 4 oz** | 174 |
| **Rabbit, domesticated** | |
| raw, whole, ready to cook, 1 lb | 581 |
| raw, meat only, 4 oz | 184 |
| stewed | |
| whole 8.6 oz (yield from 1 lb) | 529 |
| meat only | |
| 4 oz | 245 |
| 1 cup, chopped | 302 |
| 1 cup, ground | 238 |
| **Rabbit, wild** | |
| whole, ready to cook, 1 lb | 490 |
| meat only, 4 oz | 153 |
| **Raccoon, roasted, meat only, 4 oz** | 290 |
| **Reindeer, raw, lean meat only, 4 oz** | 144 |
| **Salami** | |
| dry roll | |
| 8¼ oz roll | 1,053 |
| 1 slice | 23 |
| dry slice | |
| 4 oz | 509 |
| 1 slice | 45 |
| cooked | |
| 8 oz | 706 |
| 1 slice approx 1 oz | 88 |
| **Sausage** | |
| Blood pudding | |
| 4 oz | 447 |
| 1 slice | 32 |

**7**

Polish
    4 oz        345
pork, raw
    2 oz patty        284
    1 oz link (4" x ⅞")    141
pork, cooked
    4 oz        543
    1 patty        129
    1 link        62
scrapple
    4 oz        244
    1 slice (⁹⁄₁₀ oz)    54
souse
    4 oz        205
    1 slice (1 oz)    51

**Sheep tongue**
    raw, trimmed, 8 oz    602
    braised, 4 oz    366
**Snails, raw, 4 oz**
    meat only    103
    Giant African, meat only    83
**Spleen, all types, 4 oz**    125
**Terrapin (diamondback), raw**
    in shell, 1 lb    106
    meat only, 4 oz    126
**Thuringer cervelat (summer sausage)**
    8 oz    697
    1 slice (approx 1 oz)    87
**Turtle, green, raw**
    in shell, 1 lb    97

meat only, 4 oz     101
Venison, raw, lean meat only, 4 oz     143

# MEAT, COMMERCIALLY PACKAGED

## Cured and processed meat, 1 oz unless noted

**Bacon, cooked, 1 slice**
  *Hormel*
    *Black Label*     35
    *Range Label*     45
    *Red Label*     37
  *Oscar Mayer*     40
  *Swift*     40
**Bacon bits**
  *Wilson*     140
**Beef, chopped**
  *Eckrich, 1 slice*     40
  *Wilson*     91
**Beef, corned**
  *Dinty Moore*     65
  *Libby's*     101
  *Safeway*     35

**Beef, corned brisket**
Swift                                      80
Wilson                                     45
**Beef, dried**
Swift                                      42
**Beef, roast**
Wilson                                     33
**Beef, smoked**
Safeway                                    35
spicy                                      40
**Beef steaks**
Hormel                                     92
**Bologna, 1 slice**
Eckrich                                    90
thick-sliced                              160
Hormel                                     95
Swift                                      87
Wilson                                     87
**Beef bologna**
Eckrich                                    95
Beef Smorgas                           70
Oscar Mayer                                70
**Coarse ground bologna**
Hormel                                     75
**Fine ground bologna**
Hormel                                     80
**Garlic bologna**
Eckrich                                    95
**Braunschweiger**
Oscar Mayer                               100

| | |
|---|---:|
| *Wilson* | 90 |

**Frankfurters, 1 frank**

| | |
|---|---:|
| *Eckrich* | 120 |
| Jumbo | 190 |
| Skinless | 150 |
| *Hormel* | 180 |
| Wieners | 105 |
| *Oscar Mayer* | 140 |
| *Wilson* | 140 |

**Beef frankfurters, 1 frank**

| | |
|---|---:|
| *Eckrich* | 150 |
| Jumbo | 190 |
| *Hormel* | |
| Wieners | 105 |
| *Wranglers* | 160 |
| *Oscar Mayer* | 140 |
| *Vienna* | 130 |
| *Wilson* | 136 |

**Ham, lunch meat**
cooked

| | |
|---|---:|
| *Eckrich,* 1 slice | 40 |
| *Hormel* | 35 |
| *Safeway* | 50 |
| *Oscar Mayer,* 1 slice | 30 |

chopped

| | |
|---|---:|
| *Hormel* | 70 |
| *Oscar Mayer,* 1 slice | 65 |

chopped, smoked

| | |
|---|---:|
| *Eckrich* | 40 |

**7**

**Ham, whole, canned, 1 oz**
*Amber*     110
*Oscar Mayer*     32
*Swift*     63
*Wilson*
    boned and rolled     56
    fully cooked     48
    *Tender Made*     44
**Ham, whole, packaged, 1 oz**
*Hormel*
    bone-in     52
    *Cure 82*     48
    *Curemaster*     35
*Oscar Mayer*     36
*Swift*     43
*Wilson*     48
**Ham steaks, 1 slice**
*Oscar Mayer*     70
**Ham patties, 1 patty**
*Hormel*     200
*Swift*     250
**Ham and Cheese Loaf, 1 slice**
*Oscar Mayer*     75
**Honey Loaf, 1 slice**
*Eckrich*     45
*Oscar Mayer*     40
**Liver, beef**
*Swift*     54
**Liver cheese, 1 slice**
*Oscar Mayer*     110

**Old Fashioned Loaf, 1 slice**
*Eckrich* 75
*Oscar Mayer* 65
**Olive Loaf, 1 slice**
*Oscar Mayer* 65
**Pastrami, 1 slice**
*Eckrich* 47
*Safeway* 40
**Pepperoni**
*Hormel* 140
*Swift* 150
**Pickle Loaf, 1 slice**
*Eckrich* 85
*Oscar Mayer* 65
**Polish Sausage**
*Eckrich* 100
*Frito-Lay* 73
*Hormel* 80
**Pork Butt**
*Wilson* 72
**Pork Loin**
*Eckrich* 47
**Pork Steaks**
*Hormel* 73
**Salami**
*Hormel* 327
*Oscar Mayer,* 1 slice 50
**Sausage, beef**
*Eckrich* 95

**Sausage, pork**
*Hormel*     95
*Wilson*     135

**Sausage links, 1 sausage**
*Hormel*
    *Brown 'n Serve*     78
    *Little Sizzlers*     67
    *Midget Links*     112
*Oscar Mayer*     65
*Swift*     75

**Sausage links, smoked, 1 sausage**
*Eckrich*     190
    skinless     115
    *Smok-Y-Links*     75
*Hormel*     92
*Oscar Mayer*     140

**Scrapple**
*Oscar Mayer*     45

**Sizzlean**
*Swift*     50

**Spam**
*Hormel*     85

**Summer Sausage**
*Swift*     90

**Thuringer**
*Hormel*     100

**Tripe**
*Libby's* canned     35

**Veal Steaks**
|  |  |
|---|---|
| *Hormel* | 35 |
| breaded | 60 |

**Vienna Sausage, 1 sausage**
|  |  |
|---|---|
| *Hormel* | 52 |
| *Libby's* | 84 |
| with barbecue sauce | 76 |

# Canned Meat Entrees, 1 can, various sizes

**Beef with barbecue sauce**
|  |  |
|---|---|
| *Morton House* | 240 |

**Beef, corned with cabbage**
|  |  |
|---|---|
| *Hormel* | 150 |

**Beef Goulash**
|  |  |
|---|---|
| *Hormel* | 240 |

**Beef sliced with gravy**
|  |  |
|---|---|
| *Morton House* | 190 |

**Chili con carne**
|  |  |
|---|---|
| *Hormel* | 340 |
| *Libby's* | 130 |
| *Morton House* | 340 |

**Chili con carne with beans**
|  |  |
|---|---|
| *A&P* | 440 |
| *Hormel* | 320 |
| *Libby's* | 180 |
| *Morton House* | 340 |
| *Swanson* | 310 |

**Hash, beef with potatoes**
|  |  |
|---|---|
| *Dinty Moore* | 270 |

**7**

**Hash, corned beef**

| | |
|---|---:|
| *Ann Page* | 400 |
| *Armour Star* | 435 |
| *Bounty* | 405 |
| *Broadcast* | 480 |
| *Libby's* | 160 |
| *Morton House* | 480 |
| *Wilson* | 480 |

**Hash, roast beef**

| | |
|---|---:|
| *Hormel* | 375 |

**Meatballs in gravy**

| | |
|---|---:|
| *Chef Boy-Ar-Dee* | 315 |

**Pork, sliced with gravy**

| | |
|---|---:|
| *Morton House* | 190 |

**Salisbury Steak with mushroom gravy**

| | |
|---|---:|
| *Morton House* | 160 |

**Sloppy Joe**

| | |
|---|---:|
| *Banquet* | 250 |
| *Gebhardt* | 280 |
| *Hormel* | 365 |
| *Libby's* | |
| beef | 163 |
| pork | 139 |

**Stew, beef**

| | |
|---|---:|
| *Armour Star* | 200 |
| *B & M* | 163 |
| *Bounty* | 213 |
| *Dinty Moore* | 184 |
| *Heinz* | 253 |
| *Morton House* | 312 |

| | |
|---|---|
| *James River Smithfield* | 186 |
| *Libby's* | 78 |
| *Morton House* | 240 |
| *Swanson* | 190 |
| *Wilson* | 202 |

**Stew, lamb**
| | |
|---|---|
| *B & M* | 247 |

**Stew, meatball**
| | |
|---|---|
| *Chef Boy-Ar-Dee* | 218 |
| *Libby's* | 121 |
| *Morton House* | 290 |

**Stew, Mulligan**
| | |
|---|---|
| *Dinty Moore* | 240 |

# Frozen Meat Entrees, 1 whole package, various sizes (see also pp 385-391, Frozen Dinners)

**Beef**
*Banquet*
| | |
|---|---|
| *Cookin' Bag* | 124 |
| *Buffet Supper, 32 oz* | 782 |
| *Green Giant Boil-in-Bag* | 130 |
| *Seabrook Farms* | 263 |
| *Stouffer's* | 235 |
| *Swanson* | 190 |
| *Swanson Hungry-Man* | 330 |

**Beef goulash**
Seabrook Farms 198
**Beef Pot Pie**
Banquet 412
Swanson 443
**Beef Stroganoff**
Stouffer's 390
**Green Pepper Steak**
Stouffer's 350
**Meat Loaf**
Banquet
Buffet Supper, 32 oz 1,445
Cookin' Bag 224
Man Pleaser 916
Morton 430
Swanson 330
**Noodles and Beef**
Banquet Buffet Supper, 32 oz 754
**Salisbury Steak**
Banquet 873
Green Giant Boil-in-Bag 390
Morton 490
Stouffer's 500
Swanson 370
Swanson Hungry-Man 640
**Salisbury Steak with gravy**
Banquet
Buffet Supper, 32 oz 1,454
Cookin' Bag 246

| | |
|---|---:|
| *Green Giant Oven Bake* | 290 |
| **Sausage, cheese, and tomato pie** | |
| *Weight Watchers* | 390 |
| **Sloppy Joe** | |
| *Banquet Cookin' Bag* | 199 |
| *Green Giant Boil-in-Bag* | 160 |
| **Steak** | |
| *Weight Watchers* | 390 |
| **Stew, Beef** | |
| *Banquet Buffet Supper, 32 oz* | 700 |
| *Green Giant Boil-in-Bag* | 160 |
| *Lambrecht* | 432 |
| *Seabrook Farms* | 229 |
| *Stouffer's* | 310 |
| **Stuffed Cabbage with beef** | |
| *Green Giant Oven Bake* | 220 |
| **Stuffed Green Pepper with Beef** | |
| *Green Giant Oven Bake* | 200 |

# Meat Substitutes, 1 piece or slice

| | |
|---|---:|
| *Morningstar Farms* | |
| Breakfast Links | 62 |
| Breakfast Patties | 111 |
| Breakfast Strips | 38 |

## Loma Linda

| | |
|---|---:|
| Bologna | 190 |
| Burgers | |
|     Redi-Burger | 150 |
|     Sizzle Burger | 180 |
| Frankfurters | 110 |
| Linketts | 70 |
| Little Links | 45 |
| Meatballs | 48 |
| Peanut Butter | |
|     Nuteena | 210 |
|     Proteena | 160 |
| Roast Beef | 200 |
| Salami | 210 |
| Sausage | |
|     Breakfast Links | 50 |
|     Breakfast Sausage | 140 |
| Swiss Steak | 140 |
| Tender Bits | 20 |
| Tender Rounds | 50 |
| Turkey | 190 |
| Vegeburger, 1 cup | 240 |
| Vegelona | 160 |

**7**

# POULTRY, FRESH

## Chickens, fresh

**Broilers**
broiled, with skin, giblets
| | |
|---|---|
| 7.1 oz (yield from 1 lb) | 273 |
| meat only, 4 oz | 154 |
| **Capon, raw, ready to cook, 1 lb** | 382 |

**Fryers**
| | |
|---|---|
| raw, ready to cook, 1 lb | 382 |
| fried, with skin, giblets | |
| 8 oz (yield from 1 lb) | 565 |
| fried, without skin | |
| dark meat, 4 oz | 249 |
| light meat, 4 oz | 223 |
| 1 back (approx 2 oz) | 139 |
| ½ breast (approx 3.3 oz) | 160 |
| 1 drumstick (approx 2 oz) | 88 |
| 1 neck (approx 2 oz) | 127 |
| ½ rib section (approx ¾ oz) | 41 |
| 1 thigh (approx 2.3 oz) | 122 |
| 1 wing (approx 1.8 oz) | 82 |
| skin only (approx 1 oz) | 119 |

**Roasters**
| | |
|---|---|
| raw, ready to cook, 1 lb | 791 |
| roasted, with skin, giblets | |
| 8.4 oz (yield from 1 lb) | 576 |

roasted, without skin, dark meat

| | |
|---|---|
| 4 oz | 204 |
| 1 cup, chopped | 258 |
| 1 cup, ground | 202 |

roasted, without skin, light meat

| | |
|---|---|
| 4 oz | 207 |
| 1 cup, chopped | 255 |
| 1 cup, ground | 200 |

**Stewing hens or cocks**

| | |
|---|---|
| raw, ready to cook, 1 lb | 987 |
| stewed, with skin, giblets, 8 oz (yield from 1 lb) | 708 |

stewed, without skin, dark meat

| | |
|---|---|
| 4 oz | 235 |
| 1 cup, chopped | 290 |
| 1 cup, ground | 228 |

stewed, without skin, light meat

| | |
|---|---|
| 4 oz | 204 |
| 1 cup, chopped | 252 |
| 1 cup, ground | 198 |

**Chicken gizzards**

| | |
|---|---|
| raw, 1 lb | 513 |

simmered

| | |
|---|---|
| 12 oz (yield from 1 lb) | 497 |
| 4 oz | 168 |
| 1 cup, chopped | 215 |

**Chicken hearts**

| | |
|---|---|
| raw, 4 oz | 152 |

simmered

| | |
|---|---|
| 4 oz | 221 |
| 1 cup, chopped | 283 |

**Chicken liver**

| | |
|---|---|
| raw, 1 lb | 585 |
| simmered | |
| 4 oz | 187 |
| 1 cup, chopped | 231 |
| 1 liver 2″ x 2″ x ½″ | 45 |

# Duck, fresh

**Domesticated**

| | |
|---|---|
| raw, meat only, 4 oz | 188 |
| roasted, meat only, 4 oz | 352 |

**Wild**

| | |
|---|---|
| raw, meat only, 4 oz | 157 |

# Goose, fresh, domesticated

| | |
|---|---|
| raw, whole, ready to cook, 1 lb | 1,172 |
| roasted | |
| whole, 8½ oz (yield from 1 lb) | 1,022 |
| meat only, 4 oz | 266 |
| meat and skin, 4 oz | 503 |
| Goose gizzards, raw, 1 lb | 631 |
| Goose liver, raw, 1 lb | 826 |

**7**

# Pheasant, fresh

| | |
|---|---:|
| raw, ready to cook, whole, 1 lb | 596 |
| raw, meat only, 4 oz | 184 |

# Quail, fresh, raw

| | |
|---|---:|
| whole, ready to cook, 1 lb | 686 |
| meat and skin only, 4 oz | 196 |
| giblets, 2 oz | 100 |

# Squab (Pigeon), fresh, raw

| | |
|---|---:|
| whole, dressed, 1 lb | 569 |
| meat only, 4 oz | 162 |
| light meat only, 4 oz | 143 |

# Turkey, fresh

| | |
|---|---:|
| raw, whole, ready to cook, 1 lb | 722 |
| roasted, whole, with giblets and skin 8.6 oz (yield from 1 lb) | 644 |
| roasted, dark meat without skin 4 oz | 230 |

**7**

| | |
|---|---|
| 1 cup, chopped | 284 |
| 1 cup, ground | 223 |
| **roasted, light meat without skin** | |
| 4 oz | 200 |
| 1 cup, chopped | 246 |
| 1 cup, ground | 194 |
| **roasted, skin only, 1 oz** | 256 |
| **giblets** | |
| raw, 4 oz | 170 |
| simmered | |
| 4 oz | 254 |
| 1 cup, chopped | 338 |
| **gizzards** | |
| raw, 1 lb | 712 |
| simmered | |
| 12 oz (yield from 1 lb) | 659 |
| 4 oz | 222 |
| 1 cup, chopped | 284 |
| **hearts** | |
| raw, 4 oz | 169 |
| simmered | |
| 4 oz | 245 |
| 1 cup, chopped | 313 |
| **liver** | |
| raw, 1 lb | 626 |
| simmered | |
| 4 oz | 197 |
| 1 cup, chopped | 244 |

# 7

# POULTRY, COMMERCIALLY CANNED, FROZEN, OR

**PACKAGED**: 1 package, various sizes, unless noted (see also pp 385-391, Frozen Dinners)

## Chicken

**a la King**
| | |
|---|---|
| *Banquet* | 138 |
| *Green Giant* | 170 |
| *Lambrecht* | 585 |
| *Stouffer's* | 330 |
| *Swanson* | 190 |

**Boned**
| | |
|---|---|
| *Hormel* | 110 |
| *Richardson & Robbins* | 328 |
| *Swanson* | 110 |

**Chopped, 1 slice**
| | |
|---|---|
| *Eckrich* | 47 |

**Cacciatore**
| | |
|---|---|
| *Seabrook Farms* | 248 |

**Creamed**
| | |
|---|---|
| *Stouffer's* | 300 |

**7**

**Creole**
   *Weight Watchers*     250
**Croquette**
   *Howard Johnson's*     505
**Divan**
   *Stouffer's*     335
**and Dumplings**
   *Banquet*     282
   *Morton House, 8 oz*     363
   *Swanson*     230
**Escalloped**
   *Stouffer's*     500
**Fricasse, 1 cup**
   *College Inn*     240
   *Richardson & Robbins*     229
**Fried**
   *Banquet*     259
   *Morton*     600
   *Swanson*     290
**Livers with broccoli**
   *Weight Watchers*     220
**with Noodles**
   *Banquet*     764
   *Green Giant*     250
   *Howard Johnson*     384
   *Heinz*     186
**Pot Pie**
   *Banquet*     412
   *Morton*     318
   *Stouffer's*     545

| | |
|---|---:|
| *Swanson* | 430 |
| *Swanson Hungry-Man* | 770 |
| **with Rice** | |
| *Morton House, 8 oz* | 460 |
| **Smoked** | |
| *Safeway, 1 oz* | 50 |
| **Stew, 8 oz** | |
| *B & M* | 168 |
| *Bounty* | 221 |
| *Libby's* | 88 |
| *Swanson, 7½ oz* | 180 |
| **White meat with peas and onions** | |
| *Weight Watchers* | 270 |

# Turkey

| | |
|---|---:|
| **Boned** | |
| *Hormel* | 90 |
| **with Giblet gravy** | |
| *Banquet* | 128 |
| *Banquet Buffet Supper* | 170 |
| **Pot Pie** | |
| *Banquet* | 415 |
| *Morton* | 390 |
| *Stouffer's* | 460 |
| *Swanson* | 430 |
| *Swanson Hungry-Man* | 770 |

**Slices**
  *Banquet*                                    98
  *Banquet Buffet Supper*                     564
  *Green Giant*                               100
  *Morton Country Table*                      390
  *Morton House* canned                       140
  *Swanson*                                   260
  *Swanson Hungry-Man*                        380
**Tetrazzini**
  *Stouffer's*                                480
**Smoked**
  *Eckrich,* 1 slice                           47
  *Safeway,* 1 oz                              50

# SEAFOOD, FRESH,
## 4 oz unless noted

**Abalone, raw**
  in shell                                     47
  meat only                                   111
**Barracuda, Pacific, raw**
  meat only                                   129
**Bass, black sea, raw**
  whole                                        41
  meat only                                   106

**Bass, all varieties, raw**

| | |
|---|---:|
| whole | 51 |
| meat only | 120 |

**Blackfish, see Tautug**

**Bonito, raw**

| | |
|---|---:|
| meat only | 192 |

**Butterfish, raw, meat only**

| | |
|---|---:|
| gulf | 108 |
| northern | 192 |

| | |
|---|---:|
| **Catfish, raw, fillets** | 117 |

**Caviar, sturgeon**

granular

| | |
|---|---:|
| 1 oz | 74 |
| 1 Tbsp | 42 |

pressed

| | |
|---|---:|
| 1 oz | 90 |
| 1 Tbsp | 54 |

**Clams, raw, meat only**

hard or round

| | |
|---|---:|
| 1 pt | 363 |
| 8 oz | 182 |
| 4 cherrystones or 5 littlenecks | 56 |

soft

| | |
|---|---:|
| 1 pt | 372 |
| 8 oz | 186 |

**Cod**

| | |
|---|---:|
| raw, fillets, 8 oz | 176 |

broiled, with butter

| | |
|---|---:|
| 1 steak | 352 |

| | |
|---|---:|
| 4 oz | 192 |
| dehydrated, lightly salted | 308 |
| 1 cup, shredded | 158 |
| dried, salted | 148 |
| **Crab, steamed, 8 oz** | |
| in shell | 100 |
| meat only | 211 |
| **Crab, deviled** | |
| 8 oz | 427 |
| **Crab, Imperial** | |
| 8 oz | 334 |
| **Crayfish, raw** | |
| in shell | 10 |
| meat only | 82 |
| **Croaker, Atlantic** | |
| raw, meat only | 109 |
| **Croaker, white** | |
| raw, meat only | 95 |
| **Croaker, yellow** | |
| raw, meat only | 101 |
| **Cusk** | |
| raw, meat only | 85 |
| steamed, meat only | 120 |
| **Eulachon, see Smelt** | |
| **Finnan Haddie** | |
| meat only | 117 |
| **Flounder, fillets** | |
| raw | 89 |
| baked with butter | 229 |

**Grouper, raw**
whole　42
meat only　99
**Haddock**
raw
　whole, 1 lb　172
　fillets, 1 lb　360
fried, breaded, 4 oz　187
**Halibut, Atlantic or Pacific**
raw
　whole, 1 lb　268
　fillets, 1 lb　452
broiled with butter, fillets, 4 oz　199
**Herring**
Atlantic, raw
　whole, 1 lb　405
　meat only, 4 oz　200
Pacific
　raw, meat only, 4 oz　111
　salted (in brine), 4 oz　247
　smoked, 4 oz
　　bloaters　222
　　hard　340
　　kippers　239
**Inconnu, raw**
whole　104
meat only　166
**Kingfish, raw**
whole　52

**7**

| | |
|---|---:|
| meat only | 119 |
| **Lake Herring (Cisco), raw** | |
| whole | 55 |
| meat only | 110 |
| **Lake Trout, raw** | |
| whole | 70 |
| meat only | 190 |
| **Ling Cod, raw** | |
| whole | 44 |
| meat only | 96 |
| **Lobster, northern** | |
| in shell, 1 lb | |
| raw | 107 |
| cooked | 112 |
| **Mackerel, Atlantic** | |
| raw, 1 lb | |
| whole | 468 |
| fillets | 866 |
| broiled with butter, fillets, | |
| 13 oz yield from 1 lb | 861 |
| 4 oz | 268 |
| **Mackerel, Pacific, raw** | |
| whole | 130 |
| meat only | 181 |
| **Mackerel, salted** | 345 |
| **Mackerel, smoked** | 248 |
| **Mullet, raw** | |
| whole | 88 |
| meat only | 166 |

**7**

**Muskellunge,** raw
| | |
|---|---|
| whole | 60 |
| meat only | 124 |

**Mussels, Atlantic or Pacific, raw**
| | |
|---|---|
| in shell | 38 |
| meat only | 108 |

**Ocean Perch, Atlantic**
raw
| | |
|---|---|
| whole | 31 |
| meat only | 100 |
| fried, breaded | 258 |

**Ocean Perch, Pacific, raw**
| | |
|---|---|
| whole | 29 |
| meat only | 108 |

**Octopus, raw**     83

**Oysters, raw**
Eastern
| | |
|---|---|
| in shell, 1 lb | 30 |
| meat only, 4 oz | 75 |
| 1 medium | 20 |

Pacific Western
| | |
|---|---|
| meat only, 4 oz | 105 |
| 1 medium | 55 |

**Oysters, cooked**
| | |
|---|---|
| fried, breaded, 1 medium | 25 |

**Pickerel, raw**     95

**Perch, raw**
white
| | |
|---|---|
| whole | 48 |
| meat only | 134 |

yellow
  whole   40
  meat only   103
**Pike, raw**
  blue
    whole   45
    meat only   100
  northern
    whole   26
    meat only   100
  walleye
    whole   60
    meat only   105
**Pompano, raw**
  whole   106
  meat only   188
**Porgy, raw**   52
  meat only   127
**Rockfish**
  raw   110
  steamed   115
**Roe, raw**
  carp, cod, haddock, herring, pike, and shad   148
  salmon, sturgeon, and turbot   236
**Sablefish, raw**
  whole   90
  meat only   216
**Salmon, raw**
  Atlantic
    whole   160

| | |
|---|---|
| meat only | 246 |
| King (Chinook) meat only | 252 |
| **Salmon, smoked** | 200 |
| **Sand Dab, raw** | |
| meat only | 89 |
| **Sardines, Pacific** | |
| raw, meat only | 180 |
| **Sauger, raw** | |
| whole | 34 |
| meat only | 95 |
| **Scallops, meat only** | |
| raw | 92 |
| steamed | 127 |
| **Sea Bass, white** | |
| raw, meat only | 109 |
| **Shad, raw** | |
| whole | 92 |
| meat only | 192 |
| **Sheepshead, Atlantic, raw** | |
| whole | 60 |
| meat only | 128 |
| **Shrimp** | |
| raw, whole | |
| in shell | 72 |
| shelled | 100 |
| fried, breaded | 250 |
| **Skate** | |
| raw, meat only | 111 |
| **Smelt, raw** | |
| whole | 60 |

| | |
|---|---|
| meat only | 110 |
| **Snapper, Red and Gray, raw** | |
| whole | 55 |
| meat only | 106 |
| **Sole, raw** | |
| whole | 29 |
| meat only (fillet) | 90 |
| **Spanish Mackerel, raw** | |
| whole | 142 |
| meat only | 200 |
| **Spot** | |
| raw, meat only | 250 |
| **Squid** | |
| raw, meat only | 95 |
| **Sturgeon, meat only** | |
| raw | 105 |
| steamed | 180 |
| **Sturgeon, smoked** | 170 |
| **Sucker, carp** | |
| raw | 48 |
| meat only | 125 |
| **Sucker, white and mullet, raw** | |
| whole | 195 |
| meat only | 118 |
| **Swordfish, meat only** | |
| raw | 138 |
| broiled in butter | 185 |
| **Tautug (Blackfish), raw** | |
| whole | 37 |
| meat only | 101 |

**7**

**Tilefish**
raw
    whole   46
    meat only   90
  baked, meat only   155
**Tomcod, raw**
  whole   34
  meat only   88
**Trout, Brook, raw**
  whole   56
  meat only   115
**Trout, Rainbow, raw**
  meat only   220
**Tuna, raw, meat only**
  bluefin   165
  yellowfin   150
**Turbot, Greenland, raw**
  whole   86
  meat only   166
**Weakfish**
raw
    whole   66
    meat only   138
  broiled in butter   230
**Whitefish, raw**
  whole   82
  meat only   177
  smoked   177
**Wreckfish**
  raw, meat only   130

**Yellowtail**
raw, meat only                                            157


# SEAFOOD, CANNED
# AND FROZEN


**Catfish, ocean**
*Gorton's*, 1 pkg                                           286
**Clams**
*Doxsee*
   6 oz                                                      84
   8 oz                                                     112
   12 oz                                                    147
*Howard Johnson's*
   5 oz                                                     395
   Croquettes, 1 pkg                                        608
*Mrs. Paul's* 1 cake                                        180
   Thins, 1 cake                                            155
   Sticks, 1 stick                                           48
*Sau-Sea*, 1 jar                                             99
*Snow's*                                                     60
**Cod,** 1 pkg
fillets
   *Gorton's*                                               355
   *San Juan*                                               336
   *Ship Ahoy*                                              336

sticks
| | |
|---|---|
| *Bird's Eye* | 552 |
| *Gorton's* | 830 |

**Crab**
| | |
|---|---|
| *Gold Seal*, 1 can | 185 |
| *Icy Point*, 1 can | 215 |
| *Mrs. Paul's*, 1 cake | 60 |
| *Pillar Rock*, 1 can | 216 |
| *Ship Ahoy*, 8 oz | 210 |
| *Wakefield's*, 6 oz | 160 |

**Crepes, 5½ oz**
*Mrs. Paul's*
| | |
|---|---|
| Clam | 280 |
| Crab | 240 |
| Scallop | 220 |
| Shrimp | 250 |

**Croquettes**
*Howard Johnson's*
| | |
|---|---|
| Shrimp with Newburg Sauce | 480 |

**Eel, smoked** 185
| | |
|---|---|
| *Vita* | 402 |

**Fish Au Gratin**
| | |
|---|---|
| *Mrs. Paul's* 1 pkg | 250 |

**Fish cakes, fillets and sticks, 1 piece**
| | |
|---|---|
| *Mrs. Paul's* | 105 |
| *Beach Haven* | 110 |
| Thins | 160 |

**Fish and Chips**
| | |
|---|---|
| *Swanson*, 1 pkg | 290 |

**Fish Parmesan**
  *Mrs. Paul's*, 1 pkg                               220
**Flounder**
  *Mrs. Paul's*, 1 pkg                               110
  *Weight Watchers*, 1 pkg                    160
**Gelfilte Fish, 1 oz**
  *Manischewitz*                                23
  *Mother's*                                   14
  *Rokeach*                                   19
**Haddock au Gratin**
  *Howard Johnson's*                         315
**Haddock fillets**
  *Gorton's*, 1 pkg                            360
  *Mrs. Paul's*, 1 piece                      115
**Haddock with stuffing**
  *Weight Watchers*, 1 pkg                    180
**Herring, pickled, 1 oz**
  *Vita*                                    40
**Oysters, 1 cup**
  *Bumblebee*                              172
**Perch, fried, 1 piece**
  *Mrs. Paul's*                             125
**Perch, ocean with broccoli**
  *Weight Watchers*, 1 pkg                    190
**Salmon, canned, 1 can**
  blueback
    *Icy Point*
      3¾-oz can                         181
      7¾-oz can                        376

Coho steak
*Icy Point*
3¾-oz can                                                  162
pink
*Del Monte*
7¾-oz can                                                  310
red
*Icy Point*
1-lb. can                                                  775
*Pillar Rock*
3¾-oz can                                                  181
7¾-oz can                                                  376
red sockeye
*Del Monte*
7¾-oz can                                                  340
*Bumblebee*
1 cup                                                      286
**Sardines, 1 oz**
*Del Monte*                                                44
*Underwood*
in mustard sauce                                          52
in soya bean oil                                          62
in tomato sauce                                           330
**Scallops**
*Mrs. Paul's*, 3½ oz                                       210
**Seafood combination**
*Mrs. Paul's*                                              510
**Shrimp**
*Bumblebee*, 1 can                                         90

| | |
|---|---:|
| *Icy Point*, 1 can | 148 |
| *Pillar Rock*, 1 can | 148 |
| *Mrs. Paul's*, 1 oz | 57 |
| *Sau-Sea*, 1 oz | 80 |

**Shad Roe**

| | |
|---|---:|
| *Bumblebee*, 1 can | 259 |

**Shrimp and Scallops**

| | |
|---|---:|
| *Stouffer's*, 1 pkg | 400 |

**Sole**

| | |
|---|---:|
| *Mrs. Paul's*, 4½ oz | 160 |
| *Ship Ahoy*, 1 pkg | 310 |

with peas, mushrooms, and lobster sauce

| | |
|---|---:|
| *Weight Watchers*, 1 pkg | 200 |

**Tuna, canned in oil, drained**

| | |
|---|---:|
| *Bumblebee*, 1 cup | 334 |
| *Chicken of the Sea* | |
| 3¼-oz can | 224 |
| 6½-oz can | 447 |
| 9¼-oz can | 636 |
| 12½-oz can | 860 |
| *Del Monte*, 6½-oz can | 450 |
| *Gold Seal*, 5-oz can | 278 |
| *Icy Point*, 5-oz can | 278 |
| *Pillar Rock*, 5-oz can | 278 |
| *Snow Mist*, 5-oz can | 278 |
| *Van Camp*, 6¼-oz can | 440 |

**Tuna, canned, solid, in water**

| | |
|---|---:|
| *Bumblebee*, 1 cup | 300 |
| *Chicken of the Sea*, 7-oz can | 216 |

**Tuna, creamed, with peas**
*Green Giant Boil-in-Bag* 140
**Tuna Pot Pies**
*Banquet* 478
*Morton* 385
*Star Kist* 397
**Turbot with peas and carrots**
*Weight Watchers, 1 pkg* 280

# CHAPTER 8

# *Fruits and Vegetables*

## FRESH FRUITS AND VEGETABLES

**Acerolas (West Indian Cherries)**
| | |
|---|---|
| whole, 1 lb | 104 |
| pitted, 4 oz | 32 |
| 3 cherries | 7 |

**Amaranth**
| | |
|---|---|
| whole, 1 lb | 100 |
| leaves only, 1 lb | 160 |

**Apples**
| | |
|---|---|
| with skin | |
| 1 lb | 242 |

| | |
|---|---:|
| 1 apple (3¼", 2 per lb) | 123 |
| 1 apple (2¾", 3 per lb) | 80 |
| 1 apple (2½", 4 per lb) | 61 |
| chopped, 1 cup | 73 |
| pared | |
| 1 apple (3¼", 2 per lb) | 107 |
| 1 apple (2¾", 3 per lb) | 70 |
| 1 apple (2½", 4 per lb) | 53 |
| chopped, 1 cup | 68 |

**Apples, dehydrated**
uncooked

| | |
|---|---:|
| 8 oz | 800 |
| 1 cup | 355 |

cooked, sweetened

| | |
|---|---:|
| 8 oz | 175 |
| 1 cup | 195 |

**Apples, dried**
uncooked

| | |
|---|---:|
| 8 oz | 625 |
| 1 cup | 234 |

cooked, unsweetened

| | |
|---|---:|
| 8 oz | 177 |
| 1 cup | 199 |

cooked, sweetened

| | |
|---|---:|
| 8 oz | 254 |
| 1 cup | 314 |

**Apricots**
whole

| | |
|---|---:|
| 1 lb | 217 |
| 1 apricot | 18 |

**8**

pitted, halves
  1 lb                                             231
  1 cup                                             79

**Apricots, dehydrated**
  uncooked
    8 oz                                           755
    1 cup                                          330
  cooked, sweetened
    8 oz                                           271
    1 cup                                          339

**Apricots, dried**
  uncooked
    8 oz                                           590
    1 cup                                          340
    10 medium halves                               90
  cooked, unsweetened, with liquid
    8 oz                                           195
    1 cup                                          210
  cooked, sweetened, 1 cup                         329

**Artichokes**
  raw, whole, 1 lb                                 85
  boiled, drained, 1 whole bud                     67

**Asparagus**
  raw
    whole, 1 lb                                    66
    cuts, 1 cup                                    35
  boiled, drained
    1 medium spear                                 3
    cuts, 1 cup                                    29

**8**

## Avocados, California
whole, 1 lb ..... 589
peeled and pitted, 1 average ..... 370
diced, 1 cup ..... 260
mashed, 1 cup ..... 390

## Avocados, Florida
whole, 1 lb ..... 389
peeled and pitted, 1 average ..... 200
diced, 1 cup ..... 190
mashed, 1 cup ..... 300

## Bamboo shoots, raw
8 oz ..... 61
1 cup, cuts ..... 40

## Bananas
whole
  1 large (10″) ..... 119
  1 medium (9″) ..... 103
  1 small (8″) ..... 83
1 cup
  sliced ..... 135
  mashed ..... 190

## Bananas, dehydrated
flakes, 1 cup ..... 340

## Bananas, red
whole, 1 average (7¼″) ..... 118
sliced, 1 cup ..... 135

## Bean Sprouts, mung
uncooked
  8 oz ..... 80
  1 cup ..... 37

**8**

boiled, drained
| | |
|---|---|
| 8 oz | 65 |
| 1 cup | 35 |

**Bean sprouts, soy**
uncooked
| | |
|---|---|
| 8 oz | 105 |
| 1 cup | 48 |

boiled, drained
| | |
|---|---|
| 8 oz | 86 |
| 1 cup | 48 |

**Beet greens**
| | |
|---|---|
| raw, trimmed, 1 lb | 61 |

boiled, drained
| | |
|---|---|
| 8 oz | 41 |
| 1 cup | 26 |

**Beets**
raw, trimmed
| | |
|---|---|
| 1 lb | 137 |
| whole, 1 beet (2″) | 21 |
| diced, 1 cup | 58 |

boiled, drained
| | |
|---|---|
| whole, 1 beet | 16 |
| diced, 1 cup | 58 |
| sliced, 1 cup | 66 |

**Blackberries**
| | |
|---|---|
| 1 lb | 250 |
| 1 cup | 84 |

**Blueberries**
| | |
|---|---|
| 1 lb | 260 |
| 1 cup | 90 |

**Broccoli**
raw
    whole, 1 lb     90
    trimmed, 1 lb     145
boiled, drained
    8 oz     59
    1 average stalk 6½ oz     47
    cuts, 1 cup     40
**Brussel Sprouts**
raw
    whole, 1 lb     200
    trimmed, 1 lb     190
boiled, drained
    8 oz     82
    1 cup     55
    1 average sprout     7
**Cabbage, Chinese (Celery Cabbage), raw**
    whole, 1 lb     62
    trimmed, 1 lb     65
    cuts, 1 cup     11
    strips, 1 cup     8
**Cabbage, green**
raw
    whole, 1 lb     98
    trimmed, 1 lb     110
    chopped, 1 cup     22
    sliced, 1 cup     17
    ground, 1 cup     36
  boiled, drained, 1 cup     30
**Cabbage, dehydrated, 1 oz**     87

# 8

**Cabbage, red, raw**
  whole, 1 lb    127
  trimmed, 1 lb    141
  sliced, 1 cup    22
**Cabbage, savoy, raw**
  whole, 1 lb    98
  trimmed, 1 lb    109
  sliced, 1 cup    17
**Cabbage, spoon (Bakchoy)**
  raw
    whole, 1 lb    73
    trimmed, 1 lb    70
    cuts, 1 cup    11
  boiled, drained, cuts, 1 cup    24
**Cantaloupe**
  one 5-inch melon    95
  cubed, 1 cup    48
**Carambola, raw**
  whole, 1 lb    150
  peeled and seeded, 8 oz    80
**Carissas (Natal plums), raw**
  whole, 1 lb    273
  peeled and seeded, 8 oz    155
  sliced, 1 cup    105
**Carrot**
  raw
    whole, 1 lb    156
    whole scraped
      8 oz    95
      1 medium    21

| | |
|---|---:|
| diced, 1 cup | 60 |
| slices, 1 cup | 53 |
| boiled, drained, 1 cup | 45 |
| **Carrot, dehydrated, 1 oz** | 100 |
| **Casaba melon** | |
| whole | 61 |
| cubed, 1 cup | 45 |
| **Cauliflower** | |
| raw | |
| whole, 1 lb | 48 |
| flowerets | |
| 1 lb | 120 |
| 1 cup | 27 |
| chopped, 1 cup | 30 |
| boiled, drained, 1 cup | 29 |
| **Celeriac root, raw** | |
| whole, 1 lb | 155 |
| pared, 1 root approx 1 oz | 11 |
| **Celery** | |
| raw | |
| whole, 1 lb | 58 |
| 1 large outer stalk (8″) | 7 |
| 1 small inner stalk (5″) | 3 |
| chopped, 1 cup | 20 |
| boiled, drained, 1 cup | 22 |
| **Chard, Swiss** | |
| raw | |
| whole, 1 lb | 113 |
| 1 lb, then trimmed | 104 |

**8**

boiled, drained

| | |
|---|---|
| leaves and stalks, 1 cup | 26 |
| leaves only, 1 cup | 32 |

**Chayote**

| | |
|---|---|
| raw, 1 medium squash | 56 |

**Cherimoya, raw**

| | |
|---|---|
| whole, 1 lb | 247 |
| peeled and seeded, 8 oz | 215 |

**Cherries**

sour, red

whole

| | |
|---|---|
| 1 lb | 213 |
| 1 cup | 60 |
| pitted, 1 cup | 90 |

sweet

whole

| | |
|---|---|
| 1 lb | 286 |
| 1 cup | 82 |

pitted

| | |
|---|---|
| 1 cup | 102 |
| 1 average cherry | 5 |

**Chervil**

| | |
|---|---|
| raw, 1 oz | 16 |

**Chives, raw**

| | |
|---|---|
| whole, 1 lb | 128 |
| chopped, 1 Tbsp | 1 |

**Coconut, raw**

| | |
|---|---|
| in shell, 1 coconut (4½″ and 27 oz) | 1,375 |
| shelled, meat only, 4 oz | 392 |

shredded, 1 cup

| | |
|---|---|
| loosely packed | 277 |
| firmly packed | 450 |

**Coconut, dried, shredded**

unsweetened

| | |
|---|---|
| 4 oz | 750 |
| 1 cup | 622 |

sweetened

| | |
|---|---|
| 4 oz | 622 |
| 1 cup | 515 |

**Collards**

raw

| | |
|---|---|
| whole, 1 lb | 180 |
| leaves only, 1 lb | 205 |

boiled

| | |
|---|---|
| leaves only | 60 |
| with stems, 1 cup | 43 |

**Corn, sweet**

| | |
|---|---|
| raw, on the cob, 1 lb | 240 |

boiled, drained

| | |
|---|---|
| on the cob, 1 ear (5″) | 70 |
| kernels, 1 cup | 140 |

**Corn Salad, raw**

| | |
|---|---|
| whole, 1 lb | 90 |
| trimmed, 1 lb | 95 |

**Crab apples, raw**

| | |
|---|---|
| whole, 1 lb | 280 |
| trimmed | 309 |

**Cranberries**

| | |
|---|---|
| whole, 1 lb | 200 |

⌐8

| | |
|---|---:|
| without stems, 1 cup | 52 |
| chopped, 1 cup | 50 |
| **Cranberries, dehydrated, 1 oz** | 100 |
| **Cucumber** | |
| 1 lb | 65 |
| 1 average (7½″) | 35 |
| sliced, 1 cup | 15 |
| **Currants** | |
| black | |
| whole, 1 lb | 240 |
| trimmed, 1 cup | 60 |
| red or white | |
| whole, 1 lb | 220 |
| trimmed, 1 cup | 55 |
| **Dandelion greens** | |
| raw, trimmed, 1 lb | 205 |
| boiled, drained, 1 cup | |
| loosely packed | 35 |
| firmly packed | 70 |
| **Dates, domestic** | |
| whole, 1 lb | 1,081 |
| pitted, 1 lb | 1,243 |
| chopped, 1 cup | 488 |
| 1 average date | 22 |
| **Dock (Sorrel)** | |
| raw, whole, 1 lb | 89 |
| boiled, drained, 1 cup | 38 |
| **Eggplant** | |
| raw | |
| whole, 1 lb | 92 |

| | |
|---|---:|
| diced, 1 cup | 50 |
| boiled, drained, 1 cup | 38 |
| **Elderberries** | |
| whole, 1 lb | 310 |
| without stems, 8 oz | 160 |
| **Endive (French or Belgian) bleached (Chicory)** | |
| trimmed, 1 lb | 68 |
| 1 head (6″) | 8 |
| 1 small leave | ½ |
| chopped, 1 cup | 14 |
| **Escarole** | |
| whole, 1 lb | 80 |
| large outer leaf | 5 |
| small inner leaf | ½ |
| chopped, 1 cup | 10 |
| **Fennel, raw** | |
| whole, 1 lb | 120 |
| trimmed, 2 oz | 15 |
| **Figs, raw** | |
| whole, 1 lb | 360 |
| 1 medium (2¼″) | 40 |
| dried | |
| 8 oz | 620 |
| 1 medium (2″) | 58 |
| **Garlic, raw** | |
| whole, 2 oz | 68 |
| peeled | |
| 2 oz | 80 |
| 1 clove | 3 |

**8**

**Ginger root**
| | |
|---|---|
| whole, 1 lb | 205 |
| peeled, 1 oz | 14 |

**Green (Snap) Beans, 1 cup** 31

**Gooseberries**
| | |
|---|---|
| 1 lb | 177 |
| 1 cup | 59 |

**Grapes**

American slipskin: Concord, Delaware, Niagara
| | |
|---|---|
| whole, 1 lb | 197 |

seeded
| | |
|---|---|
| 1 cup | 70 |
| 1 grape | 2 |

European close skin: Malaga, Muscat, Thompson
| | |
|---|---|
| whole, 1 lb | 270 |
| seeded, 1 cup | 100 |

seedless
| | |
|---|---|
| 1 cup | 107 |
| 1 grape | 3½ |

**Ground-cherries, raw**
| | |
|---|---|
| whole, 1 lb | 220 |

without husks
| | |
|---|---|
| 1 lb | 240 |
| 1 cup | 74 |

**Guava**
| | |
|---|---|
| whole, 1 lb | 275 |
| trimmed, 8 oz | 140 |
| 1 average | 58 |

**Honeydew Melon**
| | |
|---|---|
| whole, 1 lb | 94 |
| cubed, 1 cup | 56 |

**Jack Fruit**
| | |
|---|---|
| whole, 1 lb | 125 |
| peeled and seeded, 8 oz | 110 |

**Jujubes (Chinese dates)**
fresh
| | |
|---|---|
| whole, 1 lb | 444 |
| seeded, 8 oz | 238 |

dried
| | |
|---|---|
| whole, 1 lb | 1,160 |
| seeded, 8 oz | 650 |

**Kale**
raw
| | |
|---|---|
| whole, 1 lb | 129 |
| without stems, 1 lb | 155 |
| leaves only, 4 oz | 80 |

boiled, drained
| | |
|---|---|
| 1 cup | 31 |
| leaves only, 1 cup | 44 |

**Kohlrabi**
raw
| | |
|---|---|
| whole, 1 lb | 96 |
| pared | |
| 8 oz | 65 |
| diced, 1 cup | 40 |
| boiled, drained, 1 cup | 40 |

**Kumquats**
| | |
|---|---|
| whole, 1 lb | 274 |
| trimmed | |
| 8 oz | 150 |

⌐8

| | |
|---|---|
| 1 medium | 12 |
| **Leeks, raw** | |
| whole, 1 lb | 123 |
| bulb and lower leaf | |
| 8 oz | 116 |
| 1 medium | 17 |
| **Lettuce** | |
| Boston | |
| whole | |
| 1 lb | 47 |
| 1 head (5″) | 23 |
| 1 large, 2 medium or 3 small leaves | 2 |
| chopped, 1 cup | 8 |
| Iceberg | |
| whole | |
| 1 lb | 56 |
| 1 head (6″) | 70 |
| 1 medium leaf | 3 |
| chopped, 1 cup | 7 |
| Loose Leaf | |
| whole | |
| 1 lb | 52 |
| 3 large leaves | 15 |
| chopped, 1 cup | 10 |
| Romaine or cos | |
| whole | |
| 1 lb | 52 |
| 1 leaf | 2 |
| chopped, 1 cup | 10 |

**Limes**
| | |
|---|---:|
| whole, 1 lb | 106 |
| pulp only, 1 lime | 19 |

**Loganberries**
| | |
|---|---:|
| whole, 1 lb | 267 |
| trimmed | |
| 8 oz | 140 |
| 1 cup | 90 |

**Loqats**
| | |
|---|---:|
| whole, 1 lb | 168 |
| seeded | |
| 8 oz | 110 |
| 1 medium | 6 |

**Mangoes, whole**
| | |
|---|---:|
| 1 lb | 200 |
| 1 medium | 150 |
| 1 cup | 110 |

**Mushrooms, raw**
| | |
|---|---:|
| whole, 1 lb | 123 |
| chopped, 1 cup | 20 |

**Mustard Greens**
| | |
|---|---:|
| raw | |
| whole | |
| 1 lb | 57 |
| trimmed, 8 oz | 70 |
| boiled, drained, leaves only | |
| 8 oz | 52 |
| 1 cup | 32 |

**Mustard Spinach (Tendergreens)**
| | |
|---|---:|
| raw, whole, 1 lb | 100 |

**8**

boiled, drained
  8 oz     37
  1 cup     30
**Nectarines, whole**
  1 lb     267
  1 medium     88
**New Zealand Spinach**
raw, whole, 1 lb     86
boiled, drained
  8 oz     30
  1 cup     23
**Okra**
raw
  whole, 1 lb     140
  trimmed, 8 oz     80
boiled, drained, sliced, 1 cup     45
**Onions, mature**
raw
  whole, 1 lb     157
  trimmed
    8 oz     85
    1 medium     40
    chopped, 1 cup     65
    chopped, 1 Tbsp     4
    grated, 1 cup     90
boiled, drained, 1 cup     60
**Onions, young green**
whole, 1 lb     157
bulb and top
  trimmed, 1 lb     164

| | |
|---|---|
| chopped, 1 cup | 36 |
| chopped, 1 Tbsp | 2 |
| top only, chopped | |
| 1 cup | 27 |
| 1 Tbsp | 2 |

**Onions, Welsh**
raw
| | |
|---|---|
| whole, 1 lb | 100 |
| trimmed, 8 oz | 78 |

**Oranges**
whole
| | |
|---|---|
| 1 lb | 162 |
| 1 medium | 64 |
| diced, 1 cup | 103 |

**Papaw**
whole
| | |
|---|---|
| 1 lb | 290 |
| 1 medium | 83 |
| peeled and seeded | |
| 8 oz | 185 |
| 1 cup | 210 |

**Papayas**
whole
| | |
|---|---|
| 1 lb | 120 |
| 1 medium | 120 |
| peeled and seeded | |
| 8 oz | 90 |
| cubed, 1 cup | 55 |

**8**

**Parsley**
  whole, 1 lb                             200
  chopped
    1 cup                           26
    1 Tbsp                      2
    1 sprig                     4

**Parsnips**
  raw, whole, 1 lb              293
  boiled, drained
    diced, 1 cup             100
    mashed, 1 cup          140

**Passion Fruit**
  whole
    1 lb                        210
    1 medium               15
  shelled, 8 oz              200

**Peaches**
  whole, 1 lb                     150
  peeled, 1 medium            38
  pared, diced, 1 cup        70

**Pears, 1 pear**
  Bartlett                       200
  Bosc                         85
  D'Anjou                   120

**Peas, green immature**
  raw
    whole, 1 lb                150
    shelled
      1 lb                  380
      1 cup               120

boiled, drained

| | |
|---|---:|
| 8 oz | 160 |
| 1 cup | 115 |

**Peas, mature, dried**

raw

whole

| | |
|---|---:|
| 1 lb | 1,540 |
| 1 cup | 680 |
| split, uncoated, 1 cup | 700 |
| cooked, split, uncoated, 1 cup | 230 |

**Pea Pods (Snow Peas)**

| | |
|---|---:|
| whole, 1 lb | 228 |

**Pepper, Hot chili, green, raw**

| | |
|---|---:|
| whole, 1 lb | 120 |
| seeded, 8 oz | 85 |

**Pepper, Hot chili, red**

raw

| | |
|---|---:|
| whole, 1 lb | 400 |
| seeded, 8 oz | 145 |
| pods, dried, 1 Tbsp | 25 |

**Peppers, Sweet, green, raw**

whole

| | |
|---|---:|
| 1 lb | 80 |
| 1 pepper, fancy grade large | 35 |
| 1 pepper, No 1 grade | 15 |
| chopped, 1 cup | 33 |

**Peppers, Sweet, red, raw**

| | |
|---|---:|
| whole, 1 lb | 110 |
| seeded and cored, 8 oz | 70 |
| chopped, 1 cup | 47 |

**8**

**Persimmon**
  Japanese or Kaki
    whole, 1 lb              286
    seedless, 1 lb         295
    trimmed, 1 medium    130
  native
    whole
      1 lb             475
      1 medium        32
    trimmed and seeded, 8 oz   65

**Pigeon peas**
  raw, whole, 1 lb        210
  dried, 8 oz          760

**Pineapple**
  whole, 1 lb          125
  cubed, 1 cup         80

**Pitanga (Surinam Cherries)**
  whole
    1 lb             187
    4 medium         10
  pitted, 1 cup       87

**Plantains, raw**
  whole, 1 lb          390
  peeled, 8 oz        270
  1 banana (10″)     285

**Plums**
  Damson
    whole
      1 lb           272

| | |
|---|---:|
| 1 medium | 7 |
| pitted, 8 oz | 150 |
| **Japanese** | |
| whole | |
| 1 lb | 205 |
| 1 medium | 32 |
| pitted, 8 oz | 110 |
| **Prune type** | |
| whole | |
| 1 lb | 320 |
| 1 medium | 21 |
| pitted, 8 oz | 170 |
| **Poke Shoot (Pokeberry)** | |
| raw, 1 lb | 104 |
| boiled, drained, 1 cup | 33 |
| **Pomegranate** | |
| whole | |
| 1 lb | 194 |
| 1 medium | 100 |
| **Potatoes** | |
| raw | |
| whole, 1 lb | 280 |
| peeled, 1 cup | 114 |
| baked in skin | |
| 4 oz | 81 |
| 1 long | 145 |
| boiled in skin | |
| 4 oz | 79 |
| 1 long | 173 |
| 1 round | 104 |

boiled, peeled

| | |
|---|---:|
| 4 oz | 74 |
| 1 cup | 100 |
| fried, 4 oz | 275 |
| hash brown, 4 oz | 260 |

mashed, with milk and butter

| | |
|---|---:|
| 4 oz | 107 |
| 1 cup | 137 |
| scalloped, with cheese, 4 oz | 118 |

**Prickly Pears, raw**

| | |
|---|---:|
| whole, 1 lb | 84 |
| peeled and seeded, 8 oz | 96 |

**Prunes, dehydrated, uncooked**

| | |
|---|---:|
| 8 oz | 780 |
| 1 cup | 344 |

**Pumpkin, raw**

| | |
|---|---:|
| whole, 1 lb | 83 |
| pulp only, 8 oz | 60 |

**Purslane leaves**

| | |
|---|---:|
| raw, whole, 1 lb | 95 |
| boiled, drained, 1 cup | 27 |

**Quinces**

| | |
|---|---:|
| whole, 1 lb | 158 |
| peeled and seeded, 8 oz | 130 |

**Radishes, raw**

whole

| | |
|---|---:|
| 1 lb | 49 |
| 10 medium | 8 |
| sliced, 1 cup | 20 |

**Radishes, Oriental**

| | |
|---|---|
| whole, 1 lb | 57 |
| without tops, 1 lb | 67 |
| pared, 8 oz | 45 |

**Raisins, seedless**

| | |
|---|---|
| 8 oz | 655 |
| 1 cup loose | 420 |
| 1 cup firmly packed | 477 |

**Raspberries**

black

| | |
|---|---|
| 1 lb | 330 |
| 1 cup | 98 |

red

| | |
|---|---|
| 1 lb | 260 |
| 1 cup | 70 |

**Rhubarb**

raw

| | |
|---|---|
| whole, 1 lb | 33 |
| trimmed, 1 lb | 60 |
| diced, 1 cup | 20 |
| cooked, sweetened, 1 cup | 381 |

**Rose Apples**

| | |
|---|---|
| whole, 1 lb | 170 |
| trimmed and seeded, 8 oz | 138 |

**Rutabagas**

raw

| | |
|---|---|
| whole, 1 lb | 177 |
| trimmed, 8 oz | 105 |
| diced, 1 cup | 60 |

boiled, drained
cubes, 1 cup — 60
mashed, 1 cup — 84
**Sapodillas**
whole, 1 lb — 323
peeled and seeded, 8 oz — 202
**Shallots, raw**
whole, 1 oz — 18
peeled
1 oz — 20
1 Tbsp — 7
**Soursop, raw**
whole, 1 lb — 200
peeled and seeded, 8 oz — 149
**Soybean curd (Tofu)**
4 oz — 82
**Spinach**
raw
whole, 1 lb — 85
trimmed
leaves, 1 cup — 9
chopped, 1 cup — 14
boiled, drained, leaves, 1 cup — 41
**Squash, summer**
raw
whole, 1 lb — 85
trimmed, 8 oz — 25
diced, 1 cup — 35
boiled, drained, 1 cup — 30

**8**

**Squash, winter**
| | |
|---|---|
| raw, whole, 1 lb | 150 |
| baked, 8 oz | 120 |

**Strawberries, whole**
| | |
|---|---|
| 1 lb | 161 |
| trimmed, 1 lb | 168 |
| 1 cup | 55 |

**Sugar Apples (Sweetsop)**
| | |
|---|---|
| whole, 1 lb | 192 |
| peeled and seeded | |
| 8 oz | 220 |
| 1 cup | 235 |

**Swamp Cabbage**
| | |
|---|---|
| raw | |
| whole, 1 lb | 107 |
| trimmed, 1 lb | 132 |
| boiled, drained, 8 oz | 48 |

**Sweet Potatoes**
| | |
|---|---|
| raw, whole, 1 lb | 420 |
| baked in skin, 4 oz | 125 |

**Tamarinds**
| | |
|---|---|
| whole, 1 lb | 520 |
| shelled and seeded, 8 oz | 540 |

**Tomatoes, green**
| | |
|---|---|
| whole, 1 lb | 99 |

**Tomatoes, ripe**
| | |
|---|---|
| raw | |
| whole | |
| 1 lb | 100 |
| 1 medium | 25 |

| | |
|---|---|
| sliced, 1 cup | 40 |
| boiled, 1 cup | 63 |
| **Towel Gourd** | |
| whole, 1 lb | 70 |
| pared, 8 oz | 40 |
| **Turnip Greens** | |
| raw | |
| whole, 1 lb | 107 |
| trimmed, 1 lb | 127 |
| boiled | |
| 8 oz | 46 |
| 1 cup | 30 |
| **Turnips** | |
| raw | |
| whole, 1 lb | 117 |
| cubed, 1 cup | 39 |
| boiled, drained | |
| 8 oz | 52 |
| 1 cup | 36 |
| mashed | 53 |
| **Vinespinach (Basella), raw, 8 oz** | 44 |
| **Water Chestnuts, Chinese** | |
| raw, whole, 1 lb | 276 |
| **Watercress** | |
| whole | |
| 1 lb | 80 |
| 1 cup | 7 |
| chopped, 1 cup | 24 |
| **Watermelon** | |
| whole, 1 lb | 54 |

| | |
|---|---|
| 1 wedge (4″ x 8″) | 110 |
| diced, 1 cup | 42 |
| **Wax (Yellow) Beans** | |
| 1 cup | 29 |
| **Yam Beans, raw** | |
| whole, 1 lb | 225 |
| pared, 8 oz | 130 |
| **Yams, raw** | |
| whole, 1 lb | 395 |
| pared, 4 oz | 115 |
| **Zucchini (see Summer Squash)** | |

# FRUIT,
# COMMERCIALLY PACKAGED,
# CANNED OR FROZEN,
## ½ cup unless noted

| | |
|---|---|
| **Apples and Apricots** | |
| *Mott's* | 104 |
| **Apples and Cherries** | |
| *Mott's* | 110 |
| **Apples and Pineapples** | |
| *Mott's* | 127 |

# 8

**Apples and Raspberries**
  *Mott's*                                      105
**Applesauce**
  *Del Monte*                                    85
  *Mott's*                                       45
  *S & W*                                        48
  *Stokely-Van Camp*                             90
  *Tillie Lewis*                                 60
  *Town House*                                   85
**Apricots**
  *Del Monte*                                   100
  *Libby's*                                     100
  *Stokely-Van Camp*                            110
  *Tillie Lewis*                                 60
  *Town House*                                   80
**Blackberries**
  *S & W*                                        36
**Blueberries**
  *Seabrook Farms*                               45
**Boysenberries**
  *S & W*                                        32
**Cherries**
  *Del Monte* Light                              95
    Dark                                         90
    Dark pitted                                  95
  *Libby's*                                     100
  *S & W*                                        50
  *Stokely-Van Camp*                             50
**Cherries, maraschino**
  *Vita* 1 cherry                                20

**Cranberry and Orange**
Ocean Spray     100
**Cranberry Sauce**
Ocean Spray     90
**Currants**
Del Monte     190
**Dates**
Bordo     330
Dromedary     397
Dromedary pitted     376
**Figs**
Del Monte     100
S & W, 6 figs     49
**Fruit Cocktail**
Del Monte     85
Dole     72
Libby's     75
S & W     35
Stokely-Van Camp     95
Tillie Lewis     50
Town House     85
**Fruit Salad**
Del Monte     85
Del Monte Tropical     100
Kraft     48
Libby's     90
S & W     35
Stokely-Van Camp     95
**Fruits and Peels**
Liberty     388

## Grapefruit sections
*Del Monte*     45
*Kraft*     43
*S & W*     36
*Tillie Lewis*     45

## Mixed Fruit
*Birds Eye*     105

## Melon Balls
*Birds Eye,* 1 pkg     144

## Oranges
*Del Monte*     75
*Kraft*     52
*S & W*     27

## Peaches
*Birds Eye*     72
*Del Monte*     85
*Highway*     70
*S & W*     25
*Scotch Buy*     70
*Seabrook Farms*     105
*Stokely-Van Camp*     90
*Town House,* heavy syrup     95
*Town House,* extra heavy syrup     130

## Peaches and Strawberries
*Birds Eye*     80

## Pears
*Del Monte*     80
*Libby's*     85
*Libby's* Juice Pack     75
*Highway*     80

| | |
|---|---|
| *Scotch Buy* | 70 |
| *S & W* | 28 |
| *Stokely-Van Camp* | 105 |
| *Tillie Lewis* | 50 |

**Pineapple**

| | |
|---|---|
| *Del Monte* in juice | 70 |
| *Del Monte* in syrup | 95 |
| *Dole* in juice | 65 |
| *Dole* in syrup | 85 |
| *S & W* | 50 |
| *Town House* in juice | 75 |
| *Town House* in syrup | 95 |

**Plums**

| | |
|---|---|
| *Del Monte* | 95 |
| *Libby's* | 105 |
| *S & W* | 50 |
| *Stokely-Van Camp* | 120 |
| *Tillie Lewis* | 70 |

**Prunes**

| | |
|---|---|
| *Del Monte* | 115 |
| *Heart's Delight* | 210 |
| *Sunsweet* | 196 |

**Raspberries**

| | |
|---|---|
| *Birds Eye* | 120 |
| *Seabrook Farms* | 120 |

**Rhubarb**

| | |
|---|---|
| *Birds Eye* | 138 |

**Strawberries**

| | |
|---|---|
| *Birds Eye* | 90 |
| *Birds Eye* slices | 145 |

| | |
|---|---:|
| *Seabrook Farms* | 42 |
| *Seabrook Farms* slices | 140 |
| *S & W* | 20 |

# VEGETABLES, COMMERCIALLY PACKAGED, CANNED OR FROZEN,
## 1 cup unless noted

| | |
|---|---:|
| **Artichoke Hearts** | |
| *Birds Eye* | 53 |
| **Asparagus, cuts** | |
| *Green Giant* | 40 |
| *Kounty Kist* | 40 |
| *Lindy* | 39 |
| *Stokely-Van Camp* | 44 |
| **Asparagus, Spears** | |
| *Del Monte* | 35 |
| *Green Giant* | 40 |
| *Le Sueur* | 38 |
| *S & W* | 18 |
| *Town House* | 35 |
| **Asparagus, frozen** | |
| *Birds Eye* | 61 |
| with Hollandaise Sauce, 1 pkg | 290 |

| | |
|---|---:|
| *Green Giant* | 90 |
| *Seabrook Farms* | 46 |
| **Bamboo Shoots** | |
| *Chun King* | 30 |
| *La Choy* | 23 |
| **Bean Sprouts** | |
| *Chun King* | 40 |
| *La Choy* | 24 |
| **Beets, cut** | |
| *Del Monte* | 70 |
| *Libby's* | 70 |
| *Stokely-Van Camp* | 90 |
| **Beets, diced** | |
| *Comstock* | 82 |
| *Libby's* | 70 |
| *Stokely-Van Camp* | 70 |
| **Beets, Harvard** | |
| *Greenwood* | 104 |
| *Libby's* | 160 |
| *Lord Mott* | 80 |
| *Stokely-Van Camp* | 160 |
| **Beets, pickled** | |
| *Del Monte* | 150 |
| *Greenwood* | 150 |
| *Libby's* | 150 |
| *Lord Mott* | 150 |
| *Stokely-Van Camp* | 190 |
| *Town House* | 145 |
| **Beets, sliced** | |
| *Del Monte* | 70 |

**8**

| | |
|---|---|
| *Libby's* | 70 |
| *Lord Mott* | 50 |
| *S & W* | 56 |
| *Stokely-Van Camp* | 80 |
| **Beets, whole** | |
| *Del Monte* | 70 |
| *Libby's* | 70 |
| *Stokely-Van Camp* | 85 |
| **Beets, frozen** | |
| *Birds Eye* | 105 |
| **Broccoli, frozen** | |
| *Birds Eye* | 25 |
| with cheese | 110 |
| in hollandaise | 200 |
| *Green Giant* | 30 |
| in butter | 90 |
| in cheese sauce | 130 |
| with cauliflower and carrots | 140 |
| *Kounty Kist* | 30 |
| *Seabrook Farms* | 46 |
| *Stouffer's Au gratin* | 340 |
| **Brussels Sprouts** | |
| *Birds Eye* | 30 |
| *Green Giant* | 50 |
| in butter sauce | 110 |
| in cheese sauce | 170 |
| *Kounty Kist* | 50 |
| *Seabrook Farms* | 76 |
| **Cabbage** | |
| *Greenwood* | 150 |

| | |
|---|---|
| *Lord Mott* | 120 |
| **Carrots, diced** | |
| *Comstock* | 48 |
| *Del Monte* | 61 |
| *Libby's* | 40 |
| *S & W* | 44 |
| *Stokely-Van Camp* | 60 |
| **Carrots, sliced** | |
| *Birds Eye*, in buttersauce | 340 |
| in sugar | 194 |
| *Comstock* | 35 |
| *Del Monte* | 58 |
| *Green Giant*, in butter sauce | 100 |
| *Libby's* | 42 |
| *Lord Mott* | 50 |
| *Stokely-Van Camp* | 50 |
| **Cauliflower** | |
| *Birds Eye* | 61 |
| with cheese sauce | 130 |
| *Green Giant* | 30 |
| with cheese sauce | 130 |
| *Kounty Kist* | 26 |
| *Seabrook Farms* | 26 |
| **Collard Greens** | |
| *Birds Eye* | 30 |
| *Seabrook Farms* | 44 |
| **Corn, Yellow, canned** | |
| cream style | |
| *Birds Eye* | 170 |
| *Del Monte* | 210 |

| | |
|---|---|
| *Green Giant* | 210 |
| *S & W* | 168 |
| *Stokely-Van Camp* | 210 |
| liquid pack | |
| *Del Monte* | 170 |
| *Green Giant* | 160 |
| *Kounty Kist* | 180 |
| *Le Sueur* | 170 |
| *Libby's* | 160 |
| *S & W* | 104 |
| *Stokely-Van Camp* | 180 |
| vacuum pack | |
| *Del Monte* | 200 |
| *Green Giant* | 160 |
| *Kounty Kist* | 160 |
| *Stokely-Van Camp* | 240 |
| with peppers | |
| *Del Monte* | 190 |
| *Green Giant* | 150 |
| **Corn, Yellow, frozen** | |
| *Birds Eye* in butter sauce | 200 |
| *Green Giant* in butter sauce | 190 |
| with peppers | 180 |
| *Stouffer's*, 1 pkg | 465 |
| **Corn, White, frozen and canned** | |
| *Birds Eye* creamed | 170 |
| with peas | 140 |
| *Del Monte* creamed | 190 |
| kernels | 150 |
| *Green Giant* | 130 |

| | |
|---|---|
| *Kounty Kist* | 140 |
| **Eggplant Parmesan** | |
| *Mrs. Paul's* | 364 |
| **Eggplant slices** | |
| *Mrs. Paul's* | 613 |
| **Eggplant sticks** | |
| *Mrs. Paul's* | 254 |
| **Kale** | |
| *Seabrook Farms* | 60 |
| **Mixed Vegetables, canned** | |
| *Del Monte* | 79 |
| *La Choy* | 35 |
| *Libby's* | 78 |
| *Stokely-Van Camp* | 81 |
| *Town House* | 88 |
| **Mixed Vegetables, frozen** | |
| *Birds Eye* | 145 |
| *Chun King* | 23 |
| *Green Giant* | 90 |
| *Kounty Kist* | 89 |
| California | 30 |
| *La Choy* | 23 |
| **Mixed Vegetables, frozen, Chinese style** | |
| *Birds Eye* Cantonese | 123 |
| *Birds Eye* International | 48 |
| *Green Giant* | 130 |
| *La Choy* | 72 |
| **Mixed Vegetables, frozen, European styles** | |
| *Birds Eye* | |
| Danish | 74 |

**8**

| | |
|---|---:|
| Italian | 98 |
| Parisian | 74 |
| **Mixed Vegetables, frozen, Hawaiian style** | |
| *Birds Eye* | 98 |
| *Green Giant* | 197 |
| **Mixed Vegetables, frozen, Japanese style** | |
| *Birds Eye* | 98 |
| *Birds Eye* with seasonings | 74 |
| *Green Giant* | 130 |
| *La Choy,* 1 pkg | 71 |
| **Mixed Vegetables, frozen, American styles** | |
| *Birds Eye* | |
| New England | 150 |
| New Orleans Creole | 150 |
| Jubilee | 250 |
| Pennsylvania Dutch | 98 |
| San Francisco | 111 |
| Wisconsin | 111 |
| *Green Giant* | 130 |
| **Mushrooms** | |
| *Birds Eye* | 50 |
| *Brandywine* | 30 |
| *B & B* | 60 |
| *Dole* | 5 |
| *Green Giant* | 15 |
| **Mustard greens** | |
| *Birds Eye* | 44 |
| *Seabrook Farms* | 42 |
| **Okra** | |
| *Birds Eye* | 61 |

| | |
|---|---:|
| *Green Giant* | 211 |
| *Seabrook Farms* | 52 |
| **Onions** | |
| *Birds Eye* | 64 |
| in cream sauce | 239 |
| whole | 98 |
| *Green Giant* | 140 |
| *Lord Mott* | 60 |
| in cream sauce | 130 |
| *Ore-Ida* | 80 |
| *Seabrook Farms* | 232 |
| **Onion Rings,** 1 oz | |
| *Birds Eye* | 170 |
| *Mrs. Paul's* | 60 |
| *O & C* | 178 |
| *Ore-Ida* | 80 |
| **Peas, canned** | |
| early | |
| *Del Monte* | 110 |
| *Kounty Kist* | 139 |
| *Le Sueur* | 110 |
| *Lindy* | 138 |
| *Lord Mott* | 110 |
| *Minnesota Valley* | 109 |
| *Stokely-Van Camp* | 128 |
| sweet | |
| *Del Monte* | 101 |
| *Green Giant* | 110 |
| with onion | 105 |
| *Kounty Kist* | 131 |

| | |
|---|---|
| *Libby's* | 121 |
| *Lindy* | 130 |
| *S & W* | 70 |
| *Stokely-Van Camp* | 130 |
| with carrots | |
| *Del Monte* | 100 |
| *Libby's* | 101 |
| *Lord Mott* | 165 |
| *S & W* | 65 |
| *Stokely-Van Camp* | 120 |
| **Peas, frozen** | |
| early | |
| *Birds Eye* | 169 |
| *Green Giant* | 102 |
| *Kounty Kist* | 119 |
| *Le Sueur* | 149 |
| *Seabrook Farms* | 148 |
| sweet | |
| *Birds Eye* | 155 |
| *Green Giant* | 150 |
| *Seabrook Farms* | 104 |
| with carrots | |
| *Birds Eye* | 122 |
| *Kounty Kist* | 90 |
| *Seabrook Farms* | 82 |
| with cream sauce | |
| *Birds Eye* | 369 |
| *Green Giant* | 300 |
| with cream sauce and cauliflower | |
| *Birds Eye* | 247 |

in onion sauce
    *Seabrook Farms*              192
with onions
    *Birds Eye*              149
with onions and carrots
    *Le Sueur*              180
with potatos
    *Birds Eye*              431
with mushrooms
    *Birds Eye*              155
**Peppers, green**
    *Stouffers*, 1 pkg              225
    *Weight Watchers*, one 13-oz pkg      320
**Potatoes, canned**
    *Del Monte*              90
    *Hormel au gratin*, 7½-oz can      270
        with ham, 7½-oz can      255
    *Stokely-Van Camp*              103
**Potatoes, frozen, 3 oz unless noted**
    *Au gratin*
        *Green Giant*, 1 cup      390
        *Stouffer's*              270
    French fried
        *Birds Eye*
            Crinkle Cuts      124
            Cottage Fries      120
            Gold Crinkle Cuts      140
            French      111
            Shoestrings      138
            Steak Fries      109

*Ore-Ida*
| | |
|---|---|
| Cottage Fries | 140 |
| Golden Crinkles | 130 |
| Sizzling Fries | 157 |
| Sizzling Crinkles | 171 |
| Sizzling Shoestrings | 218 |
| Shoestrings | 170 |

Hash browns
| | |
|---|---|
| *Birds Eye* | 54 |
| O'Brien | 45 |
| *Ore-Ida* | 70 |
| in butter sauce | 120 |
| in butter sauce and onions | 130 |

with parsley
| | |
|---|---|
| *Seabrook Farms* | 208 |

Scalloped
| | |
|---|---|
| *Stouffer's* | 252 |

Shredded hash browns
| | |
|---|---|
| *Birds Eye* | 60 |
| *Ore-Ida* | 60 |

Slices
| | |
|---|---|
| *Green Giant* | 210 |

with sour cream
| | |
|---|---|
| *Green Giant* | 270 |

Stuffed
| | |
|---|---|
| *Green Giant* | |
| with cheese, 5 oz | 240 |
| with sour cream, 5 oz | 229 |

with peas
| | |
|---|---|
| *Green Giant* | 242 |

Taters and Puffs

| | |
|---|---|
| *Birds Eye Tasti Fries* | 140 |
| *Tasti Puffs* | 190 |
| *Ore-Ida Tater Tots* | 160 |
| *Tater Tots* with Bacon | 151 |
| *Tater Tots* with Onion | 165 |

With Vermicelli

| | |
|---|---|
| *Green Giant* | 399 |

Whole

| | |
|---|---|
| *Birds Eye* | 179 |
| *Ore-Ida* | 70 |
| *Seabrook Farms* | 153 |

**Potatoes, mix, ½ cup**

| | |
|---|---|
| *French's* | 120 |
| *Big Tate* | 129 |
| *Hungry Jack* | 160 |

Julienne

| | |
|---|---|
| *Betty Crocker* | 132 |

Au gratin

| | |
|---|---|
| *Betty Crocker* | 150 |
| *French's* | 190 |

Creamed

| | |
|---|---|
| *Betty Crocker* | 163 |

Hash browns

| | |
|---|---|
| *Betty Crocker* | 147 |
| *French's* | 160 |

Pancakes

| | |
|---|---|
| *French's* 3 cakes | 130 |

Potato Buds

| | |
|---|---|
| *Betty Crocker* | 132 |

**8**

Scalloped
   *Betty Crocker* — 150
   *French's* — 189
  With sour cream
   *Betty Crocker* — 144

**Pumpkin**
  *Del Monte* — 79
  *Libby's* — 80
  *Stokely-Van Camp* — 88

**Sauerkraut**
  *Del Monte* — 50
  *Libby's* — 42
  *Stokely-Van Camp* — 50
   Bavarian — 69

**Soup Greens**
  *Durkee* — 213

**Spinach, canned**
  *Del Monte* — 45
  *Libby's* — 44
  *Lord Mott* — 44

**Spinach, frozen**
  chopped
   *Birds Eye* — 47
   *Seabrook Farms* — 50
  creamed
   *Birds Eye* — 157
   *Green Giant* — 190
   *Lord Mott* — 130

|  |  |
|---|---:|
| *Seabrook Farms* | 200 |
| leaf | |
| *Birds Eye* | 47 |
| *Seabrook Farms* | 48 |
| souffle | |
| *Green Giant* | 300 |
| *Stouffer's*, 1 pkg | 400 |
| with butter sauce | |
| *Green Giant* | 89 |
| **Squash** | |
| *Birds Eye* | 100 |
| *Green Giant* | 118 |
| *Seabrook Farms* | 92 |
| **Stew, vegetable** | |
| *Dinty Moore*, 7½-oz can | 160 |
| *Ore-Ida* | 140 |
| **Succotash** | |
| *Birds Eye* | 202 |
| *Libby's* creamed | 190 |
| kernel | 151 |
| *Seabrook Farms* | 174 |
| *Stokely-Van Camp* | 170 |
| **Sweet Potatoes** | |
| *Birds Eye* | 408 |
| *Green Giant* | 341 |
| *Lord Mott* | 235 |
| *Mrs. Paul's* | 320 |
| **Tomatoes** | |
| stewed | 70 |
| whole | 50 |

8

**Tomato paste**
   *Contadina*                                200
   *Del Monte*                              200
   *Hunt's*                                   185
   *Town House*                          225
**Tomato puree**
   *Contadina*                                120
**Turnip Greens**
   *Birds Eye*                              47
   *Seabrook Farms*                    44
   *Stokely-Van Camp*              46
**Zucchini**
   *Birds Eye*                              39
   *Del Monte*                              60
   *Mrs. Paul's*                        480

# CHAPTER 9

# Condiments, Dips, Dressings, Oils and Sauces

## CONDIMENTS,
### 1 Tbsp, unless noted

217

**celery flakes, 1 tsp**
  *Wyler's* 7
**curry powder**
  *Crosse & Blackwell* 26
**garlic flavoring, 1 tsp**
  *Burton's* 42
**garlic powder, 1 tsp**
  *Wyler's* 8
**garlic spread**
  *Lawry's* 88
**horseradish**
  *Borden* 16
  *Heinz* 26
  *Kraft* 4
  *Tastee* 5
**hot sauce, 1 tsp**
  *Frank's* 10
  *Gebhardt* 4
  *Tabasco* 4
**meat sauces**
  *A-1* 12
  *Crosse & Blackwell* 21
  *Durkee* 60
  *Escoffier* 19
  *Gravymaster, 1 tsp* 8
  *Heinz 57* 14
  *Heinz Savory* 21
  *H.P.* 21
  *Maggi* 17

**9**

| | |
|---|---|
| *Steak Supreme* | 20 |
| **mustard** | |
| Brown | |
| *French's* | 15 |
| *Gulden's* | 13 |
| *Heinz* | 11 |
| *Mr. Mustard* | 11 |
| Dijon | |
| *Grey Poupon* | 15 |
| German | |
| *Kraft* | 15 |
| Horseradish | |
| *French's* | 15 |
| Hot | |
| *Gulden's Diablo* | 13 |
| *Heinz* | 11 |
| Onion | |
| *French's* | 25 |
| Yellow | |
| *French's* | 16 |
| *Gulden's* | 11 |
| *Heinz* | 10 |
| *Kraft* | 12 |
| **onion flakes, 1 tsp** | |
| *Wyler's* | 7 |
| **onion flavoring, 1 tsp** | |
| *Burton's* | 42 |
| **onion powder, 1 tsp** | |
| *Wyler's* | 1 |

**onions, minced, 1 tsp**
  *Borden's*    7
  *Wyler's*    7
**parsley flakes, 1 tsp**
  *Wyler's*    1
**pepper**
  Seasoned
    *Lawry's, 1 tsp*    16
  sweet
    *Wyler's, 1 tsp*    2
**salt, flavored, 1 tsp**
  celery    6
  garlic    6
  onion    6
**sandwich spread**
  *Hellman's*    60
  *Kraft*    56
**vinegar**
  Cider or white    1
  Wine
    *Holland House*
      Marsala    35
      Red    25
      Sherry    40
      White    25
    *Regina*
      Sauterne    1
      Sherry    10

# Flavorings, Extracts, 1 tsp

**Almond**
*Durkee* 13
*Ehlers* 5
**Anise**
*Durkee* 16
*Ehlers* 12
**Banana**
*Durkee* 15
*Ehlers* 7
**Black Walnut**
*Durkee* 45
**Brandy**
*Durkee* 15
*Ehlers* 18
**Cherry**
*Ehlers* 8
**Chocolate**
*Durkee* 8
**Coconut**
*Durkee* 7
*Ehlers* 13
**Lemon**
*Durkee* 17
*Ehlers* 14
**Maple**
*Durkee* 6
*Ehlers* 9

**Mocha**
   *Durkee*     14
**Orange**
   *Durkee*     16
   *Ehlers*     14
**Peppermint**
   *Durkee*     15
   *Ehlers*     12
**Pineapple**
   *Ehlers*     13
**Raspberry**
   *Ehlers*     10
**Rum**
   *Durkee*     14
   *Ehlers*     12
**Strawberry**
   *Durkee*     12
   *Ehlers*     11
**Vanilla**
   *Durkee*     5

# Relishes, Pickles, Olives: 1 piece unless noted

**Capers, 1 Tbsp**
   *Crosse & Blackwell*     6

**Carrots, dill**
  *Cresca* Cocktail Sticks      1
**Cauliflower, sweet**
  *Heinz*      9
  *Smucker's*      23
**ChowChow, 1 Tbsp**
  *Crosse & Blackwell*      20
**Chutney**
  Major Grey's      53
**Eggplant**
  *Cresca*      1
**Olives**
  Green, Manzanilla
    *Durkee*      4
    *Grandee*      4
  Green, Spanish
    *Vita*      11
  Green, queen
    *Durkee*      14
    *Grandee*      14
  Ripe
    *Durkee*      7
    *Grandee*      7
    *Lindsay*      6
    *Vita*      7
**Onions**
  *Cresca*      1
  *Crosse & Blackwell*      1
  *Heinz*      2
  *Heinz* Spiced      1

**Peppers, 1 oz unless noted**
Chili
 *Del Monte*         5
 *Ortega*
  Jalapeños       8
  Green        5
Hot, 1 pepper
 *Cresca*         6
 *Smucker's*       10
Mild, sweet
 *Del Monte*       5
Pickled
 *Old El Paso*      9
Red, bell
 *Ortega*        9
**Pickle Relish, 1 Tbsp**
Barbecue
 *Crosse & Blackwell*    22
 *Heinz*         31
Corn
 *Crosse & Blackwell*    15
Hamburger
 *Crosse & Blackwell*    20
 *Heinz*         17
Hot dog
 *Crosse & Blackwell*    22
 *Heinz*         2
Hot pepper
 *Crosse & Blackwell*    22

India
   *Crosse & Blackwell*               26
piccalilli
   *Crosse & Blackwell*               25
   *Heinz*                              19

**Pickles**
  Sour
     *Bond's*                       2
     *Crosse & Blackwell*            2
     *Heinz*
       Genuine Dill           10
       Kosher Dills          2
     *L & S*                      2
  Sweet
     *Bond's*                    19
     *Crosse & Blackwell*          28
       slices, 1 Tbsp        15
     *Heinz*
       Midget                5
       Sweet Gherkins      25
       Sweet Pickles       45
       Sticks               13
       Candied dill strips    35

**Pimientos, 1 oz**
  *Dromedary*                  8
  *Ortega*                     7
  *Stokely-Van Camp*        8

**Watermelon Rind, 1 Tbsp**     38

# 9

# Seasonings, 1 tsp unless noted

| | |
|---|---|
| **Accent** | 9 |
| **Bacon** | |
| *Ann Page* | 8 |
| *Baco's* | 13 |
| *Durkee* | 3 |
| *French's* | 2 |
| *Lawry's* | 13 |
| *McCormick* | |
| Bits | 10 |
| Chips | 12 |
| *Schilling* | |
| Bits | 19 |
| Chips | 13 |
| **Barbecue** | |
| *French's* | 6 |
| **Chili Powder** | |
| *Lawry's* | 9 |
| *Mexene* | 8 |
| **Cinnamon Sugar** | |
| *French's* | 16 |
| **Chutney** | |
| *Major Grey's* | 16 |
| *Spice Island* | 12 |
| **Herb** | |
| *Lawry's* | 9 |
| **Horseradish** | |
| *Reese* | 18 |

**Hot Sauce**
 *Frank's*   1
**Lemon Pepper**
 *Lawry's*   7
 *French's*   6
**Meat Tenderizer**
 *French's*   2
**Pepper**
 *French's*   8
 *Lawry's*   8
**Salad**
 *Durkee*   4
  with cheese   10
 *French's*   6
**Salt**
 *French's*
  Butter   8
  Celery   2
  Garlic   4
  Hickory Smoked   2
  Onion   6
  Parsley Garlic   6
  Seasoned   2
 *Lawry's*
  Garlic   5
  Onion   4
  Seasoned   1
**Seafood**
 *French's*   2

**Stock Base**
*French's*                                                      8


# Seasoning Mixes, 1 pkg, various sizes

**A la King**
  *Durkee*                                                   297
**Beef**
  *Lawry's*
    *Beef Olé*                                               126
    Marinade                                                  69
**Beef Stew**
  *Durkee*                                                    99
  *French's*                                                 150
  *Lawry's*                                                  131
  *McCormick*                                                 90
  *Schilling*                                                 89
**Beef Stroganoff**
  *French's*                                                 192
  *Lawry's*                                                  119
  *McCormick*                                                113
**Beef, Ground**
  *Ann Page*                                                 100
  *Durkee*                                                    91
  *French's*                                                 100
**Chili**
  *Ann Page*                                                 120
  *French's*                                                 150

| | |
|---|---:|
| Pizza | 99 |
| *French's* | 128 |
| *Lawry's* | 139 |
| *McCormick* | 167 |
| *Schilling* | 172 |
| **Rice, Fried** | |
| *Durkee* | 62 |
| **Rice, Spanish** | |
| *Durkee* | 129 |
| *Lawry's* | 125 |
| **Swiss Steak** | |
| *McCormick* | 44 |
| *Schilling* | 42 |
| **Taco** | |
| *Durkee* | 67 |
| *French's* | 150 |
| *McCormick* | 65 |
| *Schilling* | 65 |
| **Tuna Casserole** | |
| *McCormick* | 104 |

# DIPS, 1 oz

## Ready to Serve

**Bacon and Horseradish**
*Borden*                                      79
*Kraft*
  Ready                            71
  *Teez*                           57
*Lucerne*                                    63
**Bacon and Smoke**
*Sealtest*                                   47
**Barbecue**
*Borden's*                                   48
**Bean**
Chili
  *Lucerne*                        50
Jalapeño
  *Frito-Lay*                      36
  *Gebhardt*                       30
  *Granny Goose*                   37
  *Lucerne*                        35
**Blue Cheese**
*Granny Goose*                               110
*Kraft*
  Ready                            69
  *Teez*                           51

| | |
|---|---|
| *Lucerne* | 67 |
| *Sealtest* | 49 |
| **Casino** | |
| *Sealtest* | 45 |
| **Chili, Green** | |
| *Borden* | 55 |
| **Chipped Beef** | |
| *Sealtest* | 44 |
| **Clam** | |
| *Kraft* | |
| Ready | 66 |
| *Teez* | 44 |
| *Lucerne* | 34 |
| **Clam and Lobster** | |
| *Borden* | 60 |
| **Dill** | |
| *Kraft* | 67 |
| **Garlic** | |
| *Granny Goose* | 100 |
| *Kraft* | 47 |
| *Lucerne* | 58 |
| **Green Goddess** | |
| *Kraft* | 45 |
| **Guacamole** | |
| *Lucerne* | 69 |
| **Hickory Smoke** | |
| *Lucerne* | 60 |
| **Onion** | |
| *Borden* | 48 |
| *Lawry's* | 50 |

*Kraft*
  Ready     68
  *Teez*     43
  *Lucerne*     58
  *Sealtest*     46
**Tartar**
  *Borden*     48

# Unprepared Mixes

**Bacon and Onion**
  *Frito-Lay*     100
**Barbecue**
  *Salada*     120
**Blue Cheese**
  *Frito-Lay*     117
  *Lawry's*     94
**Caesar**
  *Frito-Lay*     118
  *Lawry's*     .94
**Cheddar Cheese**
  *Salada*     43
**Chili**
  *Frito-Lay*     120
**Dill**
  *Frito-Lay*     90
**Dill and Chives**
  *Salada*     130

**9**

**Garlic and Onion**
| | |
|---|---|
| *McCormick* | 126 |
| *Salada* | 100 |

**Horseradish**
| | |
|---|---|
| *Lawry's* | 86 |
| *Frito-Lay* | 105 |

**Onion**
| | |
|---|---|
| *Frito-Lay* | 87 |
| Green | 100 |
| *Lawry's* | |
| Green | 100 |
| Toasted | 82 |
| *McCormick* | 131 |
| *Salada* | 100 |

**Taco**
| | |
|---|---|
| *Frito-Lay* | 105 |

# SALAD DRESSINGS,
## 1 Tbsp unless noted

**Avocado**
| | |
|---|---|
| *Kraft* | 70 |

**Bacon**
| | |
|---|---|
| *Lawry's* | 78 |

**Blue Cheese**
| | |
|---|---|
| *Ann Page* Low Calorie | 18 |

*Kraft*
| | |
|---|---:|
| Chunky | 70 |
| Low Calorie | 14 |
| Low Calorie Chunky | 30 |

*Lawry's*
| | |
|---|---:|
| bottled | 57 |
| mix, 1 pkg | 74 |

| | |
|---|---:|
| *Nu Made* | 75 |
| *Roka* | 60 |
| *Seven Seas* | 70 |
| *Wish-Bone* | 80 |
| *Weight Watchers* | 10 |

**Caesar**

| | |
|---|---:|
| *Kraft* | 70 |

*Lawry's*
| | |
|---|---:|
| bottled | 70 |
| mix, 1 pkg | 72 |

| | |
|---|---:|
| *Nu Made* | 75 |
| *Pfeiffer* | 70 |
| Low Calorie | 10 |
| *Seven Seas* | 70 |
| *Wish-Bone* | 80 |

**Chef Style**
| | |
|---|---:|
| *Ann Page* | 20 |
| *Kraft* | 18 |

**Coach House**
| | |
|---|---:|
| *Seven Seas* | 78 |

**Coleslaw**
| | |
|---|---:|
| *Kraft* | 70 |
| Low Calorie | 30 |

**9**

**Cucumber**

*Kraft* 80

  Low Calorie 30

**French**

*Ann Page* 25

*Casino* 70

*Kraft* 60

  Casino Garlic 70

  Herb and Garlic 90

  Low Calorie 25

  Miracle 70

*Lawry's*

  bottled 50

  mix, 1 pkg 72

*Nu Made*

  Low Calorie 20

  Savory 65

  Zesty 70

*Pfeiffer* 55

  Low Calorie 18

*Seven Seas* 60

  Low Calorie 30

*Tillie Lewis* 12

*Wish-Bone*

  Deluxe 50

  French Garlic 70

  Low Calorie 25

  Sweet and Spicy 70

*Weight Watchers* 4

**9**

**Garlic**
*Kraft* 50
*Wish-Bone* 80
**Green Goddess**
*Kraft* 80
*Lawry's*
  bottled 60
  mix, 1 pkg 69
*Nu Made* 80
*Seven Seas* 80
*Wish-Bone* 60
**Green Onion**
*Kraft* 70
**Hawaiian**
*Lawry's* 75
**Herb and Garlic**
*Kraft* 83
**Herb and Spices**
*Seven Seas* 60
**Italian**
*Ann Page* 14
*Good Seasons* 8
*Kraft* 80
  Golden 70
  Low Calorie 6
*Lawry's*
  bottled 80
  mix, 1 pkg 44
  cheeses mix, 1 pkg 69

**9**

| | |
|---|---|
| *Nu Made* | 90 |
| Low Calorie | 16 |
| *Pfeiffer* | 60 |
| Low Calorie | 10 |
| *Seven Seas* | 70 |
| Family | 60 |
| Low Calorie | 35 |
| *Viva* | 70 |
| *Tillie Lewis* | 6 |
| *Weight Watchers* | 2 |
| *Wish-Bone* | 80 |
| Low Calorie | 20 |
| **Lemon garlic** | |
| *Lawry's*, 1 pkg | 65 |
| **Mayonnaise, all brands** | 100 |
| **Mayonnaise, flavored** | |
| *Durkee* | 69 |
| **Mayonnaise, imitation** | |
| *Mrs. Filbert's* | 40 |
| *Piedmont* | 50 |
| *Weight Watchers* | 40 |
| **May Lo Naise** | |
| *Tillie Lewis* | 25 |
| **Oil and Vinegar** | |
| *Kraft* | 70 |
| *Lawry's* | 55 |
| *Nu Made* | 60 |
| *Seven Seasons* | 70 |
| **Onion** | |
| *Lawry's* | 84 |

| | |
|---|---|
| *Wish-Bone* | 80 |
| **Parmesan** | |
| *Good Seasons* | 84 |
| **Roquefort** | |
| *Kraft* | 58 |
| **Red Wine** | |
| *Pfeiffer* | 40 |
|   Low Calorie | 10 |
| **Russian** | |
| *Kraft* | 30 |
| *Nu Made* | 55 |
| *Pfeiffer* | 65 |
|   Low Calorie | 15 |
| *Seven Seas* | 80 |
| *Tillie Lewis* | 12 |
| *Weight Watchers* | |
|   bottled | 50 |
|   mix | 4 |
| *Wish-Bone* | 60 |
|   Low Calorie | 25 |
| **Salad dressing** | |
| *Ann Page* | 70 |
| *Heinz* | 63 |
| *Kraft* | 65 |
| *Mrs. Filbert's* | 65 |
| *Nu Made* | 80 |
| *Piedmont* | 70 |
| *Sultana* | 50 |
| **Salad Secret** | |
| *Kraft* | 60 |

**9**

**Sea Island**
*Kraft* 93
**Sour Treat**
*Friendship* 90
**Sherry**
*Lawry's* 55
**Spin Blend**
*Hellmann's* 55
**Tahitian Isle**
*Wish-Bone* 55
**Thousand Island—**
*Ann Page* 25
*Kraft* 60
  Low Calorie 30
*Lawry's*
  bottled 65
  mix, 1 pkg 78
*Nu Made* 30
*Pfeiffer* 65
  Low Calorie 15
*Seven Seas* 50
*Tillie Lewis* 18
*Weight Watchers*
  bottled 50
  mix 12
*Wish-Bone* 70
  Low Calorie 25
**Tomato-Blue Cheese**
*Kraft* 90

**Tomato-Spice**
*Seven Seas* 45
**Whipped**
*Tillie Lewis* 25
**Yogonaise**
*Henri's* 60
**Yogowhip**
*Henri's* 60
**Yogurt, all flavors**
*Henri's* 35

# OILS, 1 Tbsp

**Corn**
*Mazola* 122
*Nu Made* 124
**Olive**
*Filippo Berio* 125
**Peanut**
*Planters* 128
**Popcorn**
*Planters* 130
**Safflower**
*Nu Made* 119
**Soybean**
*Mrs. Tucker's* 128

**9**

**Sunflower**

   *Sunlight*                          120

**Vegetable**

   *Crisco*                           120

   *Puritan*                         118

   *Swift*                            115

   *Wesson*                        120

**Vegetable and cottonseed**

   *Swift*                          120

# Shortening, 1 Tbsp unless noted

**Lard**                           115

   1 cup                       1,850

**Vegetable**

   *Crisco*                          109

   *Fluffo*                        109

   *Mrs. Tucker's*             120

   *Pam*                           7

   *Snowdrift*                   111

   *Spry*                         97

# SAUCES,
## ½ cup unless noted

**A la King**
Durkee ............................................ 66
**Barbecue, 1 Tbsp**
Chris' and Pitt's ............................. 15
Durkee with vinegar ..................... 64
French's .......................................... 14
   Hot ............................................. 27
   Smoky ........................................ 14
Open Pit .......................................... 26
   Hot 'n Spicy ............................. 27
   Hickory Smoked ...................... 27
   with onions .............................. 28
**Bearnaise**
Butternut Farm ............................ 176
**Bordelaise**
Butternut Farm ............................. 48
**Cheese**
Durkee .......................................... 168
French's ........................................ 160
McCormick ................................... 156
Schilling ....................................... 156
**Chili**
Gebhardt ...................................... 156
Heinz .............................................. 17

| | |
|---|---|
| *Hunt's* | 18 |
| *McCormick* | 92 |
| **Clam** | |
| *Buitoni* | |
| red | 102 |
| white | 114 |
| *La Rosa* | |
| red | 78 |
| white | 68 |
| **Cocktail Sauce** | |
| *Crosse & Blackwell* | 26 |
| *Tastee* | 25 |
| **Enchilada** | |
| *Gebhardt* | 68 |
| *Lawry's*, 1 pkg | 144 |
| *McCormick*, 1 pkg | 116 |
| *Old El Paso* | |
| Hot | 36 |
| Mild | 40 |
| **Hollandaise** | |
| *Durkee* | 118 |
| *French's* | 119 |
| *McCormick* | 171 |
| *Schilling* | 170 |
| **Horseradish, 1 oz** | |
| *Kraft* | 100 |
| **Italian** | |
| *Contadina* | 85 |
| *Lawry's*, 1 pkg | 86 |
| *Ragu* | 36 |

**Lemon-Butter, 1 oz**
  *Weight Watchers* — 16
**Mint Sauce, 1 tsp**
  *Crosse & Blackwell* — 16
**Mushroom, 1 oz**
  *Dawn Fresh* — 9
**Pizza**
  *Buitoni* — 92
  *Ragu* — 96
**Seafood cocktail sauce, 1 tsp**
  *Del Monte* — 18
  *Pfeiffer* — 25
**Sour Cream**
  *Durkee* — 160
  *French's* — 280
  *McCormick* — 146
  *Schilling* — 146
**Soy Sauce, 1 tsp**
  *La Choy* — 7
**Spaghetti**
  *Ann Page* — 70
  Marinara — 70
  Meat — 80
  Mix, 1 envelope — 120
  with Mushrooms — 70
  *Buitoni* — 92
  Clam, red — 108
  Clam, white — 144
  Marinara — 88
  Meat — 120

| | |
|---|---:|
| with Mushrooms | 88 |
| *Durkee* | 45 |
| with Mushrooms | 40 |
| *French's* | 80 |
| with Mushrooms | 80 |
| *Franco-American* | 95 |
| with Mushrooms | 95 |
| *Lawry's* | 147 |
| with Meatball seasoning | 316 |
| with Mushrooms | 116 |
| *La Rosa* | 74 |
| *Prince* | 90 |
| with Meat | 143 |
| with Mushrooms | 103 |
| *Ragu* | |
| Plain | 96 |
| Thick | 84 |
| Clam | 88 |
| Marinara | 96 |
| Meat | 92 |
| Thick with Meatball seasoning | 104 |
| with Mushrooms | 84 |
| **Spatini** | 51 |
| *Town House* | 80 |
| with Meat | 80 |
| with Mushrooms | 89 |
| **Stroganoff** | |
| *Durkee* | 410 |
| *French's* | 165 |
| *Lawry's*, 1 pkg | 118 |

| | |
|---|---|
| *McCormick* | 115 |
| *Schilling* | 115 |
| **Sweet and Sour** | |
| *Contadina* | 158 |
| *Durkee* | 115 |
| *French's* | 55 |
| *La Choy* | 262 |
| **Swiss Steak** | |
| *Contadina* | 48 |
| **Taco Sauce** | |
| *Gebhardt* | 3 |
| *Old El Paso* | 4 |
| **Tartar Sauce** | |
| *Best Foods* | 70 |
| *Hellman's* | 75 |
| *Kraft* | 72 |
| *Lawry's* | 67 |
| *Seven Seas* | 80 |
| **Teriyaki, 1 Tbsp** | |
| *Chun King* | 12 |
| *French's* | 17 |
| **Tomato** | |
| *Contadina* | 45 |
| *Del Monte* | 40 |
| with Bits | 40 |
| with Mushrooms | 50 |
| with Onions | 50 |
| *Hunt's* | 35 |
| Prima Salsa | 109 |
| Prima Salsa with Mushrooms | 110 |

Special 40
with Bits 35
with Cheese 71
with Herbs 80
with Meat 120
with Mushrooms 40
with Onions 45
*Stokely-Van Camp* 35
*Town House* 40
**Tomato Paste**
*Contadina* 46
*Hunt's* 108
*Lord Mott* 44
**Tuna Casserole**
*McCormick* 128
*Schilling* 128
**White**
*Durkee* 119
**Wine, 1 oz**
*Lawry's*
Burgundy 98
Sherry 94
White 113
**Worcestershire Sauce**
*Crosse & Blackwell* 15
*Heinz* 11
*French's* 10
*Lea & Perrins* 12

**9**

# Gravies, ¼ cup unless noted

**Au Jus**

| | |
|---|---:|
| *Ann Page* 1 envelope | 64 |
| *Durkee* | 8 |
| *Durkee, Roastin' Bag,* 1 pkg | 64 |
| *French's* | 8 |
| *French's Pan Rich* | 30 |
| *McCormick* | 4 |
| *Schilling* | 4 |

**Beef**

| | |
|---|---:|
| *Franco-American* | 30 |
| *Howard Johnson's* | 25 |
| *Wyler's* | 24 |

**Brown**

| | |
|---|---:|
| *Ann Page* 1 envelope | 79 |
| *Dawn Fresh* | 20 |
| *Durkee* | 15 |
| with Mushrooms | 15 |
| with Onions | 17 |
| *Franco-American* | 25 |
| *French's* | 20 |
| *French's Pan Rich* | 62 |
| *McCormick* | 26 |
| Herb | 21 |
| Lite | 10 |
| *Pillsbury* | 15 |
| *Schilling* | 26 |
| Herb | 21 |

| | |
|---|---:|
| *Weight Watchers* | 8 |
| with Mushrooms | 12 |
| with Onions | 13 |
| **Chicken** | |
| *Ann Page,* 1 envelope | 120 |
| *College Inn* | 25 |
| *Durkee* | 22 |
| Creamy | 39 |
| Roastin' Bag, 1 pkg | 122 |
| Roastin' Bag Italian, 1 pkg | 144 |
| *French's* | 25 |
| *French's Pan Rich* | 60 |
| *McCormick* | 21 |
| Lite | 10 |
| *Pillsbury* | 25 |
| *Schilling* | 21 |
| Lite | 10 |
| *Weight Watchers* | 10 |
| *Wyler's* | 24 |
| **Chicken Giblet** | |
| *Franco-American* | 35 |
| **Herb** | |
| *McCormick* | 26 |
| **Homestyle** | |
| *Durkee* | 18 |
| *French's* | 25 |
| *Pillsbury* | 15 |
| **Meatloaf** | |
| *Durkee,* 1 pkg | 130 |

**Mushroom**
  *Ann Page*, 1 envelope      79
  *Durkee*      16
  *Franco-American*      35
  *French's*      20
  *McCormick*      19
  *Schilling*      19
  *Wyler's*      15
**Mustard**
  *French's*      16
**Onion**
  *Ann Page*, 1 envelope      120
  *Durkee*      21
  *Durkee Roastin' Bag*, 1 pkg      124
  *French's*      25
  *French's Pan Rich*      50
**Pork**
  *Durkee*      18
  *Durkee Roastin' Bag*, 1 pkg      130
  *French's*      20
**Pot Roast**
  *Durkee*, 1 pkg      124
**Sparerib**
  *Durkee*, 1 pkg      162
**Swiss Steak**
  *Durkee*      11
  *Durkee Roastin' Bag*, 1 pkg      115
**Turkey**
  *Durkee*      23

# CHAPTER 10

# *Desserts, Baking and Baked Goods*

## BAKING MISCELLANY

**10**

**Baking Chocolate, 1 oz**
  Chips
    *Baker's*                                 130
    *Hershey's*                              115
    *Nestlé*                                  130
  Ground
    *Ghiradelli*                           150
  Solid
    *Baker's*
      German                         140
      semi-sweet                   130
      unsweetened                140
    *Ghiradelli*                           150
    *Hershey*                            190
**Butterscotch**
  Nestlé chips                       150
**Coconut**
  *Baker's*                              150
**Ginger**
  *Borden's* crystallized         98
  *Borden's* preserved          88
**Peanut Butter**
  *Reese* chips                      150

# CAKES, FROZEN,
## 1 whole cake

**Banana**
| | |
|---|---|
| *Pepperidge Farm* | 1,115 |
| *Sara Lee* | 1,439 |

**Banana Nut**
| | |
|---|---|
| *Sara Lee* | 1,864 |

**Black Forest**
| | |
|---|---|
| *Sara Lee* | 1,625 |

**Boston Creme**
| | |
|---|---|
| *Pepperidge Farm* | 1,070 |

**Cheesecake**
| | |
|---|---|
| *Lambrecht* | 1,530 |
| *Mrs. Smith's* | 1,230 |
| *Sara Lee* | |
| small | 860 |
| large | 1,440 |
| Cherry | 1,280 |
| French | 2,190 |
| Strawberry | 1,280 |
| Strawberry French | 2,062 |

**Chocolate**
| | |
|---|---|
| *Pepperidge Farm* | 1,238 |
| *Sara Lee* | 1,380 |

**Chocolate Bavarian**
| | |
|---|---|
| *Sara Lee* | 2,250 |

**10**

**Chocolate Fudge**
*Pepperidge Farm*     1,800
**Chocolate, German**
*Pepperidge Farm*     1,589
*Sara Lee*     1,234
**Coconut**
*Pepperidge Farm*     1,800
**Crumbcake**
*Sara Lee*     170
*Stouffer's*
    Blueberry     211
    Chocolate Chip     225
    French     200
**Cupcake**
*Stouffer's*
    Cream     240
    Yellow     190
**Devil's Food**
*Pepperidge Farm*     1,800
*Sara Lee*     1,496
**Golden**
*Pepperidge Farm*     900
*Sara Lee*     1,440
**Lemon**
*Sara Lee*     2,175
**Lemon Coconut**
*Pepperidge Farm*     1,100
**Mandarin Orange**
*Sara Lee*     1,650

**Orange**
| | |
|---|---|
| *Howard Johnson's* | 1,700 |
| *Sara Lee* | 1,440 |

**Pound**
| | |
|---|---|
| *Sara Lee* | |
| Banana Nut | 1,170 |
| Chocolate | 1,220 |
| Chocolate Swirl | 1,300 |
| Plain | 1,320 |
| Raisin | 1,270 |
| *Pepperidge Farm* | |
| Apple Nut | 1,300 |
| Butter | 1,300 |
| Carrot | 1,600 |
| Chocolate | 1,300 |

**Cherry**
| | |
|---|---|
| *Mrs. Smith's* | 2,335 |

**Strawberry**
| | |
|---|---|
| *Mrs. Smith's* | 1,830 |
| *Sara Lee* | 1,550 |
| Strawberry and Cream | 1,700 |

**Vanilla**
| | |
|---|---|
| *Pepperidge Farm* | 1,900 |

**Walnut**
| | |
|---|---|
| *Sara Lee* | 1,690 |

# CAKE MIXES, 1 whole cake

**Angel Food**
| | |
|---|---|
| *Betty Crocker* | 1,560 |
| One Step | 1,680 |
| Confetti | 1,800 |
| Strawberry | 1,800 |
| *Duncan Hines* | 1,670 |
| *Pillsbury* | 1,680 |
| *Swans Down* | 1,590 |

**Apple Raisin**
| | |
|---|---|
| *Duncan Hines* | 2,280 |
| Spicy | 1,620 |

**Applesauce Raisin**
| | |
|---|---|
| *Betty Crocker* | 1,800 |

**Banana**
| | |
|---|---|
| *Betty Crocker* | 3,140 |
| *Duncan Hines* | 2,400 |
| *Pillsbury* | 3,120 |

**Banana Nut**
| | |
|---|---|
| *Betty Crocker* | 1,800 |
| *Duncan Hines* | 1,800 |

**Bundt**
*Pillsbury*
| | |
|---|---|
| Fudge | 3,480 |
| Lemon | 3,350 |
| Macaroon | 3,950 |
| Marble | 3,960 |

| | |
|---|---|
| Pound | 3,710 |
| Triple Fudge | 3,590 |
| **Butter** | |
| *Duncan Hines* | 3,240 |
| *Pillsbury* | 2,680 |
| **Butter Brickle** | |
| *Betty Crocker* | 3,110 |
| **Butter Fudge** | |
| *Duncan Hines* | 3,240 |
| **Butter Pecan** | |
| *Betty Crocker* | 3,120 |
| **Cheesecake** | |
| *Jello-O* | 2,000 |
| *Pillsbury* | 3,120 |
| *Royal* | 1,840 |
| **Cherry** | |
| *Duncan Hines* | 2,280 |
| **Cherry Chip** | |
| *Betty Crocker* | 2,280 |
| **Chocolate** | |
| *Betty Crocker* | 1,380 |
| *Duncan Hines* | 2,400 |
| *Pillsbury* Dark | 3,120 |
| *Swans Down* | 2,240 |
| **Chocolate Almond** | |
| *Betty Crocker* | 1,890 |
| **Chocolate Chip** | |
| *Betty Crocker* | 1,980 |
| *Duncan Hines* | 1,710 |
| Double Chocolate Chip | 1,620 |

# 10

**Chocolate Fudge**
*Betty Crocker* ............ 3,240

**Chocolate, German**
*Betty Crocker* ............ 3,240
*Pillsbury* ............ 3,120

**Chocolate, Sour Cream**
*Betty Crocker* ............ 3,240
*Duncan Hines* ............ 2,400

**Chocolate, Swiss**
*Duncan Hines* ............ 2,400
*Swans Down* ............ 2,240

**Chocolate with frosting**
*Betty Crocker* ............ 1,620

**Coconut Pecan**
*Betty Crocker* ............ 1,975

**Date Nut**
*Betty Crocker* ............ 1,890

**Devil's Food**
*Betty Crocker* ............ 3,240
*Duncan Hines* ............ 2,400
*Pillsbury* ............ 3,240
*Swans Down* ............ 2,230

**Fudge Marble**
*Duncan Hines* ............ 2,400
*Pillsbury* ............ 3,240

**Gingerbread**
*Betty Crocker* ............ 1,890

**Lemon**
*Betty Crocker* ............ 3,240
Pudding Cake ............ 1,380

| | |
|---|---|
| *Duncan Hines* | 2,400 |
| *Pillsbury* | 3,240 |
| **Lemon Chiffon** | |
| *Betty Crocker* | 2,280 |
| **Marble** | |
| *Betty Crocker* | 3,280 |
| **Orange** | |
| *Betty Crocker* | 3,240 |
| *Duncan Hines* | 2,400 |
| **Pineapple** | |
| *Betty Crocker* | 2,400 |
| *Duncan Hines* | 2,400 |
| **Pound** | |
| *Betty Crocker* | 2,280 |
| **Spice** | |
| *Betty Crocker* | 3,240 |
| *Duncan Hines* | 2,400 |
| **Spice Raisin** | |
| *Betty Crocker* | 1,800 |
| **Strawberry** | |
| *Betty Crocker* | 3,240 |
| *Duncan Hines* | 2,400 |
| **Streusel** | |
| *Pillsbury* | |
| Cinnamon | 4,080 |
| Devil's Food | 3,950 |
| Fudge Marble | 4,080 |
| Chocolate | 3,950 |
| Lemon | 4,200 |

**White**

| | |
|---|---|
| *Betty Crocker* | 2,400 |
| *Duncan Hines* | 2,280 |
| *Pillsbury* | 3,000 |
| *Swans Down* | 2,120 |

**Yellow**

| | |
|---|---|
| *Betty Crocker* | 3,240 |
| Butter | 2,880 |
| with fresting | 1,380 |
| *Duncan Hines* | 2,400 |
| *Pillsbury* | 3,120 |
| *Swans Down* | 2,240 |

# CAKES FOR SNACKS, 1 cake

| | |
|---|---|
| **Big Wheels** | 170 |
| **Brownie** | |
| *Hostess* | |
| small | 150 |
| large | 240 |
| **Chocolate, cream-filled** | |
| *Yankee Doodles* | 134 |
| **Choco-Diles** | 250 |
| **Creamies, 1 pkg** | |
| *Tastykake* | |
| Chocolate | 255 |

**10**

| | |
|---|---|
| Spice | 270 |
| **Crumb Cakes** | |
| *Hostess* | 130 |
| **Cupcakes** | |
| *Hostess* | |
| Chocolate | 155 |
| Orange | 147 |
| *Tastykake, 1 pkg* | |
| Buttercream | 238 |
| Chocolate | 200 |
| Chocolate Cream | 239 |
| **Devil Dogs** | 169 |
| **Devil's Food** | |
| *Hostess* | 140 |
| *Drake's* | 135 |
| **Ding Dongs** | 170 |
| **Donuts** | |
| *Hostess* | |
| Cinnamon | 110 |
| Crunch | 100 |
| Enrobed | 130 |
| Plain | 105 |
| Powdered | 115 |
| **Funny Bones, 1 pkg** | 162 |
| **Ho-Ho's** | 120 |
| **Juniors, 1 pkg** | |
| *Tastykake* | |
| Chocolate | 307 |
| Coconut | 330 |
| Coffee cake | 310 |

**Krimpets, 1 pkg**
  *Tastykake*
    Butterscotch                              190
    Chocolate                                 255
    Jelly                                     168
    Vanilla                                   240
**Macaroons**
  *Hostess*                                   210
**Oatmeal Raisin, 1 pkg**
  *Tastykake*                                 267
**Orange Treats, 1 pkg**
  *Tastykake*                                 230
**Pound**
  *Drake's*
    Marble                                    185
    Plain                                     181
    Raisin                                    323
**Ring Ding**                                 366
**Sno Balls**                                 140
**Tandy Takes, 1 pkg**
  Chocolate                                   180
  Peanut Butter                              190
**Teens, 1 pkg**                              225
**Tempty, 1 pkg**
  Chocolate                                   196
  Lemon                                       259
**Tiger Tails**                               415
**Twinkies**                                  140

# COFFEE CAKE, 1 cake

**Almond**
| | |
|---|---|
| *Sara Lee* | 1,350 |
| *Sara Lee* Coffee Ring | 1,100 |

**Angel Food**
| | |
|---|---|
| *Howard Johnson's* | 710 |

**Apple**
| | |
|---|---|
| *Morton* | 1,130 |
| *Sara Lee* | 1,175 |

**Apple Cinnamon**
| | |
|---|---|
| *Pillsbury* | 1,880 |

**Apricot**
| | |
|---|---|
| *Sara Lee* | 1,176 |

**Banana**
| | |
|---|---|
| *Sara Lee* | 1,440 |

**Blueberry**
| | |
|---|---|
| *Sara Lee* Coffee Ring | 1,080 |
| *Sara Lee* Danish | 1,175 |

**Butter Pecan**
| | |
|---|---|
| *Pillsbury* | 2,480 |

**Butter Streusel**
| | |
|---|---|
| *Sara Lee* | 1,395 |

**Cherry**
| | |
|---|---|
| *Sara Lee* | 1,050 |

**Chocolate**
| | |
|---|---|
| *Sara Lee* | 1,375 |

**Chocolate, German**
| | |
|---|---|
| *Morton* | 1,360 |
| *Sara Lee* | 1,230 |

**Cinnamon Streusel**
| | |
|---|---|
| *Pillsbury* | 2,000 |
| *Sara Lee* | 1,230 |

**Coconut**
| | |
|---|---|
| *Pepperidge Farm* | 1,940 |

**Coffee Cake**
| | |
|---|---|
| *Aunt Jemima* | 1,360 |

**Crumb**
| | |
|---|---|
| *Drake's* | 1,460 |

**Lemon**
| | |
|---|---|
| *Drake's* | 1,030 |

**Maple Crunch**
| | |
|---|---|
| *Sara Lee* | 1,157 |

**Orange**
| | |
|---|---|
| *Sara Lee* | 1,442 |

**Pecan**
| | |
|---|---|
| *Drake's* | 1,109 |
| *Morton* | 1,368 |
| *Sara Lee* small | 764 |
| *Sara Lee* large | 1,320 |

**Raspberry**
| | |
|---|---|
| *Sara Lee* | 1,090 |

**Sour Cream**
| | |
|---|---|
| *Pillsbury* | 2,160 |

# COOKIES, 1 piece

**Adelaide**
Pepperidge Farm ... 53
**Almond**
Keebler ... 47
Stella D'Oro ... 49
**Almond Spice**
Keebler ... 50
**Angel Puffs**
Stella D'Oro ... 17
**Animal Crackers**
Keebler ... 12
Nabisco ... 12
Sunshine ... 10
**Animal Crackers Iced**
Keebler ... 52
Sunshine ... 26
**Anise**
Stella D'Oro
Anisette Sponge ... 50
Anisette Toast ... 34
**Apple**
Keebler ... 27
Nabisco ... 48
**Applesauce**
Sunshine ... 33
Iced ... 104

**Arrowroot**
*Nabisco*                                                          22
*Sunshine*                                                        16

**Assorted**
*Stella D'Oro*
  Hostess                                                          39
  Lady Stella                                                      37

**Bordeaux**
*Pepperidge Farm*                                                  37

**Breakfast Treats**
*Stella D'Oro*                                                    100

**Brown Edge**
*Nabisco*                                                          28

**Brown Sugar**
*Nabisco*                                                          25
*Pepperidge Farm*                                                 50

**Brussels**
*Pepperidge Farm*                                                 57

**Butter**
*Keebler*                                                          84
*Nabisco*                                                          37
*Pepperidge Farm*                                                 38
*Sunshine*                                                         24

**Capri**
*Pepperidge Farm*                                                 85

**Cashew**
*Nabisco*                                                          57

**Chessman**
*Pepperidge Farm*                                                 43

**Chinese Dessert**
*Stella D'Oro* 170
**Chocolate**
*Keebler*
Bavarian Fudge 80
Nut Fudge 31
Pecan Fudge 66
*Melody* 31
*Nabisco*
Wafers 28
Snaps 18
*Pepperidge Farm* 48
*Sunshine* 13
**Chocolate Almond**
*Nabisco* 55
**Chocolate Brownies**
*Pepperidge Farm* 57
**Chocolate Chip**
*Chips Ahoy* 50
*Estee* 30
*Keebler* 44
Old Fashioned 80
Rich 'N Chips 73
Townhouse 49
*Nabisco* 51
Family Favorite 33
Snaps 21
*Pepperidge Farm* 52
*Sunshine* 37
*Chip-A-Roos* 63

# 10

**Chocolate Chip Coconut**
| | |
|---|---|
| *Keebler* | 80 |
| *Nabisco* | 76 |
| *Sunshine* | 76 |

**Chocolate Strawberry Wafers**
| | |
|---|---|
| *Estee* | 90 |

**Cinnamon**
| | |
|---|---|
| *Sunshine* | 20 |

**Cinnamon Almond**
| | |
|---|---|
| *Nabisco* | 53 |

**Cinnamon Sugar**
| | |
|---|---|
| *Fun Days* | 48 |
| *Pepperidge Farm* | 52 |

**Coconut**
| | |
|---|---|
| *Keebler* | 61 |
| Old Fashioned | 83 |
| Strip | 37 |
| *Nabisco* | 16 |
| *Stella D'Oro* | 47 |
| *Sunshine* | 47 |

**Coconut, Iced**
| | |
|---|---|
| *Keebler Crunchies* | 70 |

**Coconut Chocolate**
| | |
|---|---|
| *Pepperidge Farm* | 83 |

**Creme Sandwiches**
Butterscotch
| | |
|---|---|
| *Keebler* | 85 |

Chocolate
| | |
|---|---|
| *Keebler* Dutch | 95 |

# 10

| | |
|---|---|
| *Keebler* Opera | 85 |
| *Oreo* grocery | 50 |
| *Oreo* individual | 40 |
| Chocolate fudge | |
| *Cookie Mates* | 53 |
| *Keebler* | 97 |
| *Sunshine* | 74 |
| Coconut | |
| *Nabisco* | 53 |
| *Sunshine* | 51 |
| *Wise Coco* | 39 |
| Lemon | |
| *Keebler* | 85 |
| Swiss | |
| *Nabisco* | 43 |
| Vanilla | |
| *Cameo* | 68 |
| *Cookie Mates* | 52 |
| *Keebler* | 82 |
| French | 95 |
| Opera | 85 |
| *Sunshine* | 79 |
| *Vienna Fingers* | 69 |
| *Wise* | 38 |
| **Crescents** | |
| *Nabisco* | 34 |
| **Cup Custard** | |
| *Sunshine* | 70 |
| **Danish Wedding** | |
| *Keebler* | 31 |

# 10

## Date Nut
*Pepperidge Farm*     53
*Sunshine*     82

## Devil's Food
*Keebler*     64
*Nabisco*     58
*Sunshine*     55

## Dixie Vanilla
*Sunshine*     60

## Egg Biscuits
*Stella D'Oro*     37
  Anise     135
  Egg Jumbo     43
  Rum and Brandy     135
  Sugared     135
  Vanilla     130

## Figs
*Nabisco Fig Newtons*     59
*Frito-Lay*     189
*Keebler*     71
*Sunshine*     42

## Fruit
*Stella D'Oro*     67
*Sunshine Golden Fruit*     61

## Fruit, Iced
*Nabisco*     70

## Fudge
*Keebler*
  Sticks     42

**10**

**Kichel**
   *Stella D'Oro*     64
**Lady Joan**
   *Sunshine*     42
   *Sunshine* Iced     47
**LaLanne**
   *Sunshine*     15
**Lemon**
   *Keebler*     83
   *Nabisco*     17
   *Sunshine*     76
      Lemon Coolers     29
**Lemon Nut**
   *Pepperidge Farm*     58
**Lido**
   *Pepperidge Farm*     95
**Love Cookies**
   *Stella D'Oro*     110
**Macaroons**
   *Sunshine*     85
      Butter     39
      Coconut     81
   *Bake Shop*     87
   *Nabisco*     71
**Mandel Toast**
   *Stella D'Oro*     54
**Margherite**
   *Stella D'Oro*     73
**Marigold Sandwich**
   *Keebler*     91

**Marshmallow**
  Chocolate covered
   *Keebler*
    Dainties    68
    Galaxies    82
    Treasures    83
    Tulips    83
  Coconut
   *Nabisco*    54
   *Sunshine*    70
  Iced
   *Sunshine*
    Frosted Cakes    68
    Nut Sundae    74
  Mallomars    60
   *Nabisco*
    Puffs    94
    Twirls    133
    Pinwheels    139
   *Sunshine*
    Puffs    63
    Kings    135
  Sandwich
   *Keebler*    81
   *Nabisco*    32
  Sprinkles
   *Sunshine*    71
**Milano**
  *Pepperidge Farm*    63
  Mint    70

**10**

**Raisin Bran**
*Pepperidge Farm*     53

**Shortbread**
*Keebler*     27
*Lorna Doone*     38
*Pepperidge Farm*     65
*Scottie*     39

**Shortbread with Cashews**
*Nabisco*     50

**Shortbread, Chocolate-covered**
*Nabisco*     50

**Shortbread with Coconut**     65

**Shortbread, Iced**     58

**Shortbread Pecans**
*Keebler*     77
*Nabisco*     77

**St. Moritz**
*Pepperidge Farm*     47

**Sorrento**
*Stella D'Oro*     57

**Sprinkles**
*Sunshine*     57

**Sugar**
*Eton*     50
*Keebler*
  Giant     70
  Old Fashioned     81
*Nabisco*     17
*Pepperidge Farm*     53

**Sugar Wafers**
*Nabisco Biscos*     18
  Creme Waffles     47
*Keebler*     26
*Kreemlined*     45
*Regent*     23
*Sunshine*     47

**Sugar Wafers, Chocolate-covered**
*Eton*     54
*Milco*     80
*Nabisco*     76
  Creme Stix     50
*Sunshine*     30

**Sugar Wafers, Spiced**
*Nabisco*     33

**Sunflower Raisin**
*Pepperidge Farm*     53

**Swedish Creme**     103

**Swiss Chalet**     97

**Swiss Fudge**
*Stella D'Oro*     64

**Tahiti**
*Pepperidge Farm*     85

**Taste of Vienna**
*Stella D'Oro*     85

**Tea Biscuits**
*Nabisco*     21

**Toy Cookies**
*Sunshine*     13

**Vanilla**
  *Keebler* 19
  *Nabisco*
    Snaps 13
    Wafers 18
  *Sunshine* 15
**Vanilla Thins**
  *Estee* 25
**Vienna Finger Sandwich**
  *Sunshine* 71
**Yum Yums**
  *Sunshine* 83
**Zanzibar**
  *Pepperidge Farm* 37

# PASTRY, FROZEN, MIXES, AND TOASTER, 1 piece unless noted

**Dessert mixes**
  *Pillsbury Appleasy* 160
**Donuts**
  *Morton*
    Bavarian Creme 180
    Boston Creme 205

| | |
|---|---|
| Chocolate | 150 |
| Glazed | 150 |
| Jelly | 180 |
| Mini | 120 |
| *Town House* Cinnamon | 210 |
| **Dumplings, apple** | |
| *Pepperidge Farm* | 280 |
| **Strudel, apple** | |
| *Pepperidge Farm,* 1 oz | 85 |
| **Tarts** | |
| *Kellogg's* Pop Tarts | 210 |
| *Pepperidge Farm* | |
| Apple | 280 |
| Blueberry | 285 |
| Cherry | 280 |
| Lemon | 310 |
| Raspberry | 320 |
| **Popovers (Flako)** | 166 |
| **Turnovers** | |
| *Pepperidge Farm* | 320 |
| *Pillsbury* | 180 |

# PIES, FROZEN, 1 whole pie

**Apple**
*Banquet*                                  1,440

| | |
|---|---|
| *Morton* | 1,740 |
| Mini | 590 |
| *Mrs. Smith's* | 1,768 |
| Natural | 2,881 |
| Dutch | 1,860 |
| Tart | 1,495 |

**Banana Cream**

| | |
|---|---|
| *Banquet* | 1,032 |
| *Morton* | 1,020 |
| Mini | 230 |
| *Mrs. Smith's* | 1,290 |
| Light | 1,320 |

**Blueberry**

| | |
|---|---|
| *Banquet* | 1,523 |
| *Morton* | 1,680 |
| Mini | 580 |
| *Mrs. Smith's* | 1,740 |
| Natural | 2,040 |

**Boston Cream**

| | |
|---|---|
| *Mrs. Smith's* | 1,980 |

**Cherry**

| | |
|---|---|
| *Banquet* | 1,360 |
| *Morton* | 1,805 |
| Mini | 591 |
| *Mrs. Smith's* | 1,860 |
| Natural | 2,040 |

**Chocolate**

| | |
|---|---|
| *Mrs. Smith's* | 1,500 |
| *Royal Dutch* | 2,040 |

**Chocolate Cream**

| | |
|---|---|
| *Banquet* | 1,060 |
| *Morton* | 1,200 |
| Mini | 260 |
| *Mrs. Smith's* | 1,470 |

**Coconut**

| | |
|---|---|
| *Mrs. Smith's* | 1,380 |

**Coconut Cream**

| | |
|---|---|
| *Banquet* | 1,040 |
| *Morton* | 1,140 |
| Mini | 260 |
| *Mrs. Smith's* | 1,380 |

**Coconut Custard**

| | |
|---|---|
| *Banquet* | 1,220 |
| *Morton* | |
| Mini | 370 |
| *Mrs. Smith's* | 1,590 |

**Custard**

| | |
|---|---|
| *Banquet* | 1,240 |

**Devil Cream**

| | |
|---|---|
| *Royal* | 2,280 |
| *Mrs. Smith's* | 1,470 |

**Lemon**

| | |
|---|---|
| *Mrs. Smith's* | 2,040 |
| *Royal* | 2,080 |

**Lemon Cream**

| | |
|---|---|
| *Banquet* | 1,000 |
| *Morton* | 1,000 |
| Mini | 240 |
| *Mrs. Smith's* | 1,350 |

**Lemon Crunch**
  *Mrs. Smith's*                              2,480
**Lemon Meringue**
  *Mrs. Smith's*                              1,560
**Lemon Yogurt**
  *Mrs. Smith's*                              1,200
**Mince**
  *Morton*                                    1,860
    Mini                                        590
  *Mrs. Smith's*                              2,010
**Mincemeat**
  *Banquet*                                   1,520
**Neapolitan Cream**
  *Morton*                                    1,140
  *Mrs. Smith's*                              1,440
**Nesselrode**
  *Royal*                                     2,000
**Peach**
  *Banquet*                                   1,320
  *Morton*                                    1,680
    Mini                                        560
  *Mrs. Smith's*                              1,800
    Natural                                   1,980
**Pecan**
  *Morton*
    Mini                                        580
  *Mrs. Smith's*                              2,589
**Pineapple**
  *Mrs. Smith's*                              1,800

**Pineapple-Cheese**
 *Mrs. Smith's*      1,580
**Pumpkin**
 *Banquet*      1,230
 *Morton*      1,380
  Mini      430
 *Mrs. Smith's*      1,440
**Raisin**
 *Mrs. Smith's*      1,890
**Spumoni**
 *Royal*      2,120
**Strawberry Cream**
 *Banquet*      1,020
 *Morton*      1,080
 *Mrs. Smith's*      1,320
**Strawberry and Rhubarb**
 *Mrs. Smith's*      1,890
  Natural      1,920
**Strawberry-Yogurt**
 *Mrs. Smith's*      1,220

# Pie Mixes, 1 whole pie

*Betty Crocker Boston Cream*   2,080
*Pillsbury*
 Chocolate Cream    2,460
 Lemon Chiffon    1,980
 Vanilla    2,340

# 10

## Pie Crusts and Shells, 1 piece

**Pastry Sheets**
    *Pepperidge Farm*     570
**Pastry Shells**
    *Pepperidge Farm*     240
    *Stella D'Oro*     146
**Pie Crusts**
    *Betty Crocker*     1,920
     Stick     960
    *Flako*     1,560
    *Pillsbury*     1,740
**Pie Shells**
    *Pepperidge Farm*     521
     shallow     440
     with top     760
    *Stella D'Oro*     240
**Tart Shells**
    *Pepperidge Farm*     88

## Pie Fillings, 1 whole can unless noted

**Apple**
    *Wilderness*     660
**Apricot**
    *Wilderness*     720
**Banana Cream**
    *Jell-O*     660

**Blueberry**
*Wilderness*     660

**Cherry**
*Wilderness*     650

**Lemon**
*Jell-O*     1,080
*Royal,* 1 cup     310
*Wilderness*     840

**Lime**
*Royal,* 1 cup     310

**Mince**
*Wilderness*     840

**Mincemeat**
*None Such,* 1 cup     660

**Peach**
*Wilderness*     655

**Pumpkin**
*Libby's,* 1 cup     205
*Stokely-Van Camp,* 1 cup     370

**Raisin**
*Wilderness*     720

**Strawberry**
*Wilderness*     710

# 10
# SMALL PASTRY PIES, 1 piece

**Apple**
  *Stella D'Oro*                      90
  *Hostess*                          400
  *Tastykake*                        350
  *Tastykake* French                 400
**Blueberry**
  *Hostess*                          365
**Cherry**
  *Hostess*                          420
  *Tastykake*                        380
**Fig**
  *Stella D'Oro*                     100
**Guava**
  *Stella D'Oro*                     125
**Lemon**
  *Hostess*                          420
  *Tastykake*                        355
**Peach/Apricot**
  *Stella D'Oro*                      90
**Pecan**
  *Frito-Lay*                        345
**Prune**
  *Stella D'Oro*                      92
**Puff Pastry**
  *Durkee*
    **Beef**                          47

**10**

| | |
|---|---|
| Cheese | 59 |
| Chicken | 49 |
| Chicken liver | 48 |
| Shrimp | 44 |

# PUDDINGS, MIXES AND CANNED, ½ cup, unless noted

**Banana**
| | |
|---|---|
| *Ann Page* | 250 |
| *Del Monte* | 180 |
| *Shak-A-Pudd'n* | 165 |
| *Royal* | 164 |

**Banana Cream**
| | |
|---|---|
| *Jell-O* | 175 |
| *My-T-Fine* | 175 |

**Bavarian Cream**
| | |
|---|---|
| *My-T-Fine* | 176 |

**Butter Pecan**
| | |
|---|---|
| *My-T-Fine* | 175 |

**Butterscotch**
| | |
|---|---|
| *Ann Page* | 190 |
| Instant | 170 |
| *Del Monte* | 175 |

| | |
|---|---:|
| *D-Zerta* | 25 |
| *Foremost* | 175 |
| *Jell-O* | 172 |
| *My-T-Fine* | 170 |
| *Royal* | 190 |
| *Sego* | 250 |
| **Caramel Nut** | |
| *Royal* | 195 |
| **Cherry** | |
| *Whip 'n Chill* | 139 |
| **Cherry-Plum** | |
| *Junket* | 135 |
| **Chocolate** | |
| *Ann Page* | 180 |
| *Betty Crocker* | 180 |
| *Bounty* | 174 |
| *Dannon* | 150 |
| *Del Monte* | 250 |
| *D-Zerta* | 20 |
| *Foremost* | 175 |
| *Jell-O* | 175 |
|   Instant | 190 |
| *My-T-Fine* | 185 |
| *Royal* | 190 |
|   Dark 'N Sweet | 200 |
| *Sego* | 250 |
| *Shak-A-Pudd'n* | 200 |
| *Whip 'n Chill* | 145 |
| **Chocolate Almond** | |
| *My-T-Fine* | 196 |

**Chocolate Fudge**
  *Betty Crocker* ................................ 180
  *Del Monte* ..................................... 190
  *Foremost* ...................................... 175
  *Jell-O* ......................................... 175
    Instant ....................................... 191
  *My-T-Fine* ..................................... 190
  *Sego* .......................................... 250
  *Whip 'n Chill* ................................. 139
**Chocolate Malt**
  *Shak-A-Pudd'n* ................................. 200
**Chocolate Marshmallow**
  *Sego* .......................................... 250
**Coconut**
  *Ann Page*
    Cream ......................................... 190
    Toasted ....................................... 170
  *Jell-O* ........................................ 175
    Instant ....................................... 190
  *Royal* ......................................... 185
**Currant-Raspberry**
  *Junket* ........................................ 135
**Custard**
  *Ann Page* ...................................... 150
  *Jell-O* ........................................ 165
  *My-T-Fine*
    Caramel ....................................... 145
    Vanilla ....................................... 156
  *Rice-A-Roni* ................................... 120
  *Royal* ......................................... 145

**Indian**
  *B & M* ............................................ 150
**Lemon**
  *Ann Page* ...................................... 150
  Instant ............................................ 180
  *Bounty* .......................................... 196
  *Foremost* ....................................... 197
  *Jell-O* ............................................ 178
  Instant ............................................ 179
  *My-T-Fine* ..................................... 180
  *Royal* ............................................ 180
  *Whip 'n Chill* ................................ 135
**Lemon Chiffon**
  *Jell-O* ............................................ 144
**Mocha Nut**
  *Royal* ............................................ 190
**Pineapple Cream**
  *Jell-O* ............................................ 165
  Instant ............................................ 179
**Pistachio**
  *Ann Page* ...................................... 180
  *Royal* ............................................ 180
**Plum**
  *Crosse & Blackwell* ....................... 255
  *R & R* ........................................... 300
**Rice**
  *Betty Crocker* ............................... 150
  *Bounty* .......................................... 195
**Strawberry**
  *Junket* ........................................... 135

| | |
|---|---|
| *Shak-A-Pudd'n* | 160 |
| *Whip 'n Chill* | 135 |
| **Tapioca** | |
| Chocolate | |
| *Ann Page* | 180 |
| *Jell-O* | 165 |
| *Royal* | 185 |
| Lemon | |
| *Jell-O* | 166 |
| Orange | |
| *Jell-O* | 166 |
| Vanilla | |
| *Ann Page* | 170 |
| *Betty Crocker* | 150 |
| *Jell-O* | 166 |
| *My-T-Fine* | 144 |
| *Royal* | 170 |
| **Vanilla** | |
| *Ann Page* | 170 |
| *Betty Crocker* | 190 |
| *Bounty* | 128 |
| *Dannon* | 150 |
| *Del Monte* | 190 |
| *D-Zerta* | 30 |
| *Foremost* | 175 |
| *Jell-O* | 164 |
| Instant | 178 |
| *My-T-Fine* | 170 |
| *Royal* | 165 |
| Instant | 180 |

# CHAPTER 11

# Jellies, Syrups, Toppings and Spreads

## DESSERT TOPPINGS, 1 Tbsp

**Black Cherry**
  *No-Cal*      0
**Black Raspberry**
  *No-Cal*      0
**Butterscotch**
  *Hershey's*      55
  *Kraft*      60
  *Smucker's*      69
**Caramel**
  *Kraft*
    chocolate      56

|  |  |
|---|---|
| vanilla | 57 |
| *Smucker's* | 69 |
| peanut butter | 75 |
| **Cherry** | |
| *Smucker's* | 65 |
| **Chocolate** | |
| *Bosco* | 50 |
| *Hershey's* | 45 |
| *Kraft* | 50 |
| *No-Cal* | 6 |
| *Smucker's* | 65 |
| *Tillie Lewis* | 16 |
| **Chocolate Fudge** | |
| *Hershey's* | 45 |
| *Kraft* | 70 |
| *Smucker's* | 65 |
| Swiss | 72 |
| **Chocolate Mint** | |
| *Hershey's* | 61 |
| *Smucker's* | 67 |
| **Chocolate Peanut Butter** | |
| *Hershey's* | 60 |
| **Coffee** | |
| *No-Cal* | 6 |
| **Cola** | |
| *No-Cal* | 0 |
| **Cream, whipped** | |
| *Reddi-Whip* | 8 |
| *Top-Whip* | 7 |

**Grape**
  *No-Cal*     0
**Hard Sauce**
  *Crosse & Blackwell*     64
**Marshmallow**
  *Kraft*     35
**Pecans in Syrup**
  *Kraft*     82
  *Smucker's*     65
**Pineapple**
  *Kraft*     50
  *Smucker's*     62
**Strawberry**
  *Kraft*     45
  *No-Cal*     0
  *Smucker's*     60
**Walnut**
  *Kraft*     88
**Walnuts in Syrup**
  *Smucker's*     65
**Whip, non-dairy**
  *Cool Whip*     14
  *D-Zerta*     8
  *Dream Whip*     10
  *Kraft*     9
  *Lucky Whip*     11
  *Pet*     16
  *Reddi-Whip*     9

# FROSTINGS, 1 can

**Betty Crocker**
| | |
|---|---|
| Chocolate Fudge | 1920 |
| Coconut Pecan | 1310 |
| White, creamy | 1920 |
| White, fluffy *Lite* | 720 |
| All other flavors | 1800 |

**Pillsbury**
| | |
|---|---|
| Coconut Pecan | 1800 |
| White, fluffy | 840 |
| All other flavors | 2040 |

# GELATIN, ½ cup

**Borden's**
| | |
|---|---|
| Cherry | 80 |
| Fruit Cocktail | 109 |
| Mandarin Orange | 89 |
| Perfection | 81 |
| Pineapple-papaya | 78 |
| Pineapple-raspberry | 77 |
| Strawberry | 75 |

*Jell-O*
| | |
|---|---|
| 1-2-3 | 81 |
| Best | 77 |
| *Knox* unflavored, dry, 1 envelope | 28 |
| *Royal* | 80 |

# JELLIES AND BUTTERS, 1 Tbsp

**Apple Butter**
| | |
|---|---|
| *Bama* | 31 |
| *Smucker's* | |
|   Cider | 39 |
|   Spiced | 39 |
|   Peach | 45 |
| *Ma Brown* | 32 |
| *Musselman's* | 33 |

**Jams**
| | |
|---|---|
| *Ann Page* | 51 |
| *Bama* | 51 |
| *Diet Delight* | 22 |
| *Kraft* | 49 |
| *S & W* | 10 |
| *Smucker's* | 54 |
|   Slenderella | 24 |
|   artificially sweetened | 1 |

**11**

## Jellies

| | |
|---|---:|
| Ann Page | 54 |
| Bama | 51 |
| Crosse & Blackwell | 51 |
| Diet Delight | 21 |
| Home Brands | 54 |
| Kraft | 48 |
|   Low Calorie | 22 |
| Ma Brown | 49 |
| Musselman's | 53 |
| S & W | 12 |
| Smucker's | 51 |
|   Slenderella | 24 |
|   Single Service | 50 |
| Welch's | 50 |

## Marmalade

| | |
|---|---:|
| Ann Page | 54 |
| Bama | 54 |
| Kraft | 54 |
|   Low Calorie | 25 |
| S & W | 11 |
| Smucker's | 49 |
|   Slenderella | 24 |

## Preserves

| | |
|---|---:|
| Ann Page | 54 |
| Bama | 51 |
| Crosse & Blackwell | 59 |
| Empress | 54 |
| Home Brands | 54 |
| Kraft | 48 |

| | |
|---|---:|
| Low Calorie | 25 |
| Regular | 55 |
| *Ma Brown* | 51 |
| *S & W* | 11 |
| *Smucker's* | 54 |
| *Welch's* | 54 |
| **Spreads** | |
| *Smucker's* | 24 |
| *Tillie Lewis* | 12 |

# SPREADS, 1 Tbsp

**Anchovy Paste**

| | |
|---|---:|
| *Crosse & Blackwell* | 20 |
| **Chicken** | |
| *Swanson* | 35 |
| *Underwood* | 32 |
| **Chicken Salad** | |
| *Carnation* | 31 |
| **Corned Beef** | |
| *Underwood* | 28 |
| **Ham** | |
| *Carnation* | 26 |
| *Hormel* | 35 |
| *Libby's* | 100 |
| *Underwood* | 48 |

**Liverwurst**
Underwood ... 46
**Peanut Butter**
Ann Page ... 105
Bama ... 100
  and jelly ... 82
Datetree ... 93
Home Brands ... 100
Jif ... 93
Kitchen King ... 95
Peter Pan ... 94
Planters ... 95
Roberts ... 93
Skippy ... 95
Smucker's ... 95
  Goober Grape ... 63
Sultana ... 101
**Potted Meat**
Libby's ... 140
**Roast Beef**
Underwood ... 29
**Sandwich Spread**
Best Foods ... 60
Hellman's ... 58
Mrs. Filbert's ... 53
Nu Made ... 51
Oscar Mayer ... 33
**Spam**
Hormel ... 40

**Tuna**
  *Carnation*        26
**Turkey Salad**
  *Carnation*        27

# SUGAR, SYRUPS, SWEETENERS AND HONEY

| | |
|---|---:|
| **Honey, 1 Tbsp** | 64 |
|   1 cup | 1,031 |
| **Sugar, 1 cup** | |
|   Brown | |
|     loosely packed | 540 |
|     firmly packed | 820 |
|   Maple | 790 |
|   Powdered | 460 |
|     sifted | 385 |
|   White, granulated | 770 |
|     1 Tbsp | 45 |
| **Sweeteners, Sugar Substitutes** | |
|   *Dia-Mel Sugar-Like*, 1 gram pkt | 3 |
|   *Dia-Mel Sweet'n-it* Liquid | 0 |
|   *Featherweight Sug'r Like*, 1 tsp | 2 |
|   *Pillsbury Sprinkle Sweet*, 1 tsp | 2 |

| | |
|---|---:|
| *Pillsbury Sweet 10* | 0 |
| *Sweet'n Low,* 1 gram pkt | 3½ |
| *Weight Watchers Sweet'ner,* 1 gram pkt | 3 |
| *Whitlock Suprose,* 1 gram pkt | 4 |
| **Syrup, 1 Tbsp** | |
| *Aunt Jemima* | 53 |
| *Cary's Diet* | 10 |
| *Cary's Maple* | 60 |
| *Diet Delight* | 15 |
| *Golden Griddle* | 50 |
| *Karo* | 60 |
|   Corn | 58 |
|   Maple | 54 |
| *Log Cabin* | |
|   Buttered | 52 |
|   Country Kitchen | 53 |
|   Maple | 46 |
|   Maple-Honey | 55 |
| *Mrs. Butterworth's* | 54 |
| *S & W* | 12 |
| *Tillie Lewis* | 14 |
| Molasses | |
|   dark | 45 |
|   light | 50 |
| Sorghum | 55 |

# CHAPTER 12

# *Candies, Ice Cream and Nuts*

## CANDY, 1 oz

| | |
|---|---|
| Baby Ruth | 135 |
| Butterfinger | 130 |
| Butter mint | |
| *Kraft* | 8 |
| Caramel | |
| *Curtiss* | 113 |
| *Kraft* | 114 |
| *Sugar Daddy* | 113 |
| *Sugar Babies* | 113 |
| Caramel, chocolate-coated | |
| *Kraft* | 124 |

| | |
|---|---|
| *Milk Duds* | 111 |
| *Nestlé's Caramel Cream* | 124 |
| *Poms Poms* | 119 |
| **Certs** | |
| clear | 8 |
| pressed | 6 |
| **Cherry, chocolate-coated** | |
| *Welch's* | 115 |
| **Chewels** | 10 |
| **Chocolate, milk** | |
| *Ghiràdelli* | 150 |
| *Hershey* | 152 |
| *Nestlé's* | 148 |
| *Welch's* | 116 |
| **Chocolate, mint** | |
| *Welch's* | 142 |
| **Chocolate, semi-sweet** | |
| *Eagle* | 142 |
| *Hershey* | 147 |
| *Nestlé's* | 141 |
| **Chocolate, candy-coated** | |
| *Hershey* | 133 |
| **Chocolate with fruit or nuts** | |
| *Chunky* | 135 |
| *Chunky Pecan* | 135 |
| *Ghiradelli* | 152 |
| *Hershey* | 154 |
| *Mr. Goodbar* | 153 |
| *Nestlé's* | 149 |

**12**

**12**

**Jellied Candy**

| | |
|---|---|
| Dots | 100 |
| Jujubes | 50 |
| Jujyfruits | 94 |
| Mason | 99 |
| Quaker City | 93 |
| Red Hot Dollars | 94 |

**Licorice**

| | |
|---|---|
| Black Crows | 101 |
| Diamond Drops | 98 |
| Good & Plenty | 99 |
| Heide Pastilles | 96 |
| Switzer | 97 |

| | |
|---|---|
| **Lifesavers, 1 piece** | 7 |

**Malted Milk**

| | |
|---|---|
| Walter Johnson | 131 |

| | |
|---|---|
| **Mars** | 126 |

**Marshmallows**

| | |
|---|---|
| Campfire | 100 |
| Curtiss | 97 |
| Kraft | 96 |
| Jet Puff | 125 |
| Macaroon | 110 |

| | |
|---|---|
| **Milky Way** | 119 |

**Mints**

| | |
|---|---|
| Kraft | 105 |
| Richardson | 110 |

**Mints, chocolate-coated**

| | |
|---|---|
| Mason | 203 |

# GUM, 1 piece

| | |
|---|---:|
| *Adams* | 9 |
| *Beeman* | 10 |
| *Beech-Nut* | 9 |
| *Beechies* | 6 |
| *Black Jack* | 9 |
| *Bubble Yum* | 25 |
| *Bubblicious* | 24 |
| *Care Free* | 8 |
| *Chiclets* | 6 |
| *Clorets* | 6 |
| *Clove* | 5 |
| *Dentyne* | 5 |
| *Estee* | 3 |
| *Freshen-Up* | 9 |
| *Fruit Stripe* | 9 |
| *Orbit* | 8 |
| *Trident* | 5 |
| *Wrigley's* | 10 |

**12**

# ICE CREAM, 1 cup (½ pint)

**Black Raspberry**
  *Breyer's*                                              264
**Black Walnut**
  *Meadow Gold*                                           329
**Butter Almond**
  *Sealtest*                                              326
**Butter Almond and Chocolate**
  *Breyer's*                                              318
**Butter Brickle**
  *Sealtest*                                              299
**Butter Pecan**
  *Meadow Gold*                                           300
  *Sealtest*                                              322
**Butterscotch Pecan**
  *Breyer's*                                              302
**Caramel Pecan**
  *Breyer's*                                              320
**Cherry**
  *Sealtest*                                              276
**Cherry-Vanilla**
  *Breyer's*                                              280
  *Meadow Gold*                                           280
  *Sealtest*                                              265
**Chocolate**
  *Borden's*                                              255
  *Breyer's*                                              314

**12**

| | |
|---|---|
| *Howard Johnson's* | 414 |
| *Meadow Gold* | 281 |
| *Sealtest* | 254 |
| *Swift's* | 242 |
| **Vanilla** | |
| *Bordens* | 246 |
| *Breyer's* | 299 |
| *Carnation* | 250 |
| *Howard Johnson's* | 500 |
| *Meadow Gold* | 280 |
| *Sealtest* | 289 |
| *Swift's* | 267 |
| *Sealtest* | 280 |
| **Vanilla-Fudge** | |
| *Breyer's* | 300 |
| **Vanilla-Raspberry** | |
| *Sealtest* | 279 |

## Ice Milk, 1 cup     200

## Sherbet, 1 cup     260

**12**

# Ice Cream Bars, 1

| | |
|---|---|
| *Bi-sicle* | 110 |
| *Creamsicle* | 78 |
| *Dreamsicle* | 70 |
| *Dreamstick* | 180 |
| *Drumstick* | 183 |
| *Fudgesicle* | 100 |
| *Good Humor* | |
| Almond | 218 |
| Chocolate | 222 |
| Ice | 50 |
| Chocolate-covered vanilla | 169 |
| Whammy | 105 |
| *Popsicle* | 72 |
| *Sealtest* | |
| Orange Cream | 71 |
| Orange Treat | 89 |

# Ice Cream Cones and Cups, 1 item

| | |
|---|---|
| *Comet* | |
| cone | 19 |
| cone, rolled sugar | 35 |
| cup | 20 |

# 12

# Take-Out Ice Cream, 1 item

**Baskin Robbins**

| | |
|---|---|
| *Banana Daiquiri Ice* | 129 |
| *Butter Pecan* | 195 |
| *Chocolate Fudge* | 229 |
| *Chocolate Mint* | 189 |
| *Jamoca* | 182 |
| *Mango Sherbert* | 132 |
| *Peach* | 165 |
| *Rocky Road* | 205 |
| *Strawberry* | 168 |
| *Vanilla* | 217 |

**Bridgeman's**

| | |
|---|---|
| Plain cone | 170 |
| Sugar cone | 200 |

**Dairy Queen**

| | |
|---|---|
| Banana Split | 540 |
| Cone | |
| large | 340 |
| medium | 230 |
| small | 110 |
| Float | 330 |
| Freeze | 520 |
| Malt | |
| large | 840 |
| medium | 600 |
| small | 340 |
| Parfait | 460 |
| Sandwich | 140 |

**[12**

Sundae
   large                                400
   medium                          300
   small                             170

*Friendly's*
Fribble
   chocolate                    470
   vanilla                       420
Sundae
   vanilla fudge           420
   vanilla strawberry    340

# NUTS AND SEEDS, 1 oz

**Almonds**
   *Blue Diamond*         179
   *Franklin*               154
   *Granny Goose*         155
   *Planters*               170
**Cashews**
   *A & P*                  170
   *Frito-Lay*             170
   *Franklin*              145
   *Granny Goose*         170
   *Planters*               170
   *Skippy*                163

**Filberts**
*Franklin* 164
**Mixed**
*A & P* 190
*Excel* 190
*Franklin* 160
   with peanuts 156
*Granny Goose* 168
*Planters* 180
   with peanuts 185
*Skippy* 172
**Peanuts**
*A & P* 180
   in shell 170
*Excel* 180
*Frito-Lay* 175
   in shell 160
   Spanish 170
*Granny Goose* 168
*Planters* 170
   Spanish, dry roasted 162
   *Peanut Crisps* 150
*Skippy* 165
*Tavern Nuts* 171
**Pecans**
*A & P* 200
*Granny Goose* 203
*Planters* 190
**Pistachios**
*Frito-Lay* 174

*Granny Goose*                                        176
*Planters*                                            169
**Sesame Mix**
*Planters*                                            163
**Soybeans**
*Malt-O-Meal*
  dry roasted                               132
  oil roasted                               141
**Planters**                                          133
**Sunflower Seeds**
  whole, 1 lb                             1,371
  whole, 1 cup                              257
  hulled, 1 cup                             810

# CHAPTER 13

# *Fast Foods and Snacks*

## CHIPS, PUFFS, CRISPS, ETC.
### 1 oz unless noted

**Jalapeño Corn Toots**
  *Granny Goose* 161
**Munchos**
  *Frito-Lay* 154
**Onion Rings**
  *Old London* 136
  *Wise* 123
**Potato Chips**
  *Frito-Lay* 157
  *Granny Goose* 160
  *Planters* 149
  *Pringles* 153
    Country Style 158
  *Wise* 159
**Potato Sticks**
  *Kobey's* 157
  *O & C* 161
  *Wise* 136
**Rinds, Bacon**
  *Wise* 160
  *Wonder* 140
**Rinds, Pork**
  *Frito-Lay, Baken-Ets* 139
  *Granny Goose* 152
**Shapies**
  *Nabisco* 152
**Sticks**
  *Pepperidge Farm*
    Pumpernickel 109

**13**

| | |
|---|---|
| Salted | 121 |
| Sesame | 119 |
| Whole wheat | 122 |

**Taco Chips**
*Old London* — 127

**Tortilla Chips**
*Doritos*
| | |
|---|---|
| Nachos | 137 |
| Tacos | 142 |

*Granny Goose* — 144
*Planters*
| | |
|---|---|
| Nachos | 128 |
| Tacos | 132 |

**Wheat Chips**
*Bakon Snacks* — 147

# PIZZA, FROZEN, 1 whole
## pizza unless noted

**Beef and Cheese**
*El Chico*
| | |
|---|---|
| with enchilada | 1,010 |
| with taco | 990 |

**Bacon**
*Tostino's* — 704

**Cheese**
  *Buitoni*        276
  *Celeste*        473
    large        1,280
    Sicilian        1,395
    with mushroom, small        459
    with mushroom, large        1,205
  *Chef Boy-Ar-Dee*        798
    small        160
  *Jeno's*        840
    Deluxe        1,470
    Junior        165
    Mix        838
  *Kraft*        822
    Pee Wee        170
  *Lambrecht*        909
  *La Pizzeria*        1,230
  *Lean Cuisine*        170
  *Roman*        891
  *Stouffer's*        330
  *Tostino's*        882

**Cheese and Refried Beans**
  *El Chico*        902

**Cheese and Chili**
  *El Chico*        1,039

**Combinations**
  *Celeste*        600
    large        1,480
  *Jeno's* Deluxe        1,667

| | |
|---|---:|
| *La Pizzeria* | 830 |
| large | 1,529 |
| *Stouffer's* | 789 |
| *Tostino's* | 1,683 |
| Classic | 1,675 |
| **Hamburger** | |
| *Jeno's* | 888 |
| *Tostino's* | 910 |
| Crisp | 955 |
| **Open Face** | |
| *Buitoni* | 250 |
| **Pepperoni** | |
| *Celeste* | 540 |
| large | 1,438 |
| *Chef Boy-Ar-Dee* | 175 |
| *Jeno's* | 901 |
| *La Pizzeria* | 1,322 |
| *Roman* | 889 |
| *Stouffer's* | 800 |
| *Tostino's* | 923 |
| Crisp | 960 |
| Classic | 1,792 |
| Classic with mushrooms | 1,497 |
| **Rolls** | |
| *Jeno's* | |
| Cheeseburger | 268 |
| Pepperoni | 262 |
| Sausage | 259 |
| Shrimp | 214 |

**Sausage**

| | |
|---|---|
| *Celeste* | 561 |
| large | 1,500 |
| *Jeno's* | 899 |
| Deluxe | 1,495 |
| Mix | 1,058 |
| *Kraft* | 1,000 |
| *Pee Wee* | 190 |
| *Lambrecht* | 1,005 |
| *La Pizzeria* | 860 |
| large | 1,515 |
| *Roman* | 233 |
| *Tostino's* | 938 |
| Crisp | 981 |
| Classic | 1,799 |

# POPCORN AND PRETZELS

**Popcorn, 1 cup**

| | |
|---|---|
| *Jiffy Pop* | 31 |
| *Jolly Time* | 31 |
| *King Korn* | |
| Cheese | 40 |
| Seasoned | 42 |
| *Pops-Rite* | 38 |

| | |
|---|---|
| *Presto-Pop* | 37 |
| *3 Minute* | 38 |
| *TNT* | 52 |
| *Wise* | 43 |
|   Cheese-flavored | 49 |
| *Wonder* | 45 |
| **Pretzels, 1 piece** | |
| *Bachman* | |
|   B's | 8 |
|   Beer | 55 |
|   Medium | 20 |
|   Teeny | 11 |
|   Thin | 18 |
| *Old London* | 5 |
| *Nabisco Mister Salty* | |
|   Dutch | 51 |
|   3-Ring | 12 |
|   Veri-Thin | 20 |
|   Pretzelettes | 6 |
| *Sunshine* | 19 |

# FAST FOODS

*Arby's*
| | |
|---|---|
| Beef and Cheese Sandwich | 450 |
| Club Sandwich | 560 |

**13**

| | |
|---|---:|
| Ham and Cheese Sandwich | 380 |
| Junior Roast Beef Sandwich | 220 |
| Roast Beef Sandwich | 350 |
| Super Roast Beef Sandwich | 620 |
| Swiss King Sandwich | 660 |
| Turkey Deluxe Sandwich | 510 |
| Turkey Sandwich | 410 |

*Arthur Treacher's*

| | |
|---|---:|
| Chicken | 271 |
| Chicken Sandwich | 265 |
| Chips | 243 |
| Chowder | 66 |
| Cole Slaw | 144 |
| Fish | 241 |
| Fish Sandwich | 282 |
| Krunch Pup | 358 |
| Lemon Luvs | 324 |
| Shrimp | 380 |

*Brazier (Dairy Queen)*

| | |
|---|---:|
| Hamburger | 260 |
| Cheeseburger | 320 |
| *Big Brazier* | 460 |
| *Big Brazier* with Cheese | 550 |
| *Big Brazier* with Lettuce and Tomato | 470 |
| *Super Brazier (The Half-Pounder)* | 780 |
| Hot Dog | 270 |
| Hot Dog with Chili | 330 |
| Hot Dog with Cheese | 330 |
| Fish Sandwich | 400 |
| Fish Sandwich with Cheese | 440 |

**13**

| | |
|---|---|
| French Fries | 200 |
| French Fries, large | 320 |
| Onion Rings | 300 |
| **Burger Chef** | |
| Chocolate Shake | 310 |
| *Big Chef* | 542 |
| Cheeseburger | 304 |
| Double Cheeseburger | 434 |
| Double Hamburger | 325 |
| French Fries | 187 |
| Hamburger | 258 |
| Mariner Platter | 680 |
| Rancher Platter | 640 |
| Shake | 326 |
| *Skipper's Treat* | 604 |
| *Super Chef* | 600 |
| **Burger King** | |
| *Whopper* | 650 |
| Double Beef *Whopper* | 850 |
| *Whopper* with Cheese | 760 |
| Double Beef *Whopper* with Cheese | 970 |
| *Whopper Junior* | 360 |
| *Whopper Junior* with Cheese | 420 |
| *Whopper Junior* with Double Meat | 490 |
| *Whopper Junior* Double Meat with Cheese | 550 |
| Hamburger | 310 |
| Hamburger with Cheese | 360 |
| Double Meat Hamburger | 440 |
| Double Meat Hamburger with Cheese | 540 |

**13**

| | |
|---|---|
| Steak Sandwich | 600 |
| *Whaler* | 660 |
| *Whaler* with Cheese | 770 |
| Onion Rings, large | 330 |
| Onion Rings, regular | 230 |
| French Fries, large bag | 360 |
| French Fries, regular bag | 240 |
| Chocolate Milkshake | 380 |
| Vanilla Milkshake | 360 |
| Apple Pie | 240 |

## Carl's Jr.

| | |
|---|---|
| *Famous Star* Hamburger | 480 |
| *Super Star* Hamburger | 660 |
| *Old Time Star* Hamburger | 440 |
| *Happy Star* Hamburger | 290 |
| Steak Sandwich | 630 |
| California Roast Beef Sandwich | 380 |
| Fish Fillet Sandwich | 550 |
| Original Hot Dog | 340 |
| Chili Dog | 360 |
| Chili Cheese Dog | 400 |
| American Cheese | 40 |
| Salad with Condiments 11 oz | 170 |
| Dressing, 2 oz | |
|    Blue Cheese | 200 |
|    Thousand Island | 190 |
|    Lo-Cal Italian | 48 |
| French Fries | 220 |
| Apple Turnover | 330 |

**13**

| | |
|---|---:|
| Carrot Cake | 380 |
| Shake | 310 |
| Soft Drinks | 200 |

***Church's Fried Chicken*, 1 piece, boned**

| | |
|---|---:|
| Dark | 305 |
| White | 327 |

***Dunkin' Donuts***

| | |
|---|---:|
| Cake and Chocolate Cake Donuts | |
| rings, sticks, crullers, etc. | 240 |
| Yeast-raised Donuts | 160 |
| Glazed Yeast-Raised Donuts | 168 |
| Fancies | |
| coffee rolls, danish, etc. | 215 |
| Fancies with Filling and Topping | 260 |
| *Munchkins*, Yeast-raised | 26 |
| *Munchkins*, Cake and Chocolate Cake | 66 |
| *Munchkins* with Filling and Topping | 79 |

***Gino's***

| | |
|---|---:|
| Apple Pie | 238 |
| Cheeseburger | 300 |
| Cheese Hero | 738 |
| Cheese Sirloiner | 532 |
| Coke | 117 |
| Fish Platter | 650 |
| Fish Sandwich | 450 |
| French Fries | 156 |
| Giant | 569 |
| Hamburger | 254 |
| Hero | 647 |
| Hot Chocolate | 90 |

# 13

### Hardees

| | |
|---|---|
| Apple Turnover | 282 |
| Big Twin | 447 |
| Cheeseburger | 335 |
| Deluxe | 675 |
| Double Cheeseburger | 495 |
| Fish Sandwich | 468 |
| French Fries, large | 381 |
| French Fries, small | 239 |
| Hamburger | 305 |
| Hot Dog | 346 |
| Milkshake | 391 |
| Roast Beef Sandwich | 390 |

### Jack-in-the-Box

| | |
|---|---|
| Apple Turnover | 411 |
| Breakfast Jack | 301 |
| Cheeseburger | |
| *Deluxe* | 310 |
| *Jumbo Jack* | 628 |
| Double Cheese Omelet | 423 |
| French Fries | 270 |
| French Toast | 537 |
| Hamburger | |
| *Bonus Jack* | 461 |
| *Deluxe* | 260 |
| *Jumbo Jack* | 551 |
| Ham and Cheese Omelet | 425 |
| Jack Burrito | 448 |
| Jack Steak | 428 |
| Lemon Turnover | 446 |

| | |
|---|---|
| *Moby Jack* | 455 |
| Onion Rings | 351 |
| Pancakes | 626 |
| Ranchero Omelet | 414 |
| Scrambled Eggs | 719 |
| Shakes, Chocolate | 365 |
| Strawberry | 380 |
| Vanilla | 342 |
| Taco | 189 |
| Taco Super | 285 |

**Kentucky Fried Chicken**
Chicken Dinner
(3 pieces chicken, potatoes, cole slaw, roll)

| | |
|---|---|
| Original Recipe Dinner | 830 |
| Extra Crispy Dinner | 950 |

Individual Pieces

| | |
|---|---|
| Wing | 151 |
| Drumstick | 136 |
| Keel | 253 |
| Rib | 242 |
| Thigh | 276 |

**Long John Silver's**

| | |
|---|---|
| Breaded Clams | 465 |
| Breaded Oysters | 460 |
| Chicken planks | 458 |
| Cole Slaw | 138 |
| Corn on the Cob | 174 |
| Fish with Batter, 2 pieces | 318 |
| Fries | 375 |

| | |
|---|---|
| Hush Puppies | 153 |
| Ocean Scallops | 257 |
| *Peg Leg* | 514 |
| Shrimp | 268 |
| *Treasure Chest* | 467 |

**McDonald's**

| | |
|---|---|
| Apple Pie | 300 |
| *Big Mac* | 541 |
| Cheeseburger | 306 |
| Cherry Pie | 298 |
| Chocolate Shake | 364 |
| *Egg McMuffin* | 352 |
| English Muffin, Buttered | 186 |
| Fillet O' Fish | 402 |
| French Fries | 211 |
| Hamburger | 257 |
| Hot Cakes, with Butter or Syrup | 472 |
| *McDonaldland* Cookies | 294 |
| Quarter-pounder | 418 |
| Quarter-pounder with Cheese | 518 |
| Sausage | 184 |
| Scrambled eggs | 162 |
| Shake, Strawberry | 345 |
| Shake, Vanilla | 323 |

**Pizza Hut, 1 slice, Thin**

Standard

| | |
|---|---|
| Cheese | 180 |
| Pepperoni | 202 |
| Pork and Mushroom | 196 |

| | |
|---|---|
| Super Supreme | 266 |
| Superstyle | |
|   Cheese | 213 |
|   Pepperoni | 233 |
|   Pork and Mushroom | 230 |
| Supreme | 216 |
| ***Ponderosa*, Entree** | |
| Chopped Beef | 324 |
| Double Deluxe | 362 |
| Extra-cut Prime Rib | 409 |
| Extra-cut Ribeye | 358 |
| Fillet of Sole | 251 |
| Fillet of Sole Sandwich | 125 |
| Junior Patty | 98 |
| Prime Rib | 286 |
| Ribeye | 259 |
| Ribeye/Shrimp | 400 |
| Shrimp | 220 |
| Steakhouse Deluxe | 181 |
| Strip Sirloin | 277 |
| Super Sirloin | 383 |
| T-Bone | 374 |
| ***Poppin' Fresh*** | |
| Chef's Salad | 800 |
| Custard Pie, 1 slice | 380 |
| Dairy Salad | 650 |
| Dinner Salad | 250 |
| Doughboy Salad | 530 |
| Pumpkin Pie, 1 slice | 390 |

| | |
|---|---|
| Shrimp Salad | 640 |
| Tuna Salad | 640 |

**Steak 'N Shake**

| | |
|---|---|
| Steakburger | 276 |
| Steakburger with Cheese | 352 |
| Super Steakburger | 375 |
| Super Steakburger with Cheese | 451 |
| Triple Steakburger | 474 |
| Triple Steakburger with Cheese | 625 |
| Low Calorie Platter | 293 |
| Baked Ham Sandwich | 451 |
| Toasted Cheese Sandwich | 250 |
| Ham & Egg Sandwich | 434 |
| Egg Sandwich | 275 |
| French Fries | 211 |
| Chili and Oyster Crackers | 337 |
| Chili | 402 |
| Baked Beans | 173 |
| Lettuce and Tomato Salad with 1 oz Thousand Island Dressing | 168 |
| Chef Salad | 313 |
| Cottage Cheese | 93 |
| Apple Danish | 391 |

Sundaes

| | |
|---|---|
| Strawberry | 329 |
| Hot Fudge Nut | 530 |
| Brownie Fudge | 645 |
| Apple Pie | 407 |
| Cherry Pie | 334 |

**13**

| | |
|---|---|
| Cheesecake | 368 |
| Brownie | 259 |
| *Taco Bell* | |
| Bean Burrito | 343 |
| Beef Burrito | 466 |
| Beefy Tostada | 291 |
| *Bellbeefer* | 221 |
| *Bellbeefer* with Cheese | 278 |
| Burrito Supreme | 457 |
| Combination Burrito | 404 |
| Enchirito | 454 |
| Pintos Cheese | 168 |
| Taco | 186 |
| Tostada | 179 |
| *Wendy's* | |
| Cheeseburger | |
| Single cheese | 580 |
| Double cheese | 800 |
| Triple cheese | 1,040 |
| Chili | 230 |
| French Fries | 330 |
| Frosty | 390 |
| Hamburger | |
| Single | 470 |
| Double | 670 |
| Triple | 850 |
| *White Castle* | |
| Cheeseburger | 185 |
| Fish | 192 |

**Fast Foods and Snacks**

| | |
|---|---|
| French Fries | 225 |
| Hamburger | 160 |
| *Zantiago* | |
| Burrito | 345 |
| Enchirito | 391 |
| Frijoles | 231 |
| Taco | 146 |
| Tostada | 206 |

# CHAPTER 14

# *Home Cooked, Restaurant and Frozen*

## HOME COOKED AND RESTAURANT DISHES,
### 1 average portion unless noted

| | |
|---|---:|
| Abalone with mushrooms | 526 |
| Abalone with oyster sauce | 283 |
| Abalone steaks | 215 |
| Aioli sauce, 1 Tbsp | 125 |
| Almond tarts, each | 70 |
| Alu Bhaji | 130 |

**14**

| | |
|---|---|
| Ambrosia | 126 |
| Ambrosia salad | 542 |
| Anchovy butter, 1 Tbsp | 127 |
| Angel Food Cake | 120 |
| Apples, baked | 225 |
| Apples, stuffed | 265 |
| Apple Brown Betty | 547 |
| Apples, candied | 355 |
| Apple Caramel | 488 |
| Apple cinnamon rings | 180 |
| Apple curried rings | 155 |
| Apple fried rings | 165 |
| Apple, pickled, 1 apple | 50 |
| Applesauce | 225 |
| Apple turnovers | 400 |
| Apricot, Brown Betty | 498 |
| Armenian style mussels, stuffed with rice, currants and piñon nuts | 528 |
| Arroz con Pollo | 655 |
| Artichoke, boiled | 146 |
| Artichoke hearts, marinated | 75 |
| Artichokes, Jerusalem boiled | 163 |
| Artichoke moutarde | 374 |
| Artichoke, Provencal-style, braised | 127 |
| Artichoke vinaigrette | 446 |
| Asparagus, buttered | 90 |
| Asparagus, Chinese-style | 150 |
| Asparagus Divan, 4 spears | 375 |
| Asparagus vinaigrette | 170 |

**14**

| | |
|---|---:|
| **Beef and Asparagus** | 929 |
| and Bean Curd | 682 |
| and Bean Sprouts | 646 |
| and Broccoli | 585 |
| Congee | 896 |
| Consommé, 1 cup | 33 |
| Fondue Bourguignonne | 479 |
| and Green Pepper | 444 |
| Lo Mein | 1,042 |
| and Mushrooms | 435 |
| and Noodles in Brown Bean Sauce | 685 |
| and Oyster Sauce | 689 |
| with Pea Pods and Water Chestnuts | 648 |
| and Mushroom Pirog | 720 |
| Picadillo | 400 |
| **Beef Brisket** | 530 |
| **Beef Heart, stuffed** | 475 |
| **Beef Kidneys, braised** | 275 |
| **Beef Roasts** | |
| Pot-au-feu | 555 |
| Pot Roast | 600 |
| Pot Roast, French-style | 715 |
| Pot Roast, German-style | 650 |
| Sauerbraten | 569 |
| Yankee Pot Roast | 746 |
| **Beef Short Ribs** | 485 |
| **Beef Steak** | |
| Bracioulini | 423 |
| Chicken-fried | 935 |
| Chinese-style | 345 |

**Beets**

| | |
|---|---|
| harvard in sour cream | 170 |
| in horseradish | 120 |
| pickled, 1 beet | 10 |
| **Beignet d 'Aubergines, 4 oz** | 200 |
| **Beurre Manié, 1 Tbsp** | 98 |
| **Bhendi Bhaji** | 85 |
| **Bernaise Sauce, 1 Tbsp** | 46 |
| **Billi-Bi** | 222 |
| **Biscuit Tortoni** | 284 |
| **Biscuit, Baking Powder, 1 piece** | 83 |
| **Black Bean dip, 1 Tbsp** | 36 |
| **Black-eyed peas, Southern-style** | 550 |
| **Black forest cake** | 758 |
| **Blancmange** | 162 |
| **Blanquette de Veau** | 699 |
| **Blini, 1 piece** | 87 |
| with butter | 184 |
| with caviar | 204 |
| **Blintzes, cheese, 1 piece** | 177 |
| **Blood Sausage, 6 oz** | 708 |
| **Blueberry muffins** | 133 |
| **Blueberry waffles** | 259 |
| **Bocconcini** | 524 |
| **Bordelaise sauce, 1 Tbsp** | 23 |
| **Borscht** | 400 |
| **Boston Baked beans** | 534 |
| **Boston Brown Bread, 1 slice** | 86 |
| **Bougatsa, 1 piece** | 401 |
| **Bouillabaisse** | 600 |

**14**

**Cabbage**

| | |
|---|---|
| Austrian | 227 |
| Baked | 106 |
| Colcannon | 144 |
| Creole | 133 |
| Flemish Red, with Apples | 268 |
| Pennsylvania Dutch | 155 |
| Pickled, 1 cup | 200 |
| Polish | 400 |
| Rolls Stuffed with Lamb | 372 |
| Sweet and Sour | 150 |

| | |
|---|---|
| **Cacciucco** | 414 |
| **Cacik** | 100 |
| **Caesar salad** | 299 |

**Cake**

| | |
|---|---|
| Applesauce | 205 |
| Cheesecake | 424 |
| Cheesecake, Italian style | 520 |
| Chocolate | 230 |
| Cinnamon and Coffee | 135 |
| Coconut cream | 240 |
| Devil's food | 240 |
| Lemon Chiffon | 300 |
| Light Fruit | 266 |
| Genoese | 120 |
| Marble | 195 |
| Petits fours, 1 piece | 251 |
| Pineapple Upside-down | 255 |
| Rainbow | 210 |
| Sachertorte | 362 |

**14**

| | |
|---|---:|
| Celeri Rémoulade, 4 oz | 303 |
| Celeriac, creamed | 213 |
| Ceviche | 308 |
| Champ | 157 |
| Champignon farci gratinée, 1 piece | 135 |
| Chantilly Sauce, 1 Tbsp | 75 |
| Chard, pureed | 107 |
| Char shu ding | 300 |
| Charlotte Russe | 458 |
| Chasseur Sauce, 1 Tbsp | 31 |
| Cheese Boreks | 138 |
| Cheese Dumplings, 1 piece | 95 |
| Cheese Fondue | 1,000 |
| Cheese straws, 10 pieces | 283 |
| Cheese sauce, 1 Tbsp | 38 |
| Cheese soufflé | 327 |
| Cherries Jubilee | 200 |
| Chestnuts | |
| creamed | 400 |
| pureed | 327 |
| roasted, 6 oz | 245 |
| Chicken | |
| and Almonds | 750 |
| and Asparagus | 510 |
| Barbecued with Skin and Bones | 405 |
| Bhuna | 219 |
| and Black Bean Sauce | 748 |
| Burmese, in Peanut and Coconut Sauce | 845 |
| Cacciatore | 468 |
| and Cashews | 750 |

**14**

| | |
|---|---:|
| Musallam | 227 |
| with Mushrooms | 528 |
| Pancake, Chinese-style | 899 |
| Parmigiana | 510 |
| Pizziola | 290 |
| Roumanian-style, with Apricots | 468 |
| Salad | 423 |
| with Snow peas | 520 |
| Stew | 560 |
| stuffed with rice and mushrooms | 362 |
| Sub Gum | 638 |
| Sweet and Sour | 1,150 |
| Tandoori | 366 |
| Teriyaki | 878 |
| Tetrazzini | 878 |
| Chinese-style, with vegetables | 670 |
| Velvet | 742 |
| Vino bianco | 300 |
| with walnuts | 929 |
| Yakitori | 253 |
| Zingara | 500 |
| and tomato salad | 199 |
| **Chili** | 448 |
| **Chiles con Queso** | 327 |
| **Chiles Rellenos** | 442 |
| **Chiles de Frijoles** | 544 |
| **Chimichango** | 288 |
| **Chinese style** | |
| Beef | 343 |
| Cabbage, quickfried | 200 |

**14**

| | |
|---|---:|
| Cabbage, steamed | 85 |
| Cabbage, Sweet and Sour | 200 |
| Carp, Sweet and Sour | 300 |
| Mustard Sauce, 1 Tbsp | 5 |
| Egg roll | 145 |
| Fried eggs and Rice | 324 |
| Fried puffs, 1 piece | 86 |
| Fried rice | 301 |
| Pork with rice | 277 |
| Shrimp with ginger | 274 |
| Snow peas | 115 |
| Spareribs | 565 |
| Sweet and sour sauce, 1 Tbsp | 15 |
| Cucumber and soy sauce | 62 |

**Chocolate**

| | |
|---|---:|
| Chiffon Cake, 1 slice | 318 |
| Chip Cookie, 1 piece | 75 |
| Eclairs | 282 |
| Mousse | 316 |
| Profiteroles, 1 piece | 153 |
| Sauce, 1 Tbsp | 86 |
| Hot Soufflé | 339 |

| | |
|---|---:|
| **Chinese fried puffs, 1 piece** | 86 |
| **Chopped Chicken liver, ½ cup** | 262 |
| **Chorizos, 1 link** | 147 |

**Chutney, 1 Tbsp**

| | |
|---|---:|
| Coconut | 17 |
| Green Tomato | 25 |
| Mango | 63 |

| | |
|---|---:|
| Mint | 10 |
| Tomato | 30 |
| **Clams** | |
| Bisque | 200 |
| in Black Bean Sauce, Chinese-style, 1 | 39 |
| Casino, 1 dozen | 536 |
| New England Pie | 325 |
| Origanata, 1 dozen | 440 |
| Red Sauce | 301 |
| White Sauce | 142 |
| **Cockaleekie** | 95 |
| **Cocoa** | 175 |
| **Coconut Macaroon, 1 piece** | 57 |
| **Cod Kedgeree** | 333 |
| **Coleslaw and caraway salad** | 238 |
| **Court Bouillon** | 4 |
| **Couscous, Boiled** | 305 |
| Beef | 567 |
| Chicken | 653 |
| Lamb | 600 |
| **Coquilles Saint-Jacques** | 475 |
| **Cornbread, 1 slice** | 100 |
| **Corn Fritters** | 249 |
| relish, 1 Tbsp | 16 |
| sticks, per stick | 100 |
| **Corned beef and cabbage** | 600 |
| **Corned beef hash** | 400 |
| **Coulibiac** | 288 |
| **Crab** | |
| Cakes, Maryland-style | 257 |

**14**

| | |
|---|---|
| Cocktail, ½ cup | 92 |
| Deviled | 398 |
| Legs, Alaska King | 297 |
| Louis | 767 |
| Meunière, 2 | 278 |
| Mornay | 513 |
| Newburg Imperial | 426 |
| **Cranberry Nut Bread, 1 slice** | 136 |
| **Cranberry Relish, 1 Tbsp** | 44 |
| **Cranberry sauce, 1 Tbsp** | 28 |
| **Cream Cheese Dip, with Bacon and Horseradish, 1 Tbsp** | 74 |
| **Cream Puff, 1 piece** | 251 |
| **Creme brulee** | 655 |
| **Creme Caramel** | 280 |
| **Crepes, au champignon, 1 piece** | 178 |
| **Crepes, au jambon gratinée, 1 piece** | 156 |
| **Crepes Suzette, 1 piece** | 208 |
| **Crispy Bass, Chinese-style** | 484 |
| **Croissant, 1 piece** | 90 |
| **Croque Madame** | 710 |
| **Croque Monsieur** | 710 |
| **Croquettes de crevette** | 263 |
| **Croquettes de volaille** | 493 |
| **Cucumber and yogurt sauce, 1 Tbsp** | 5 |
| **Crumpet, 1 piece** | 80 |
| **Cumberland sauce, 1 Tbsp** | 40 |
| **Curried** | |
| Beef | 415 |
| Beef Triangles, 1 piece | 154 |

| | |
|---|---:|
| Lamb | 656 |
| Lamb and dhal | 870 |
| Cold lobster | 493 |
| Shrimp | 504 |
| **Custard, baked** | 162 |
| **Custard, floating island** | 253 |
| **Custard, rennet** | 107 |
| **Custard sauce** | 27 |
| **Danish pastry** | 144 |
| **Datenut bread, 1 slice** | 88 |
| **Dhal** | 229 |
| **Deviled Ham, 1 Tbsp** | 38 |
| **Diable sauce, 1 Tbsp** | 20 |
| **Dijonnaise sauce, 1 Tbsp** | 93 |
| **Dips, 1 Tbsp** | |
| Black bean | 37 |
| Chili | 18 |
| Clam in Cream Cheese | 75 |
| Cream cheese, bacon and horseradish | 71 |
| Curry | 40 |
| Deviled clam | 80 |
| Taramasalata | 102 |
| **Divinity, 1 piece** | 38 |
| **Dolma** | 225 |
| **Doughnut** | |
| chocolate, 1 piece | 175 |
| jelly | 147 |
| old fashioned | 135 |
| **Duck** | |
| with Cherry sauce | 400 |

| | |
|---|---|
| Crispy, Chinese style, 4 oz | 820 |
| Eight precious, 4 oz | 905 |
| with Orange sauce | 490 |
| Peking, 4 oz | 835 |
| Pressed, 4 oz | 399 |
| Wild roast | 256 |
| Szechuan, 4 oz | 1,000 |
| Tangerine peel, Chinese-style | 782 |
| **Dumplings, Chinese-style, 1 piece** | 95 |
| **Dumplings, Peking fried, 1 piece** | 76 |
| **Duxelles sauce, 1 Tbsp** | 19 |
| **East Indian Lentils and Rice** | 264 |
| **Eclairs, 1 piece** | 285 |
| **Eel, jellied** | 605 |
| **Eel and egg pie** | 623 |
| **Eggs** | |
| in Aspic, 1 | 130 |
| Benedict, 1 | 286 |
| Custard, steamed Chinese-style | 226 |
| Deviled, 1 | 148 |
| Florentine, 1 | 165 |
| Foo Yong, 1 foo | 322 |
| Fried rice, 1 cup | 335 |
| Huevos rancheros, 1 | 177 |
| Salad | 403 |
| Scotch, 1 | 498 |
| **Eggnog, nonalcoholic** | 243 |
| **Eggplant** | |
| Basque-style with peppers and tomatoes | 155 |
| Dip, 1 Tbsp | 45 |

| | |
|---|---|
| Fried | 281 |
| Greek-style | 195 |
| Greek-style, stuffed | 180 |
| Ismir | 246 |
| Parmigiana | 598 |
| Pisto | 135 |
| Ratatouille | 510 |
| Stuffed with mushrooms and chickpeas | 228 |
| Stuffed with pilaf and raisins | 188 |
| Turkish | 327 |
| **Egg Rolls, Chinese, 1 piece** | 145 |
| **Empanada, with beef** | 244 |
| **Empanada, with chicken** | 220 |
| **Enchilada** | |
| Beef | 299 |
| Cheese | 270 |
| Chicken | 330 |
| Chorizo | 267 |
| **Escalopes de veau cordon bleu** | 680 |
| **Escargot de bourgogne, 6 pieces** | 418 |
| **Escarole, sautéed** | 74 |
| **Esterhazy steak** | 994 |
| **Falafel** | 263 |
| **Fennel, braised** | 116 |
| **Fettuccine Alfredo** | 1,550 |
| **Fettuccine con Baccala** | 653 |
| **Figs, fresh stewed** | 195 |
| **Finnan Haddie** | 257 |
| **Fish balls, Chinese-style, 8 oz** | 319 |

**14**

| | |
|---|---|
| Fish, Jade Chinese-style, 6 oz | 547 |
| Lemon Chinese-style, 8 oz | 754 |
| Fish mousse | 286 |
| Fish piquant en papillote | 199 |
| Fish soufflé | 300 |
| Flan | 263 |
| Flemish red cabbage and apples | 248 |
| Floating island | 257 |
| Florentines, 1 piece | 118 |
| Flounder fillet in black bean sauce | 600 |
| Fondue de Gruyère | 478 |
| Fragrant noodles with shrimp, Chinese-style | 810 |
| Franks in blankets, 1 piece | 46 |
| French-fried onion rings | 165 |
| French-fried potatoes | 227 |
| Frijoles fritos | 325 |
| Frijoles Mexicanos | 194 |
| Frikadeller | 384 |
| Fruit cake, light, 1 slice | 264 |
| Fudge, chocolate, 1 piece | 78 |
| Fudge Sauce, hot, 1 Tbsp | 100 |
| Garlic bread, 1 slice | 88 |
| Garlic sauce, 1 Tbsp | 11 |
| Gefilte fish | 183 |
| Giblet gravy, 1 Tbsp | 16 |
| Gingersnaps, 1 piece | 97 |
| Gingerbread, 1 slice | 206 |
| Gingerbread boys, 1 boy | 132 |
| Gnocchi, Cheese | 410 |

**14**

| | |
|---|---|
| Farina parmigiana | 385 |
| Potato | 314 |
| Goose, Braised with chestnuts and onions | 525 |
| German style stuffed with potatoes | 488 |
| Roasted with apples and sauerkraut stuffing | 842 |
| Goulash | 394 |
| Grand Marnier soufflé | 262 |
| Grand Marnier with strawberries | 110 |
| Granite, 1 cup | 263 |
| Grasshopper pie | 680 |
| Gravy, 1 Tbsp | |
| au jus | 4 |
| giblet | 15 |
| mushroom | 22 |
| Greek Salad | 235 |
| Greek Gyro | 246 |
| Green Olives, 2 large | 20 |
| Green Beans with garlic, Chinese-style | 205 |
| Green Goddess dressing, 1 Tbsp | 89 |
| Grenouilles a l'Anglaise | 385 |
| Meuniere | 485 |
| Provencale | 423 |
| Green pepper, Stuffed | 190 |
| with beef and kidney beans | 356 |
| Mexican-style | 444 |
| Green sauce, 1 Tbsp | 82 |
| Grits | 150 |
| Guacamole, 1 Tbsp | 28 |
| Gumbo, corn | 172 |

**14**

| | |
|---|---|
| Horseradish cream sauce, 1 Tbsp | 77 |
| Horseradish, fresh, 1 Tbsp | 5 |
| Hot Chocolate | 275 |
| Hot Cross Bun, 1 piece | 105 |
| Huevos Rancheros, 1 egg | 186 |
| Humus with tahini, ½ cup | 364 |
| Hushpuppies, 1 piece | 67 |
| Indian Corn Fritters, 1 piece | 50 |
| Indian Pudding | 371 |
| Indian Rice Pilaf | 395 |
| Irish Soda Bread, 1 slice | 114 |
| Irish Stew | 710 |
| Japanese Salad | |
|    autumn | 150 |
|    cucumber | 48 |
|    cucumber and fish | 135 |
|    cucumber and seaweed | 64 |
|    lotus root | 87 |
| Jelly, homemade, 1 Tbsp | 45 |
| Jelly Roll | 187 |
| Jhinga Bhajia, 1 piece | 37 |
| Jhinga Kari, 10-12 shrimp | 609 |
| Jhonnycake, 1 piece | 98 |
| Kasha, buckwheat | 355 |
|    appel-almond | 400 |
| Katsudon | 829 |
| Kebabs, Indian lamb | 231 |
| Kedgeree | 318 |
| Keema curry | 246 |
| Keftedakia Marinata | 410 |

**14**

| | |
|---|---|
| **Keftedes** | 248 |
| **Keftedes Avgolemono** | 200 |
| **Khiri Pachadi** | 122 |
| **Kibbeh** | 964 |
| **Kidneys, braised** | 289 |
| **Kielbasa, fried, 3 oz** | 350 |
| **Kissel** | 240 |
| **Knockwurst, sauteed, 6 oz** | 538 |
| **Korma curry** | 344 |
| **Koulebiaka** | 1,300 |
| **Kourabiedes, 1 piece** | 75 |
| **Kreplach, 1 piece** | 34 |
| **Kugelhupf, 1 slice** | 187 |
| **Ladyfingers, 1 piece** | 52 |
| **Lamb** | |
| braised | 490 |
| breast | 425 |
| cassoulet | 1,050 |
| crown roast | 270 |
| dolma | 232 |
| kidneys in sour cream | 485 |
| riblets, barbecued | 840 |
| shanks | 372 |
| shish kebab | 686 |
| stew | 403 |
| **Lancashire Hot Pot** | 552 |
| **Lasagne, with cheese** | 605 |
| with meat | 408 |
| with meat balls | 1,095 |
| **Lebkuchen, 1 piece** | 84 |

**14**

| | |
|---|---:|
| Leek pie | 562 |
| Lemon curd, 1 Tbsp | 50 |
| Lemonade | 118 |
| Lemon Ice | 140 |
| Lemon sauce, 1 Tbsp | 28 |
| Lemon Sherbet, 1 cup | 290 |
| Lentils, boiled | 364 |
| Linguini alla Romana | 763 |
| Linzertorte, Viennese, 1 slice | 304 |
| Liver, Broiled | 280 |
| and onions | 306 |
| alla Veneziana | 314 |
| Chicken, sautéed | 247 |
| Chicken pâté | 294 |
| Lo mein pork | 333 |
| Lobster | |
| a l'Americaine | 503 |
| Cantonese | 393 |
| Fra diavolo | 586 |
| Mousse | 300 |
| Newburg | 483 |
| Thermidor | 483 |
| London Broil | 389 |
| Lotus Root Cake | 70 |
| Louisiana Rice and Kidney Beans | 483 |
| Lyonnaise sauce, 1 Tbsp | 31 |
| Macaroni, Beef and Tomato Casserole | 656 |
| and cheese | 482 |
| salad | 471 |
| Macaroon, 1 piece | 44 |

**14**

| | |
|---|---:|
| Moo goo gai pan | 244 |
| Mornay sauce, 1 Tbsp | 33 |
| Moules | |
| farcis provencale, 8–10 pieces | 324 |
| gratinées Normande, 8–10 pieces | 285 |
| Marseille, 8–10 pieces | 450 |
| salade de, 8–10 pieces | 461 |
| vinaigrette, 8–10 pieces | 230 |
| Moussaka | 818 |
| Mousse, Avocado | 196 |
| Chocolate | 306 |
| Fish | 282 |
| Mozzarella cheese, breaded and fried | 231 |
| Muffin, 1 piece | 108 |
| Bran | 140 |
| Corn | 148 |
| Raisin bran | 162 |
| Mushroom gravy, 1 Tbsp | 26 |
| Mushrooms | |
| creamed | 200 |
| in madeira | 236 |
| marinated | 51 |
| sauteed | 187 |
| Mushrooms with bamboo shoots | 295 |
| Mu shu pork, 2 pancakes | 874 |
| Mustard sauce, 1 Tbsp | 41 |
| Nachos, 1 piece | 40 |
| Nantua sauce, 1 Tbsp | 24 |
| Napoleons, 1 piece | 402 |

| | |
|---|---|
| **Napolitos** | 100 |
| **New England boiled dinner** | 735 |
| **Nockerln** | 163 |
| **Noodles in brown bean sauce and pork** | 891 |
| **Noodles in oyster sauce** | 463 |
| **Normandy rock cornish game hen, 1 bird** | 700 |
| **Oatmeal Bread, 1 slice** | 120 |
| **Octopus Mediterranean** | 350 |
| **Okra, fried** | 175 |
| **Omelet** | |
| with caviar, 1 egg | 180 |
| Greek, 1 egg | 130 |
| Lorraine, 1 egg | 167 |
| Lyonnaise, 1 egg | 136 |
| with mushroom and tomato, 1 egg | 135 |
| Onion frittata, 1 egg | 200 |
| Piperade, 1 egg | 215 |
| Soufflé, 1 egg | 111 |
| Spanish, 1 egg | 127 |
| **Onion Rings, french-fried** | 184 |
| **Onions, baked, 1 piece** | 155 |
| **Onions, creamed** | 209 |
| sautéed | 150 |
| stuffed | 186 |
| **Oshi tashi** | 34 |
| **Osso buco** | 905 |
| **Oysters casino, 1 dozen** | 540 |
| **Oysters en Brochette** | 215 |
| **Oysters Rockefeller, 1 dozen** | 1,000 |

| | |
|---|---|
| **Oyster Sauce, 1 Tbsp** | 35 |
| **Paella** | |
| with lobster | 620 |
| with sausage | 630 |
| Valenciana | 548 |
| **Pakora (Indian fritters)** | |
| Baigon | 41 |
| Gobhi | 38 |
| Mixed vegetable | 54 |
| **Pancakes, 1 piece** | |
| apple | 95 |
| blueberry | 87 |
| buckwheat | 82 |
| buttermilk | 73 |
| pecan | 135 |
| plain | 85 |
| wholewheat | 89 |
| **Panettone, 1 slice** | 322 |
| **Paper-wrapped Chicken, Chinese-style, 1 piece** | 98 |
| **Parsley sauce, 1 Tbsp** | 22 |
| **Parsnips, roasted** | 211 |
| **Pashka** | 300 |
| **Pastitsio** | 820 |
| **Pâté** | |
| de Campagne | 584 |
| de Canard | 1,076 |
| de Foie Gras | 648 |
| de Poisson au Asperges | 478 |
| **Peach** | |
| cardinal | 230 |

| | |
|---|---|
| cobbler | 500 |
| Melba | 354 |
| **Peanut brittle, 1 piece** | 77 |
| **Peanut butter cookies, 1 piece** | 70 |
| **Pea pods with water chestnuts** | 307 |
| **Pea pods with mushrooms** | 261 |
| **Pear Helene** | 602 |
| **Peking custard** | 464 |
| **Penuche, 1 piece** | 41 |
| **Pepper, Greek stuffed green** | 120 |
| **Pepper, Greek stuffed with rice** | 160 |
| **Peppermint sauce, 1 Tbsp** | 46 |
| **Pepperoni, 1 slice** | 26 |
| **Pfeffernusse, 1 piece** | 82 |
| **Picadillo** | 400 |
| **Piccalilli, 1 Tbsp** | 12 |
| **Pie** | |
| Apple, country | 410 |
| Apple, deep dish | 445 |
| Banana Cream | 626 |
| Blueberry | 475 |
| Boston Cream | 265 |
| Chocolate cream | 610 |
| Coconut cream | 462 |
| Coconut custard | 400 |
| Key Lime | 693 |
| Lemon Meringue | 545 |
| Nesselrode | 516 |
| Peach | 400 |
| Pecan | 585 |

|  |  |
|---|---|
| Pumpkin | 400 |
| Shoofly | 528 |
| **Pigeon Pie** | 587 |
| **Pig's feet, 1 foot** | 251 |
| **Pigs in blanket** | 200 |
| **Pilaf** | |
| Bulgur | 306 |
| Lamb | 572 |
| Rice | 312 |
| **Piquante sauce, 1 Tbsp** | 19 |
| **Pirog, Beef and Mushroom** | 727 |
| **Piroshki** | 155 |
| **Pissaladiere** | 474 |
| **Pita bread** | 247 |
| **Pizza, 1 slice** | |
| Plain | 450 |
| Green peppers | 452 |
| Mushrooms | 462 |
| Pepperoni | 587 |
| **Plantains** | 136 |
| **Plum pudding, Steamed** | 451 |
| **Plum sauce, 1 Tbsp** | 30 |
| **Polenta** | 88 |
| **Pollo en Salsa verde** | 244 |
| **Pollo molé verde** | 367 |
| **Popcorn balls, 1 ball** | 249 |
| **Poppy seed bread sticks, 1 piece** | 18 |
| **Pork** | |
| Balls, steamed, Chinese-style | 488 |
| Barbecued | 357 |

Barbecued with vegetables, Chinese-style    640
Breaded, Italian-style    423
Choucroute garnie    1,000
    with rice, Spanish-style    481
Crown roast    584
Loin, stuffed with apples and prunes    685
Lo mein    849
Red, cooked with chestnuts, Chinese-style    432
Sliced, Chinese-style    306
Sliced with green pepper, Chinese-style    411
Soong    666
Spareribs, barbecued    415
Spareribs, Chinese    555
Stuffed with oysters    400
Subgum chow mein    322
Suckling pig    1,100
Sweet and sour, Chinese-style    643
Sweet and sour stew    629
Szechuan-style with bean curd    576
Tenderloin, roast    345
Twice cooked in brown sauce    625
Twice cooked in Hoisin sauce    548
Teriyaki    453
**Portugese Filhos, 1 piece**    45
**Potato Bread, 1 slice**    70
**Potatoes**
   Anna    186
   Au Gratin    310
   Dauphine    268
   Duchess    209

| | |
|---|---|
| French-fried | 232 |
| Hash Brown | 230 |
| Lyonnaise | 289 |
| Pancakes | 144 |
| Potage Saint-Germain | 102 |
| Rosti | 162 |
| Salad | 475 |
| Salad, German-style | 270 |
| Scalloped | 215 |
| **Pot-au-feu** | 547 |
| **Poulet** | |
| a l'Estragon | 435 |
| Bonne Femme | 410 |
| Cordon Bleu | 502 |
| Roti Chasseur | 428 |
| Roti Normande | 463 |
| **Pound Cake, 1 slice** | 363 |
| **Pralines, 1 piece** | 173 |
| **Profiteroles, 1 piece** | 97 |
| **Prosciutto and melon** | 120 |
| **Pudding** | |
| Bread and butter | 258 |
| Chocolate | 312 |
| Indian | 374 |
| Plum, steamed | 442 |
| Rice | 255 |
| Tapioca | 220 |
| **Pumpernickel Bread, 1 slice** | 84 |
| **Quenelles, Chicken** | 493 |
| Fish | 148 |

| | |
|---|---:|
| Subgum, fried, 1 cup | 436 |
| **Roghan Josh** | 278 |
| **Roquefort dressing, 1 Tbsp** | 71 |
| **Rum Custard** | 208 |
| **Rum sauce, 1 Tbsp** | 36 |
| **Russian dressing, 1 Tbsp** | 80 |
| **Rutabaga, boiled** | 153 |
| **Rye Bread, 1 slice** | 64 |
| **Sachertorte** | 363 |
| **Salad** | |
| Caesar | 302 |
| Chef's | 413 |
| de Saucisson | 410 |
| Green Bean | 185 |
| Nicoise | 305 |
| Spinach with bacon dressing | 147 |
| Tabbouleh | 262 |
| Three Bean | 310 |
| Waldorf | 888 |
| **Salami, Italian, 1 slice** | 87 |
| **Salisbury Steak** | 583 |
| **Salmon** | |
| Fume au natural | 154 |
| Loaf | 230 |
| mousse | 312 |
| poached | 426 |
| soufflé | 335 |
| **Salsa, 1 cup** | 253 |
| **Salsa Verde, 1 cup** | 120 |
| **Salsify, creamed** | 237 |

| | |
|---|---|
| Saltimbocca | 520 |
| Sandwiches | |
|   Bacon, lettuce, and tomato | 268 |
|   Bagel with cream cheese | 255 |
|   Bagel with lox and cream cheese | 355 |
|   Bologna | 355 |
|   Cheese, grilled | 400 |
|   Cheese, grilled with bacon | 543 |
|   Cheese, grilled with tomato | 415 |
|   Chopped liver | 382 |
|   Corned beef | 446 |
|   Fried egg | 225 |
|   Lobster salad | 255 |
|   Meatball with tomato sauce | 400 |
|   Meatloaf | 300 |
|   Monte Cristo | 920 |
|   Pastrami | 560 |
|   Roast beef, overstuffed | 490 |
|   Reuben | 582 |
|   Salami | 394 |
|   Shrimp salad | 250 |
|   Steak | 353 |
|   Tongue, overstuffed | 475 |
|   Tuna fish salad | 324 |
|   Turkey club | 505 |
| Sangria | 93 |
| Sardine Fraiches Marines, 4 oz | 328 |
| Sashimi, assorted, 4 oz | 100 |
|   tako, 4 oz | 87 |
| Sate | 500 |

| | |
|---|---|
| Sauce Supreme, 1 Tbsp | 34 |
| Saucisson rémoulade | 631 |
| Sauerbraten | 570 |
| Sauerkraut, with juniper berries, braised | 257 |
| with caraway seeds | 72 |
| Sausage and Peppers, 2 pieces | 882 |
| Scallops, broiled | 210 |
| en Brochette | 254 |
| Scampi | 178 |
| Scrapple | 288 |
| Scungilli marinara | 269 |
| Sfogliatelli | 244 |
| Shabu-shabu | 448 |
| Shepherd's Pie | 500 |
| Shish kebab | 679 |
| Shortbread, Scottish | 152 |
| Shortcake, strawberry | 591 |
| Shrimp | |
| Ajillo, 8 large | 466 |
| in almond sauce, 8 large | 333 |
| Balls, Chinese-style | 286 |
| Batter-fried, Chinese-style, 1 piece | 84 |
| with bean curd, 12 medium | 980 |
| with black bean sauce, Chinese-style | 464 |
| Braised, Chinese-style 12 medium | 905 |
| Butterfly, Japanese-style | 250 |
| with cashews | 536 |
| creole | 344 |
| Egg foo yong | 356 |
| Fried in shell, Chinese-style, 12 medium | 674 |

**14**

| | |
|---|---|
| Clam chowder, New England | 283 |
| Chicken noodle | 78 |
| Chicken and rice | 78 |
| Chicken with bean curd, Japanese-style | 74 |
| Consommé | 42 |
| Escarole | 138 |
| Garlic | 197 |
| Gazpacho | 192 |
| Hungarian cherry | 375 |
| Hungarian cream of barley | 204 |
| Minestrone | 243 |
| Miso with bean curd | 79 |
| Miso with fish balls | 142 |
| Mulligatawny | 304 |
| Mushroom, cream of | 272 |
| Oxtail | 329 |
| Pastina | 134 |
| Peanut, cream of | 520 |
| Potato | 209 |
| Pumpkin | 150 |
| Sauerkraut | 128 |
| Senegalese | 314 |
| Stracciatelli | 125 |
| Stschy | 167 |
| Tortellini | 210 |
| Turtle, home style | 278 |
| Vegetable, cream of | 340 |
| **Sour cream and chive, 1 Tbsp** | 29 |
| **Sour Dough Bread, 1 slice** | 65 |
| **Souvlaki** | 291 |

**Spaghetti, 1 cup**

| | |
|---|---:|
| Alfredo | 405 |
| Bolognese | 357 |
| with butter, cream and parmesan | 401 |
| Carbonara | 860 |
| Clam sauce, red | 300 |
| Clam sauce, white | 344 |
| Fagioli | 348 |
| with meatballs in sauce | 853 |
| Paglia e fieno | 506 |
| al pesto | 980 |
| Pomodoro | 268 |
| with sausage | 471 |
| **Spatzle** | 165 |
| **Spiedini with anchovy** | 386 |
| **Spinach au gratin** | 275 |
| **Spinach, creamed** | 144 |
| **Spoon bread** | 632 |
| **Spumoni, 1 cup** | 510 |
| **Squid, Mediterranean** | 390 |
| Stuffed with Rice, Greek-style | 354 |
| **Squirrel Stew** | 500 |
| **Steamed Chinese sausage** | 778 |
| **Steamed Scallops with cabbage, Chinese-style,** | |
| **8 pieces** | 300 |
| **Steamed Whole Fish, Chinese-style, 1 lb** | 902 |
| **Stifado** | 228 |
| **Stollen, 1 slice** | 145 |
| **Strawberries Romanoff** | 322 |
| **Strawberry Shortcake** | 500 |

**Strudel**
| | |
|---|---|
| Almond | 398 |
| Apple | 360 |
| Cheese | 410 |
| Cherry | 405 |
| Poppy seed | 400 |

**Stuffing, 1 cup**
| | |
|---|---|
| Chestnut and mushroom | 472 |
| Corn bread | 700 |
| Herbed | 210 |
| Rice | 263 |
| Sage and onion | 220 |

| | |
|---|---|
| **Submarine, 1 roll** | 381 |
| **Sukiyaki** | 348 |

**Sushi**
| | |
|---|---|
| Chirashi | 460 |
| Norimaki | 468 |
| Tekka maki | 400 |

| | |
|---|---|
| **Sweet and Sour Chinese meatballs** | 936 |
| **Sweet and Sour fish, 1 lb** | 902 |
| **Sweet and Sour sauce, 1 Tbsp** | 20 |
| **Tabbouleh** | 304 |

**Tacos**
| | |
|---|---|
| Bean | 275 |
| Cheese | 205 |
| Chicken | 245 |
| Chili | 348 |
| Chorizo | 367 |

| | |
|---|---|
| **Taffy, 1 piece** | 50 |
| **Tahini sauce, ¼ cup** | 167 |

| | |
|---|---|
| Tamale pie | 268 |
| Tandoori fish | 300 |
| Shrimp, 10–12 | 288 |
| Taramasalata, 1 Tbsp | 100 |
| Tartar sauce, 1 Tbsp | 92 |
| Tarte au champignon | 382 |
| au Oignons | 570 |
| Tea Eggs, 1 egg | 85 |
| Tempura | 590 |
| Tempura sauce, 1 Tbsp | 5 |
| Teriyaki | |
| Beef | 213 |
| Chicken | 380 |
| Pork | 462 |
| Teriyaki sauce, 1 Tbsp | 15 |
| Toad in the Hole | 700 |
| Toast, French, 1 slice | 143 |
| Toll House Cookies, 1 piece | 60 |
| Tomato Aspic | 73 |
| Tomatos, broiled | 126 |
| Tomato sauce, 1 Tbsp | 10 |
| Bolognese, 1 cup | 330 |
| Italian-style, 1 cup | 215 |
| with red clam, 1 cup | 300 |
| Tomatos, stewed | 43 |
| Tortellini with butter and parmesan | 582 |
| with ricotta and cream | 600 |
| Tortillas, 1 piece, plain | 75 |
| Chili | 196 |
| Chorizo | 500 |

Sweetbreads

| | |
|---|---|
| braised | 300 |
| creamed | 535 |
| with mushrooms | 575 |
| sauteed | 200 |
| with sherry | 585 |
| Terrine of Veal and Ham | 250 |
| Vitello Tonnata | 850 |
| a la zingara | 602 |
| **Venison Burgers** | 360 |
| Ragout of | 437 |
| Roast saddle of | 205 |
| **Vichyssoise** | 410 |
| **Vinaigrette, 1 Tbsp** | 100 |
| **Weiner Schnitzel** | 415 |
| a la Holstein | 457 |
| **White sauce, 1 cup** | 400 |
| **Wild Boar, pot roast** | 500 |
| **Wild Duck, roasted** | 265 |
| **Won ton, fried sweet, 1 piece** | 59 |
| **Yakinasu, 4 oz** | 38 |
| **Yakitori** | 263 |
| **Yakitori donburi** | 781 |
| **Yam, candied** | 315 |
| **Yankee pot roast** | 775 |
| **Yogurt kholodnyk** | 40 |
| **Yogurt sauce, 1 Tbsp** | 9 |
| **Yorkshire Pudding** | 78 |
| **Yorkshire Scones, 1 piece** | 150 |
| **Yudofu** | 83 |

| | |
|---|---|
| **Zabaglione** | 177 |
| **Zeppole, 1 piece** | 42 |
| **Zucchini, Fried, 1 strip** | 37 |
|   Italian style | 100 |
|   Sautéed, ½ cup | 71 |
| **Zuppa di pesce** | 458 |
| **Zuppa Inglese** | 378 |

# FROZEN DINNERS,

## 1 complete dinner (see also pp 141-144 and pp 150-153)

| | |
|---|---|
| **Beans and Franks** | |
|   *Banquet* | 591 |
|   *Morton* | 530 |
|   *Swanson* | 550 |
| **Beef** | |
|   *Banquet* | 312 |
|     Chopped | 443 |
|   *La Choy* | 342 |
|   *Lean Cuisine* Oriental | 280 |
|   *Morton* | 270 |
|     Chopped | 340 |

| | |
|---|---|
| *Country Table* | 540 |
| *Steak House* | 920 |
| *Swanson* | 370 |
| *3-Course* | 490 |
| Chopped | 460 |
| *Hungry Man* | 540 |
| *Hungry Man* 18 oz | 730 |
| *Weight Watchers* 10 oz | 387 |
| *Weight Watchers* 16 oz | 586 |
| **Beef and Beans** | |
| *Swanson* | 500 |
| **Beef Stroganoff** | |
| *Stouffer's* | 390 |
| **Chicken** | |
| *La Choy* | 354 |
| *Morton* | 240 |
| *Swanson* boneless | 730 |
| *Weight Watchers* | 330 |
| **Chicken and Biscuits** | |
| *Green Giant* | 200 |
| **Chicken Croquettes** | |
| *Morton* | 410 |
| **Chicken Cacciatore** | |
| *Stouffer's* | 313 |
| *Weight Watchers* | 356 |
| **Chicken and Dumplings** | |
| *Banquet* | 282 |
| *Morton* | 280 |
| **Chicken, fried** | |
| *Banquet* | 530 |

| | |
|---|---:|
| *Man Pleaser* | 1,026 |
| *Morton* | 470 |
| *Country Table* | 710 |
| *Swanson* | 570 |
| *3-Course* | 630 |
| *Hungry Man* | 620 |
| *Hungry Man*, 15¼ oz | 910 |
| *Hungry Man*, Barbecue | 760 |
| Crispy Fried | 650 |
| **Chicken, glazed** | |
| *Lean Cuisine* | 270 |
| **Chicken with noodles** | |
| *Morton* | 260 |
| **Chicken, oriental** | |
| *Weight Watchers* | 320 |
| **Chicken Parmigiana and Spinach** | |
| *Weight Watchers* | 200 |
| **Chicken and vegetables** | |
| *Lean Cuisine* | 260 |
| **Chop Suey** | |
| *Banquet* | 282 |
| **Chow Mein** | |
| *Banquet* | 282 |
| *Green Giant* | 130 |
| *Lean Cuisine* | 240 |
| **Enchilada** | |
| *Banquet* | |
| Beef | 479 |
| Cheese | 459 |
| *El Chico* | 680 |

| | |
|---|---|
| *Swanson* | 570 |
| *Van de Kamp* | |
| Beef | 420 |
| Cheese | 430 |
| **Fish** | |
| *Banquet* | 382 |
| Haddock | 419 |
| Perch | 434 |
| *Lean Cuisine* | 200 |
| *Morton* | 270 |
| *Weight Watchers* | |
| Flounder | 240 |
| Haddock | 250 |
| Perch | 320 |
| Sole | 240 |
| Turbot | 490 |
| **Fish and Chips** | |
| *Swanson* | 450 |
| *Hungry Man* | 760 |
| **Ham** | |
| *Banquet* | 369 |
| *Morton* | 440 |
| *Swanson* | 380 |
| **Hash** | |
| *Banquet* | 372 |
| **Italian** | |
| *Banquet* | 446 |
| *Swanson* | 420 |
| **Lasagna** | |
| *Lean Cuisine* Zucchini Lasagne | 260 |

| | |
|---|---|
| *Lean Line* | 270 |
| *Swanson* | 740 |
| **Macaroni and beef** | |
| *Banquet* | 394 |
| *Morton* | 260 |
| *Swanson* | 400 |
| **Macaroni and cheese** | |
| *Banquet* | 326 |
| *Morton* | 320 |
| *Swanson* | 390 |
| **Manicotti** | |
| *Lean Line* | 270 |
| **Meat Loaf** | |
| *Banquet* | 412 |
| *Morton* | 340 |
| *Country Table* | 480 |
| *Swanson* | 530 |
| **Meatball** | |
| *Swanson* | 400 |
| **Mexican** | |
| *Banquet* | 571 |
| Combination | 571 |
| *El Chico* | 820 |
| *Swanson* | 600 |
| **Pepper** | |
| *La Choy* | 349 |
| **Polynesian** | |
| *Swanson* | 490 |
| **Pork** | |
| *Swanson* | 470 |

**Queso**
   *El Chico*     810
**Salisbury Steak**
   *Banquet*     390
   *Morton*     290
     *Country Table*     430
   *Swanson*     790
     *3-Course*     490
     *Hungry Man*     870
**Saltillo**
   *El Chico*     790
**Sausage with veal, 1 link**
   *Lean Line*     90
**Stuffed Shells**
   *Lean Line*     260
**Shrimp**
   *La Choy*     325
**Spaghetti with beef**
   *Lean Cuisine*     280
**Spaghetti and meatball**
   *Banquet*     450
   *Morton*     360
   *Swanson*     410
     *Hungry Man*     660
**Swiss Steak**
   *Swanson*     350
**Tacos, beef**
   *El Chico*     410
**Turkey**
   *Banquet*     293

| | |
|---|---|
| *Man Pleaser* | 620 |
| *Morton* | 350 |
| *Country Table* | 600 |
| *Swanson* | 360 |
| *3-Course* | 520 |
| *Hungry Man* | 740 |
| *Weight Watchers* | 400 |
| **Veal Parmigiana** | |
| *Banquet* | 421 |
| *Morton* | 330 |
| *Swanson* | 520 |
| *Hungry Man* | 910 |
| *Weight Watchers* | 230 |
| **Western** | |
| *Banquet* | 417 |
| *Morton* | 410 |
| *Swanson* | 460 |
| *Hungry Man* | 890 |
| **Ziti, baked** | |
| *Lean Line* | 270 |

# CHAPTER 15

# *Fingertip Low Calorie Guide*

## OVER 350 CALORIES

### Frozen entrees (at less than 30 calories per ounce)

| | |
|---|---:|
| *Banquet Buffet Supper* Beef and Noodles, 32 oz | 754 |
| *Banquet Buffet Supper* Beef Stew, 32 oz | 700 |
| *Banquet Buffet Supper* Chicken and Noodles, 32 oz | 764 |
| *Banquet Buffet Supper* Beef sliced with gravy, 32 oz | 782 |
| *Banquet Buffet Supper* Turkey, 32 oz | 564 |
| *La Choy* Chicken | 354 |

*Morton Country Table* Salisbury Steak, 15 oz     430
*Swanson Hungry-Man* Turkey, 13¼ oz     380
*Weight Watchers* Turkey Tetrazzini, 13 oz     380

# 200-350 CALORIES

## Frozen entrees (at less than 30 calories per ounce)

**Beef**
   *Banquet*, 11 oz     312
   *Lean Cuisine*, 9⅛ oz     280
   *Morton*, 10 oz     270
**Chicken**
   *Morton*, 10 oz     240
   *Stouffer's*
      Chicken a la King, 9½ oz     330
      Creamed Chicken, 6½ oz     300
      Chicken Divan, 8½ oz     335
   *Weight Watchers*, 15 oz     330
**Chicken and Biscuits**
   *Green Giant*, 7 oz     200
**Chicken Creole**
   *Weight Watchers*, 13 oz     250
**Chicken and Dumplings**
   *Banquet*, 12 oz     282
   *Morton*, 11 oz     280

**Chicken with Noodles**
  *Green Giant*, 9 oz                          250
  *Morton*, 10½ oz                             260
**Chicken Oriental**
  *Weight Watchers*, 16 oz                     320
**Chicken Parmigiana and Spinach**
  *Weight Watchers*, 9 oz                      200
**Chicken and Vegetables**
  *Lean Cuisine*, 12¾ oz                       260
**Chicken White Meat with Peas**
  *Weight Watchers*, 9 oz                      270
**Chop Suey**
  *Banquet*, 12 oz                             282
**Chow Mein**
  *Banquet*, 12 oz                             282
  *Lean Cuisine*, 11¼ oz                       240
**Eggplant Parmigiana**
  *Weight Watchers*, 13 oz                     280
**Fish**
  *Lean Cuisine*, 9 oz                         200
  *Morton*, 9 oz                               270
  *Weight Watchers*
    Flounder, 16 oz                            240
    Haddock, 16 oz                             250
    Perch, 16 oz                               320
    Sole, 16 oz                                240
    Sole with peas, mushrooms and
      lobster sauce, 9½ oz                     200
**Green Peppers with Beef**
  *Green Giant*, 7 oz                          200

**Lasagne**
  *Lean Line,* 10 oz     270
**Lasagne, Zucchini**
  *Lean Cuisine,* 11 oz     260
**Macaroni with Beef**
  *Green Giant,* 9 oz     240
  *Morton,* 10 oz     260
**Macaroni and Cheese**
  *Banquet,* 12 oz     326
  *Morton,* 11 oz     320
**Manicotti**
  *Lean Line,* 11 oz     270
**Salisbury Steak**
  *Banquet,* 11 oz     390
  *Morton,* 11 oz     290
**Shells, Stuffed**
  *Lean Line,* 11 oz     260
**Spaghetti with Beef**
  *Lean Cuisine,* 11½ oz     280
**Turkey**
  *Banquet,* 11 oz     293
  *Swanson* Turkey Slices, 8¾ oz     260
**Ziti, Baked**
  *Lean Line,* 10 oz     270
**Ziti with Veal and sauce**
  *Weight Watchers,* 13 oz     350
**Veal Parmigiana with Zucchini**
  *Weight Watchers,* 9½ oz     230

# Canned Entrees (at less than 30 calories per ounce)

**Pasta, one can**
  Ravioli
    *Franco-American* Beef, 7½ oz                        220
  Rotini
    *Franco-American*, 7½ oz                             200
  Macaroni
    *Franco-American*, 7½ oz                             220
  Macaroni and Meatballs
    *Franco-American*, 7½ oz                             220
**Meat, one can**
  Beef Goulash
    *Hormel*, 7½ oz                                      240
  Ham, whole
    *Hormel*, 6 oz                                       312
  Tuna, in water, drained
    *Chicken of the Sea* solid white, 7 oz can           216


# Fish, Fresh

Crab, steamed, meat only, 8 oz                          211
Haddock, fillets, 8 oz                                  180
Halibut, fillets, 8 oz                                  226
Oysters, Pacific and Western, meat only, 8 oz           207

# 15

## Meat

### Beef

**Chuck**

| | |
|---|---|
| boneless, lean only, braised, 4 oz | 219 |
| boneless, lean only, stewed, 4 oz | 243 |
| Flank steak, boneless, all lean, braised, 4 oz | 222 |
| ground, lean with 10% fat, 4 oz | 203 |
| porterhouse steak with 9% bone, lean only, broiled, 4 oz without bone | 254 |
| round steak, boneless, lean only, braised or broiled, 4 oz | 296 |
| sirloin steak, 7% bone, lean only, broiled, 4 oz without bone | 235 |
| T-bone, 11% bone, lean only, broiled, 4 oz without bone | 253 |

### Ham

fresh, lean only

| | |
|---|---|
| baked, without bone and skin, 4 oz | 246 |
| light cured, lean only | |
| baked, without bone and skin, 4 oz | 328 |

### Lamb

| | |
|---|---|
| Leg, lean only, roasted, boneless, 4 oz | 211 |
| loin chops, with bone, lean only, broiled, 4 oz | 213 |
| rib chops, with bone, lean only, broiled, 4 oz | 239 |
| shoulder, lean only, roasted, boneless, 4 oz | 233 |

**Pork**
> Picnic, without bone and skin, lean only, baked
> or roasted, 4 oz                                        239

**Veal**
> loin cuts, lean with fat, braised or broiled,
> without bone, 4 oz                                       245
> round with rump (roasts and leg cutlets),
> lean with fat, braised or broiled, without
> bone, 4 oz                                               245

## Poultry

**Chicken**
> roasted, without skin, 4 oz                              204
> stewed, light meat without skin, 4 oz                    207

**Turkey, roasted, light meat without skin, 4 oz     200**

# 101-200 CALORIES

## Pasta

**All pasta, dry, one cup**
> cooked till tender, (approx)                             190
> cooked till firm, (approx)                               155

**Canned, 1 can**

*Franco-American* macaroni and cheese, 7½ oz 184
*Franco-American* spaghetti with cheese, 7⅜ oz 170
*Franco-American* spaghetti with cheese
   sauce, 7⅜ oz 160

# Meat Entrees (at less than 30 calories per ounce)

**Frozen**

Beef, chipped, creamed
   *Banquet,* 5 oz 124
Beef, sliced
   *Banquet,* barbecue sauce, 5 oz 126
   *Banquet,* with gravy, 5 oz 116
   *Green Giant,* 5 oz 130
Beef Stew
   *Green Giant Boil-in-Bag,* 9 oz 160
   *Green Giant,* with biscuits, 7 oz 190
Veal steaks
   *Hormel,* 4 oz 130

# Meat Entrees, canned (at less than 30 calories per ounce), 1 can

| | |
|---|---|
| **Beef, corned with cabbage** | |
| Hormel, 8 oz | 150 |
| **Beef stew** | |
| Dinty Moore, 7½ oz | 184 |
| Swanson, 7½ oz | 190 |
| **Pork, sliced, with gravy** | |
| Morton House, 6¼ oz | 190 |

# Poultry entrees

| | |
|---|---|
| **Frozen (at less than 30 calories per ounce)** | |
| Chicken a la King | |
| Banquet, 5 oz | 138 |
| **Canned, 1 can** | |
| Chicken stew | |
| Swanson, 7½ oz | 180 |
| Turkey slices | |
| Morton House, 6¼ oz | 140 |
| Chicken, fresh | |
| Broiled, meat only, 4 oz | 154 |

# 15 Seafood

**Clams, canned, drained, 1 can**
Doxsee, 8 oz ... 112
Doxsee, 12 oz ... 147
**Shrimp marinara, with shells, frozen**
Buitoni, 4 oz ... 116

## Fish, fresh, 4 oz, meat only

**Abalone** ... 111
**Black Sea Bass** ... 106
**Butterfish, gulf** ... 108
**Catfish, fresh water** ... 117
**Croaker, Atlantic** ... 109
**Lake Herring (Cisco)** ... 109
**Lobster** ... 109
**Mussels** ... 108
**Ocean Pearch, Pacific** ... 108
**Red or Grey Snapper** ... 106
**Sea bass, white** ... 109
**Shrimp** ... 103
**Sturgeon** ... 107
**Tautog (Blackfish)** ... 101

# 51-100 CALORIES

## Miscellaneous

| | |
|---|---|
| *Pabst Extra Light* Beer | 70 |
| Whipped butter, 1 Tbsp | 65 |
| Farina, *Pillsbury,* ⅓ cup | 80 |
| Grits, *Quaker* Instant, 1 packet | 79 |
| One Egg, raw or boiled | |
|     extra large | 94 |
|     large | 82 |
|     medium | 72 |
| Canned Spaghetti with meatballs, *Libby's,* 1 cup | 84 |
| Canned Spanish rice, *Libby's,* 1 cup | 57 |

## Chinese dishes

| | |
|---|---|
| Chow mein, canned, 1 cup | |
|   *La Choy* | |
|     beef | 72 |
|     chicken | 68 |
|     mushroom | 85 |
|     pepper | 89 |
|     shrimp | 61 |
| Chow mein, frozen | |
|   *Banquet,* 1 bag | 89 |

| | |
|---|---|
| *La Choy* beef, 1 cup | 97 |
| *La Choy* shrimp, 1 cup | 73 |
| **Pea pods, frozen, 1 package** | |
| *La Choy* | 90 |
| **Won Ton, frozen, 1 cup** | |
| *La Choy* | 92 |

# Dairy

| | |
|---|---|
| **Cottage Cheese, low fat, ½ cup** | |
| *Borden* | 90 |
| *Breakstone* | 90 |
| *Friendship* | 100 |
| *Lucerne* | 100 |
| *Viva* | 100 |
| *Weight Watchers* | 90 |
| **Milk, 8 ounces** | |
| Buttermilk | |
| .1% fat *Borden* | 88 |
| .2% fat *Sealtest* skim | 71 |
| .5% fat *Borden* | 90 |
| .8% fat *Golden Nugget* | 92 |
| .8% fat *Light 'n Lively* | 95 |
| Dry, non-fat milk, reconstituted | 81 |
| Skin or low-fat | |
| no fat *Lucerne* | 90 |
| .1% fat *Borden* | 81 |

| | |
|---|---|
| fortified | 81 |
| .1% fat *Sealtest* | 79 |
| **Yogurt, plain, ½ cup** | |
| *Borden Lite-Line* lowfat | 70 |
| *Sealtest Light 'n Lively* lowfat | 70 |
| ***Danny On-A-Stick*, uncoated** | 65 |

# Meat, canned

| | |
|---|---|
| **Beef stew** | |
| *Libby's*, 1 cup | 78 |
| **Ham, whole** | |
| *Wilson's* certified boned and rolled, 1 oz | 56 |

# Poultry

| | |
|---|---|
| **Chicken stew with dumplings, canned** | |
| *Libby's*, 1 cup | 88 |
| **Turkey with gravy, frozen** | |
| *Banquet*, 5 oz | 98 |
| *Green Giant*, 5 oz | 100 |

# 15

## Seafood, canned

**Clams**
| | |
|---|---:|
| *Snow's,* ½ cup | 60 |
| *Sau-Sea,* 4 oz | 99 |

**Gefilte Fish**
| | |
|---|---:|
| *Manischewitz,* 3 oz piece | 53 |
| *Manischewitz* whitefish and pike, 3 oz piece | 64 |
| *Mother's,* 4 oz piece | 55 |

**Oysters**
| | |
|---|---:|
| *Bumblebee,* ½ cup | 86 |

**Shrimp**
| | |
|---|---:|
| *Bumblebee,* 4½ oz can | 90 |

## Seafood, fresh, meat only, 4 oz

| | |
|---|---:|
| **Clams** | 92 |
| **Cod** | 88 |
| **Crayfish** | 82 |
| **Croaker, white** | 95 |
| **Flounder** | 89 |
| **Ocean Perch, Atlantic** | 100 |
| **Oysters** | 75 |
| **Pickerel** | 95 |
| **Pike** | 100 |
| **Sand Dab** | 89 |
| **Sauger** | 95 |
| **Scallops** | 92 |
| **Sole** | 90 |
| **Squid** | 95 |
| **Tilefish** | 90 |

# Fruits and Vegetables

**Artichokes**
boiled, drained, 1 whole bud      67
**Beets**
raw, diced, 1 cup      58
**Broccoli**
boiled, drained, 8 oz      59
**Carrots**
raw, slices, 1 cup      53
**Chayote**
raw, 1 medium squash      56
**Cranberries**
fresh, without stems, 1 cup      52
**Currants, red or white**
trimmed, 1 cup      55
**Dock or Sorrel**
raw with stems, 1 lb      89
**Endive, French or Belgian**
trimmed, 1 lb      68
**Escarole**
untrimmed, 1 lb      80
**Grapefruit**
pink or red, with seeds
    whole, with skin, 1 lb      87
    sections, 1 cup      80
pink or red, seedless
    whole, with skin, 1 lb      93
    sections, 1 cup      80

white, with seeds
  whole, with skin, 1 lb    84
  sections, 1 cup    82
white, seedless
  whole, with skin, 1 lb    87
  sections, 1 cup    78
**Honeydew Melon**
whole, with rinds and seeds, 1 lb    94
cubed or diced, 1 cup    56
**Lettuce**
Iceberg
  whole, 1 lb    56
Loose Leaf
  whole, 1 lb    52
Romaine or cos
  whole, 1 lb    52
**Pawpaw**
peeled and seeded, 4 oz    96
**Papaya**
peeled and seeded, cubed, 1 cup    55
**Peaches**
pared, sliced, 1 cup    65
**Raspberries**
black, 1 cup    98
red, 1 cup    70
**Strawberries**
whole, 1 cup    55
**Watermelon**
whole, with rind, 1 lb    54

# 20-50 CALORIES

## Breads, Buns and Rolls

**Bread, 1 slice**
**Gluten**
*Thomas*     32
**Protein**
*Thomas*     45
**Rice Cakes**
*Spiral*     36
**Wheat**
*Thomas*     50
**White**
*Arnold Melba* Thin     40
*Fresh Horizons*     50
*Pepperidge Farm* Very Thin     40
*Weight Watchers*     35
**Buns and Rolls, 1 piece**
*Pepperidge Farm* Old-Fashioned     37
*Pepperidge Farm* Party     35
**Margarine, 1 Tbsp**
*Blue Bonnet* Diet     50
*Fleischmann* Diet     50
Imitation     50

# 15

## Candy, 1 piece

*Rolo*       28

## Cheese, 1 oz

**Farmer's**
  *Friendship*       38
**Ricotta**
  *Borden*       42
**Imitation Cream Cheese**
  *Philadelphia*       50
**American, grated**
  *Borden*       30

## Chinese Dishes

**Apple-Cinnamon roll, frozen**
  *La Choy,* 1 piece       38
**Bamboo Shoots, canned**
  *La Choy,* 8 oz       23
**Bean sprouts, canned**
  *La Choy,* 8 oz       24
**Chow Mein, canned, 1 cup**
  *Chun King*       44
  *La Choy,* meatless       47

**Egg Rolls, frozen**
   *La Choy* chicken, 1 piece        30
   *La Choy* lobster, 1 piece        27
**Mixed vegetables, canned**
   *La Choy*, 1 cup        35

# Cream

**Half & Half, 1 Tbsp**        20
   *Lucerne* Real Cream topping, 1 whipped oz   20

# Dips, 1 oz

**Bean, Jalapeño**
   *Frito-Lay*        36
   *Gebhardi*        30
   *Granny Goose*        37
   *Lucerne*        36
**Clam**
   *Lucerne*        34
**Gelatin**
   *Knox* gelatin, 1 envelope        28
**Gravy**
   *French's* Pork, mix, ½ cup        40

# Jelly, 1 Tbsp

**Apple**
 *Kraft*, Low Calorie                                    22
 *Diet Delight*                                          22
**Apricot Pineapple Jam**
 *Diet Delight*                                          21
**Blackberry Apple**
 *Kraft*, low calorie                                    22
**Blackberry Jam**
 *Diet Delight*                                          21
**Grape**
 *Kraft*, Low Calorie                                    22
 *Diet Delight*                                          21
**Raspberry Jam**
 *Diet Delight*                                          21


# Meat, 1 oz, canned

**Beef**
 Corned, canned
  *Safeway*                                              35
 Dried
  *Swift*                                                42
 Smoked
  *Safeway*                                              35
  *Safeway spicy*                                        40

Beef roast
*Wilson*                                          33
**Ham**
*Wilson* certified fully cooked        48
*Wilson* certified *Tender Made*     44
*Wilson* certified festival ham        48
**Pastrami**
*Safeway*                                      40
**Scrapple**
*Oscar Mayer* in tube                    50
*Oscar Mayer* Philadelphia style     45

# Olives

Green, 10 large                            45
Manzanillo Black, 10 large          50

# Popcorn, 1 cup

*Pops-Rite*, popped                        38
*Wise*, cheese-flavored, ready to eat      49

## Poultry

| | |
|---|---|
| *Safeway* smoked chicken, 1 oz | 50 |
| *Safeway* smoked turkey, 1 oz | 50 |

## Pudding, ½ cup

**D-Zerta**
| | |
|---|---|
| butterscotch | 25 |
| chocolate | 20 |
| vanilla | 30 |

## Salad Dressing, 1 Tbsp

**French**
| | |
|---|---|
| *Ann Page* Low Calorie | 25 |
| *Kraft* Low Calorie | 25 |
| *Nu Made* Low Calorie | 20 |

**Italian**
| | |
|---|---|
| *Wish-Bone* Low Calorie | 20 |

**May Lo Naise**
| | |
|---|---|
| *Tillie Lewis* | 25 |

**Russian**
| | |
|---|---|
| *Wish-Bone* Low Calorie | 25 |

**Thousand Island**
   *Ann Page* Low Calorie            25
   *Wish-Bone* Low Calorie       25
**Whipped**
   *Tillie Lewis*                 25

# Sauces & Spreads

Crosse & Blackwell Anchovy Paste 1 Tbsp   20
*Hunt's* Tomato Sauce, 4 oz         35
   with mushrooms, 4 oz         40
*Open Pit* Barbecue, 1 Tbsp        26

# Vegetables, canned and frozen

**Artichoke Hearts**
   *Birds Eye*, 3 oz             20
**Asparagus, 1 cup, canned**
   cuts                       40
   spears                   40
   spears and tips          35
   whole                   50
**Asparagus, frozen**
   *Birds Eye*, 3.3 oz           25
   *Seabrook Farms*, ½ cup     23

**Beans, green canned, 1 cup**
**french**

| | |
|---|---|
| *Del Monte* | 40 |
| *Green Giant* | 30 |
| *Kounty Kist* | 40 |
| *Libby's* | 35 |

**whole**

| | |
|---|---|
| *Del Monte* | 35 |
| *Green Giant* | 30 |
| *Kounty Kist* | 40 |
| *Libby's* | 35 |
| *Stokely-Van Camp* | 40 |

**Beans, green, frozen**

| | |
|---|---|
| *Birds Eye*, 3.3 oz | 25 |
| *Kounty Kist*, 1 cup | 30 |
| *Seabrook Farms*, 1 cup | 42 |

**Beans, wax or yellow, 1 cup**

| | |
|---|---|
| *Del Monte* | 35 |
| *Libby's* | 40 |
| *Stokely-Van Camp* | 45 |

**Broccoli, frozen**

| | |
|---|---|
| *Birds Eye* 3.3 oz | 25 |
| *Green Giant*, 1 cup | 30 |
| *Kounty Kist*, 1 cup | 30 |
| *Seabrook Farms*, 1 cup | 46 |

**Brussels Sprouts, frozen**

| | |
|---|---|
| *Birds Eye*, 3.3 oz | 30 |
| *Green Giant*, 1 cup | 50 |
| *Kounty Kist*, 1 cup | 50 |

**Carrots, canned, 1 cup**
*Libby's*     40
*S & W*     44
**Cauliflower, frozen**
*Birds Eye* 3.3 oz     25
*Green Giant,* 1 cup     25
*Kounty Kist,* 1 cup     25
**Collard Greens**
*Birds Eye,* 3.3 oz     30
*Seabrook Farms,* 1 cup     44
**Mixed Vegetables**
*Kounty Kist,* California, 1 cup     30
**Mustard Greens**
*Seabrook Farms,* ½ cup     21
**Sauerkraut, canned, 1 cup**     50
**Spinach, canned, 1 cup**     45
**Spinach, frozen, 1 cup**     50
**Tomatoes, canned**
*Hunt's* stewed, 4 oz     30
*Libby's* whole, 1 cup     45
*S & W* whole, 1 cup     42
*Stokely-Van Camp,* whole     50
*Townhouse,* whole     50
**Turnip Greens**
*Birds Eye* 3.3 oz     20
*Seabrook Farms,* ½ cup     22
*Stokely-Van Camp,* ½ cup     22

# Fruits and Vegetables, fresh, 1 cup unless noted

| | |
|---|---|
| **Asparagus** | |
| cut spears | 35 |
| **Bamboo shoots** | |
| cuts | 41 |
| **Bean Sprouts** | 37 |
| **Beans, green or snap** | |
| cuts | 34 |
| **Beans, wax or yellow** | |
| cuts | 30 |
| **Beet Greens** | 26 |
| **Cabbage, red or green, chopped** | 22 |
| **Cantelope, cubed** | 48 |
| **Casaba Melon, cubed** | 45 |
| **Cauliflower, flowerets** | 27 |
| **Swiss Chard, leaves only** | 32 |
| **Eggplant, diced** | 50 |
| **Radish, diced** | 20 |
| **Rhubarb, raw diced** | 20 |
| **Summer Squash, diced** | 35 |
| **Tomatos, sliced** | 40 |
| **Turnips, cubed** | 39 |

# Fruit and Vegetable drinks, 6 oz

| | |
|---|---|
| **Cranberry** | |
| *Ocean Spray* low calorie | 35 |

**Cranberry apple**
*Ocean Spray* cranapple low calorie          30
**Sauerkraut**
*Libby's*          20
**Tomato**
*Campbell's*          35
*Del Monte*          35
*Heinz*          38
*Hunt's*          43
*Libby's*          39
*S & W*          22
*Sacramento*          35
*Stokely-Van Camp*          33
*Townhouse*          35
*Welch's*          38
**Tomato cocktail**
*Ortega Snap-E-Tom*          38
**Vegetable cocktail**
*S & W*          21
*Townhouse*          35
*V-8*          35

# UNDER 20 CALORIES

## Beverages

Note: virtually all sodas that are called *low-calorie*, *sugar-free* or *dietetic* contain 2 calories or less.

# Bouillon, 1 cube

**Beef**
| | |
|---|---|
| *Herb-Ox* | 6 |
| *Maggi* | 6 |
| *Wyler's* | 7 |
| *Wyler's* Instant | 10 |

**Chicken**
| | |
|---|---|
| *Herb-Ox* | 6 |
| *Maggi* | 7 |
| *Wyler's* | 8 |
| *Wyler's* Instant | 6 |

**Onion**
| | |
|---|---|
| *Herb-Ox* | 10 |
| *Wyler's* | 6 |

**Vegetable**
| | |
|---|---|
| *Herb-Ox* | 6 |
| *Wyler's* | 6 |

# Breath Mints, 1 piece

| | |
|---|---|
| *Certs* clear | 8 |
| *Certs* pressed | 6 |
| *Chewels* | 10 |
| *Clorets* mints | 6 |
| *Dentyne* dynamints | 2 |
| *Lifesavers* | 7 |
| *Trident* mints | 8 |

# Broth, 1 packet

*Herb-Ox*

| | |
|---|---|
| Beef | 8 |
| Chicken | 12 |
| Onion | 14 |
| Vegetable | 12 |

# Candy, Dietetic

*Estee*, 1 piece

| | |
|---|---|
| chocolate covered raisins | 6 |
| gum drops | 3 |
| hard candies | 12 |
| mint candies | 4 |

# Cocktail Mix, non-alcoholic, 1 oz

| | |
|---|---|
| *Holland House* Bloody Mary | 6 |
| *Holland House* Whiskey Sour | 9 |

# Coffee, 1 cup

| | |
|---|---|
| ground | 2 |
| instant | 4 |

# 15

## Condiments, 1 Tbsp

| | |
|---|---|
| **A-1** sauce | 12 |
| **Catsup** | |
| *Del Monte* | 15 |
| **Chili sauce** | |
| *Heinz* | 17 |
| **Horseradish** | 2 |
| **Mustard** | |
| *French's* Brown | 15 |
| *French's* Yellow | 16 |
| *Grey Poupon Dijon* | 15 |
| **Soy sauce** | |
| *La Choy* | 8 |
| **Taco sauce** | |
| *Old El Paso* | 4 |
| **Vinegar** | 1 |
| **Worcestershire** | 10 |

## Cookies, 1 piece

| | |
|---|---|
| **Angel Puffs** | |
| *Stella D'Oro* Dietetic | 17 |
| **Arrowroot** | |
| *Sunshine* | 16 |
| **Royal Nuggets** | |
| *Stella D'Oro* | 1 |

**Vanilla Snaps**
   *Nabisco*     13
**Vanilla Wafers**
   *Sunshine*     15
   *Nabisco*     18
**Zuzu Ginger Snaps**
   *Nabisco*     16

# Cough Drops     9

# Crackers, 1 cracker

**Cheez-It**
   *Sunshine*     6
**Cheeze**
   *Keebler*     11
**Flings Curls**
   *Nabisco*     10
**Matzos**
   *Manischewitz Tam Tams*     14
**Melba Toast**
   *Old London*
     Garlic     9
     Onion     10
     Pumpernickel     17
     Rye     17
     Sesame     10
     Wheat     17
     White     17

**Oyster**
| | |
|---|---|
| *Keebler* | 3 |
| *Sunshine* | 3 |

**Ritz**
| | |
|---|---|
| *Nabisco* | 16 |

**Saltines**
| | |
|---|---|
| *Keebler Zesta* | 12 |
| *Nabisco Premium* | 12 |
| *Sunshine Krispy* | 11 |

**Sociables**
| | |
|---|---|
| *Nabisco* | 10 |

**Triangle Thins**
| | |
|---|---|
| *Nabisco* | 8 |

**Wheat Thins**
| | |
|---|---|
| *Nabisco* | 9 |

# Creamers, Non-Dairy, 1 tsp

| | |
|---|---|
| *Coffee-Mate, Carnation, 1 pkt* | 11 |
| *Coffee-Tone* | 12 |
| *Cremora, Pet* | 11 |

# Gelatin, mix, ½ cup

| | |
|---|---|
| *D-Zerta* | 8 |
| *Royal Sweet As You Please* | 6 |

# Gravy, ¼ cup, mix

**Au Jus**
| | |
|---|---|
| *Durkee* | 8 |
| *French's* | 8 |
| *McCormick* | 4 |
| *Schilling* | 4 |

**Brown**
| | |
|---|---|
| *Durkee* | 15 |
| *Durkee* with mushrooms | 15 |
| *Durkee* with onions | 17 |
| *McCormick Lite* | 10 |
| *Weight Watchers* | 8 |
| with mushrooms | 12 |
| with onions | 13 |

**Chicken**
| | |
|---|---|
| *Durkee home style* | 18 |
| *McCormick Lite* | 10 |
| *Pillsbury home style* | 15 |
| *Schilling Lite* | 10 |
| *Weight Watchers* | 10 |

**Mushroom**
| | |
|---|---|
| *McCormick* | 19 |
| *Schilling* | 19 |

**Pork**
| | |
|---|---|
| *Durkee* | 18 |

**Mushroom Steak**
| | |
|---|---|
| *Dawn Fresh* | 4 |

**Swiss Steak**
| | |
|---|---|
| *Durkee* | 11 |

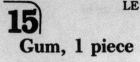

# Gum, 1 piece

| | |
|---|---|
| *Adams* | 9 |
| *Beeman* | 10 |
| *Beech-Nut* | 9 |
| *Beechies* | 6 |
| *Black Jack* | 9 |
| *Care Free* | 8 |
| *Chiclets* | 6 |
| *Clorets* | 6 |
| *Clove* | 5 |
| *Dentyne* | 5 |
| *Estee* | 3 |
| *Freshen-Up* | 9 |
| *Fruit Stripe* | 9 |
| *Orbit* | 8 |
| *Trident* | 5 |
| *Wrigley's* | 10 |

# Jelly, 1 tsp

| | |
|---|---|
| *Ann Page*, all flavors | 18 |
| *Diet Delight* Strawberry | 18 |
| *Kraft*, all flavors | 16 |
| *S & W*, all flavors | 10 |
| *Smuckers Slenderella*, all flavors | 8 |

# Oil

*Pam* Vegetable spray    7


# Pickles

**Capers, 1 Tbsp**
  *Crosse & Blackwell*    6
**Onions, cocktail, 1 Tbsp**
  *Crosse & Blackwell*    1
**Peppers, 1 oz**
  Chile Green, *Ortega*    5
  Hot Pickled, *Old El Paso*    9
**Dill Pickles, spears, 1 piece**
  *Bond's*    2
  *Del Monte*    7
  *Heinz*    7
  *Smucker's*    8
**Sour Pickles, 1 piece**
  *Del Monte*    10


# Salad dressings, 1 Tbsp

**Blue Cheese**
  *Ann Page* Low Calorie    18
  *Kraft* Low Calorie    14

| | |
|---|---|
| *Tillie Lewis* | 12 |
| *Weight Watchers* | 10 |
| **Caesar** | |
| *Pfeiffer* Low Calorie | 10 |
| **French** | |
| *Pfeiffer* Low Calorie | 18 |
| *Weight Watchers* | 4 |
| *Tillie Lewis* | 12 |
| **Italian** | |
| *Ann Page* Low Calorie | 14 |
| *Kraft* Low Calorie | 6 |
| *Nu Made* Low Calorie | 16 |
| *Pfeiffer* Low Calorie | 10 |
| *Tillie Lewis* | 6 |
| *Weight Watchers* | 2 |
| **Red Wine** | |
| *Pfeiffer* Low Calorie | 10 |
| **Russian** | |
| *Pfeiffer* Low Calorie | 15 |
| *Tillie Lewis* | 12 |
| *Weight Watchers* | 12 |
| **Thousand Island** | |
| *Pfeiffer* Low Calorie | 15 |
| *Tillie Lewis* | 18 |
| *Weight Watchers* | 12 |

# Sauces, 1 Tbsp

**Barbecue**
  *French's*    14
**Enchilada**
  *Old El Paso* hot    9
  *Old El Paso* mild    10
**Lemon-Butter**
  *Weight Watchers*    8

# Sugar, 1 tsp    15

# Pancake Syrup, 1 Tbsp

*Cary's* **Diet**    10
*Diet Delight*    15
*S & W*    12
*Tillie Lewis*    14

# Tea, 1 cup    1

**lemon-flavored**
  *Nestea*    2

# 15

## Toppings, 1 Tbsp

*No-Cal*
    all flavors except chocolate and coffee    **0**
    *No-Cal* chocolate & coffee    **6**
**whipped mix**
    *D-Zerta*    **8**
    *Dream Whip*    **10**

## Vegetables and Fruits, Fresh

**Cabbage**
    Chinese, cuts, 1 cup    11
    spoon (Bakchoy), cuts, 1 cup    11
**Celery**
    1 large outer stalk    7
    3 small inner stalks    9
**Chicory greens**
    cuts, 1 cup    11
    10 inner leaves    5
**Endive, French or Belgian**
    1 head, 5-7"    8
    10 small leaves    5
    chopped, 1 cup    14
**Escarole, cuts, 1 cup**    10
**Mushrooms, chopped, 1 cup**    20
**Pepper, sweet, green, sliced, 1 cup**    18

| | |
|---|---|
| **Pickles** | |
| dill, 1 large | 15 |
| sour, 1 large | 14 |
| **Spinach, trimmed and chopped, 1 cup** | 14 |
| **Watercress, 1 cup** | 7 |